jQuery 2.0
Development
Cookbook

Over 80 recipes providing modern solutions to web
development problems with real-world examples

Leon Revill

BIRMINGHAM - MUMBAI

jQuery 2.0 Development Cookbook

First published: February 2014

Production Reference: 1140214

Published by Packt Publishing Ltd.
Livery Place
35 Livery Street
Birmingham B3 2PB, UK.

ISBN 978-1-78328-089-6

www.packtpub.com

Cover Image by Karl Moore (karl.moore@ukonline.co.uk)

Credits

Author

Leon Revill

Reviewers

Gary Gilbert

Joni Halabi

Acquisition Editors

Akram Hussain

Sam Wood

Content Development Editor

Arvind Koul

Technical Editors

Dennis John

Pankaj Kadam

Gaurav Thingalaya

Copy Editors

Tanvi Gaitonde

Dipti Kapadia

Aditya Nair

Project Coordinator

Joel Goveya

Proofreaders

Maria Gould

Ameesha Green

Paul Hindle

Indexer

Rekha Nair

Production Coordinator

Alwin Roy

Cover Work

Alwin Roy

About the Author

Leon Revill has over five years' commercial web development experience with PHP5 and MySQL technologies on large and small projects. His development skillset extends over many JavaScript technologies, such as jQuery, AngularJS, and NodeJS. Being an all-round tech enthusiast, some of Leon's spare time is spent working on personal projects to allow him get to grips with new technologies quickly. Leon runs a web development blog (`http://www.revillweb.com/`), where he shares his knowledge in the form of articles and tutorials.

I would like to thank my friends and family, who have been incredibly supportive while writing this book. A special thanks goes to Allýce Wolverson, whose support during long days and difficult times has given me the opportunity to complete this title.

Finally, I would like to thank everyone at Packt Publishing for all their hard work in making this book possible.

About the Reviewers

Gary Gilbert first got his start with programming, hacking on Ti 99/4a and VIC-20 systems in his early teens in Canada, and was instantly hooked. After graduating from University, Gary moved to England to work for an IT consultancy, where he developed desktop applications. Two years and seven addresses later, Gary found himself working for a government contractor in Washington DC, building web applications using a variety of client/server technologies, such as HTML and pure JavaScript. In early 2007, Gary was introduced to jQuery 1.1 and in 2010, he began developing web applications with jQuery full time.

Gary Gilbert is currently Deputy Manager of software development at CONTENS Software GmbH in Munich, Germany, where he helps develop the company's next-generation content management software.

> I would like to personally thank the jQuery team for their dedication and hard work in developing the library; their tireless efforts have made my work much, much easier. I would also like to thank Packt Publishing for giving me the opportunity to review this book.

Joni Halabi is a Senior User Experience Developer at Optaros with over 10 years' experience in frontend website development. In this role, she has worked with a wide variety of clients to provide them with robust and user-focused solutions.

Joni's technical expertise includes the frontend development of complex website designs on a variety of popular frameworks, including Magento, Hybris, Drupal, and WordPress. Her talents also include JavaScript and jQuery development, as well as code optimization to meet cross-browser and mobile browser requirements.

Prior to Optaros, Joni managed and developed with a team of talented U/I engineers for a Cambridge-based online gaming company and taught web development and graphic design at several elementary schools in upstate New York. Joni is also a certified Magento frontend developer.

www.PacktPub.com

Support files, eBooks, discount offers and more

You might want to visit www.PacktPub.com for support files and downloads related to your book.

Did you know that Packt offers eBook versions of every book published, with PDF and ePub files available? You can upgrade to the eBook version at www.PacktPub.com and as a print book customer, you are entitled to a discount on the eBook copy. Get in touch with us at service@packtpub.com for more details.

At www.PacktPub.com, you can also read a collection of free technical articles, sign up for a range of free newsletters and receive exclusive discounts and offers on Packt books and eBooks.

http://PacktLib.PacktPub.com

Do you need instant solutions to your IT questions? PacktLib is Packt's online digital book library. Here, you can access, read and search across Packt's entire library of books.

Why Subscribe?

- ▶ Fully searchable across every book published by Packt
- ▶ Copy and paste, print and bookmark content
- ▶ On demand and accessible via web browser

Free Access for Packt account holders

If you have an account with Packt at www.PacktPub.com, you can use this to access PacktLib today and view nine entirely free books. Simply use your login credentials for immediate access.

Table of Contents

Preface

jQuery 2.0 Development Cookbook will provide you with many reusable code recipes to create common and unique website and web application elements, plugins, and interfaces using the most popular client-side framework, jQuery. Following the step-by-step instructions for each of the recipes will not only provide you with useable code, but also the understanding needed to extend and improve on it.

What this book covers

Chapter 1, Document Object Model Manipulation, covers how to use jQuery to manipulate the 186 web page's HTML code on the client to create a rich and visual user experience.

Chapter 2, Interacting with the User by Making Use of jQuery Events, harnesses the power of jQuery to detect and respond to user interactions, which creates intuitive user interfaces.

Chapter 3, Loading and Manipulating Dynamic Content with AJAX and JSON, utilizes jQuery's AJAX functionality with JSON-formatted data to bring pages to life by updating content without the need for a page refresh.

Chapter 4, Adding Attractive Visuals with jQuery Effects, explains how to add shine to your website or web application with jQuery's effects and basic animations to create unforgettable designs.

Chapter 5, Form Handling, covers how to use jQuery to build robust client-side validation and an intuitive user experience for web forms.

Chapter 6, User Interface, covers how to break the mold and create powerfully intuitive interfaces from scratch and engage the user with a high level of interactivity.

Chapter 7, User Interface Animation, covers how to extend upon jQuery's built-in animation and combine CSS with jQuery to create fabulous website modules for use with any website.

Chapter 8, *Understanding Plugin Development*, explains how to create reusable code that provides solutions to a range of common website and web application problems.

Chapter 9, *jQuery UI*, covers how to empower your website or web application with jQuery's user interface library to create attractive and user-friendly page elements and interfaces.

Chapter 10, *Working with jQuery Mobile*, covers how to create a mobile and cross-platform-ready website using jQuery's powerful mobile framework.

What you need for this book

For all the recipes in this book, you will require an IDE to write JavaScript, HTML, and CSS code, and a web browser to execute your code. For some of the more advanced recipes in this book, you will require a web server running MySQL and PHP.

Who this book is for

This book is for anyone who is either new to jQuery and looking to learn some basics, or familiar with jQuery and looking to expand their knowledge and create some advanced components for their website or web application. This book is an excellent resource for web developers of all skill and experience levels.

Conventions

In this book, you will find a number of styles of text that distinguish between different kinds of information. Here are some examples of these styles, and an explanation of their meaning.

Code words in text, database table names, folder names, filenames, file extensions, pathnames, dummy URLs, user input, and Twitter handles are shown as follows: "Any code within `$(function(){ });` will be automatically executed by jQuery when the page is loaded."

A block of code is set as follows:

```
<!DOCTYPE html>
<html>
<head>
  <title>Creating DOM elements</title>
  <script src="jquery.min.js"></script>
  <script></script>
</head>
<body>
<div id="container">
  <ul id="myList">
    <li>List Item 1</li>
```

```
      <li>List Item 2</li>
      <li>List Item 3</li>
    </ul>
  </div>
 </body>
 </html>
```

New terms and **important words** are shown in bold. Words that you see on the screen, in menus or dialog boxes for example, appear in the text like this: "This will display a pop-up window to the user that has the message **Are you sure you want to delete this user?**"

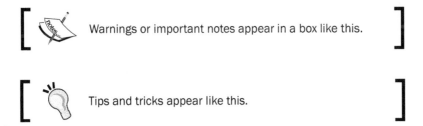

Warnings or important notes appear in a box like this.

Tips and tricks appear like this.

Reader feedback

Feedback from our readers is always welcome. Let us know what you think about this book—what you liked or may have disliked. Reader feedback is important for us to develop titles that you really get the most out of.

To send us general feedback, simply send an e-mail to feedback@packtpub.com, and mention the book title via the subject of your message.

If there is a topic that you have expertise in and you are interested in either writing or contributing to a book, see our author guide on www.packtpub.com/authors.

Customer support

Now that you are the proud owner of a Packt book, we have a number of things to help you to get the most from your purchase.

Downloading the example code

You can download the example code files for all Packt books you have purchased from your account at http://www.packtpub.com. If you purchased this book elsewhere, you can visit http://www.packtpub.com/support and register to have the files e-mailed directly to you.

Downloading the color images of this book

We also provide you a PDF file that has color images of the screenshots/diagrams used in this book. The color images will help you better understand the changes in the output. You can download this file from `https://www.packtpub.com/sites/default/files/downloads/0896OS_GraphicsBundle.pdf`.

Errata

Although we have taken every care to ensure the accuracy of our content, mistakes do happen. If you find a mistake in one of our books—maybe a mistake in the text or the code—we would be grateful if you would report this to us. By doing so, you can save other readers from frustration and help us improve subsequent versions of this book. If you find any errata, please report them by visiting `http://www.packtpub.com/submit-errata`, selecting your book, clicking on the **errata submission form** link, and entering the details of your errata. Once your errata are verified, your submission will be accepted and the errata will be uploaded on our website, or added to any list of existing errata, under the Errata section of that title. Any existing errata can be viewed by selecting your title from `http://www.packtpub.com/support`.

Piracy

Piracy of copyright material on the Internet is an ongoing problem across all media. At Packt, we take the protection of our copyright and licenses very seriously. If you come across any illegal copies of our works, in any form, on the Internet, please provide us with the location address or website name immediately so that we can pursue a remedy.

Please contact us at `copyright@packtpub.com` with a link to the suspected pirated material.

We appreciate your help in protecting our authors, and our ability to bring you valuable content.

Questions

You can contact us at `questions@packtpub.com` if you are having a problem with any aspect of the book, and we will do our best to address it.

1
Document Object Model Manipulation

In this chapter, we will cover:

- ▶ Selecting elements
- ▶ Finding and selecting sibling elements
- ▶ Creating DOM elements
- ▶ Inserting content into an element
- ▶ Modifying the DOM element properties
- ▶ Adding and removing CSS classes to dynamically change their style
- ▶ Enabling and disabling buttons by changing their properties
- ▶ Updating an image within a page
- ▶ Populating list elements
- ▶ Understanding pagination
- ▶ Removing DOM elements
- ▶ Re-using DOM elements

Introduction

This chapter looks at the fundamental principles of jQuery—finding, selecting, and manipulating DOM elements. jQuery makes it easy for JavaScript developers to select single or multiple HTML page elements using a variety of methods.

Once the developer has selected these elements, jQuery provides the ability to manipulate each of these elements in order to create a richer user experience through attribute modifications such as style, disabled, and class.

Selecting elements

There are many ways in which you can use jQuery to select DOM elements. We will explore the main methods here. For developers familiar with CSS, it is possible to use the same syntax when selecting elements with jQuery (that is, `#content`, `.content`, and so on).

Getting ready

Open a blank HTML document within your text editor or IDE of choice. Ensure that you have the latest version of jQuery downloaded and is easily accessible for inclusion into this HTML document. When creating new HTML files within this chapter, ensure that they are all within the same directory as the jQuery library file, making it easy to include into the HTML document.

How to do it...

To understand how you can use jQuery to select a variety of DOM elements, perform each of the following recipe steps:

1. Create a web page using the following HTML and JavaScript code:

```
<!DOCTYPE html>
<html>
<head>
    <title>Selecting Elements with jQuery</title>
    <script src="jquery.min.js"></script>
    <script>
        $(function(){
            var content = $("#content"); //Select the content
                div
            var span = $(".span-element"); //Select the span
                element
            var listelements = $("li"); //Select all the list
                elements
        });
    </script>
</head>
<body>
<div class="division-container">Some text within a div
    which has a class</div>
```

```
<div id="content">Some text within a div which has an ID
    attribute</div>
<a href="#">A link</a>
<a href="#" rel="dofollow">A second link</a>
<ul class="info-list">
    <li>List Item 1</li>
    <li>List Item 2</li>
    <li>List Item 3</li>
</ul>
<button>Button 1</button>
<span class="span-element">Span 1</span>
</body>
</html>
```

2. To select any of these elements, use the jQuery's $ () function. We can use this function in conjunction with an identifier or CSS selector for an element we would like to select; for example, its HTML tag li and ID #content or a class .content.

Downloading the example code

You can download the example code files for all Packt books you have purchased from your account at http://www.packtpub.com. If you purchased this book elsewhere, you can visit http://www.packtpub.com/support and register to have the files e-mailed directly to you.

How it works...

The simplest method of selecting a DOM element is by its ID. We know that all IDs within a HTML document should be unique; therefore, by selecting an element with its ID, you will be selecting a single element.

In reference to the preceding HTML document, if you wanted to select <div>, which has an ID content, you can use the following jQuery code to select it:

```
$(function(){
    var content = $('#content');
});
```

This would make the DOM element available within the content variable. More on what this means is covered later in the chapter.

Any code within $ (function() { }); will be automatically executed by jQuery when the page is loaded.

We can also select elements in the same way using their class. The code is very similar to the preceding example, except that we use the class prefix (.) instead of the ID prefix (#), illustrated as follows:

```
$(function(){
    var span = $('.span-element');
});
```

Not only can we select elements based on some identifier we specify (that is, class or ID), but we can also select elements based on their tag name. If you wanted to select all the li elements within a page, you would use $('li'), illustrated as follows:

```
$(function(){
    var listelements = $('li');
    var i = 1;
    listelements.each(function(){
        console.log("Loop: " + i);
        i++;
    });
});
```

The preceding example uses the jQuery selector to select all the list elements within the page. To demonstrate that listelements now contains multiple elements, we loop through these and output some information to the console.

 .each() is a jQuery function. Learn more about its uses in *Chapter 3, Loading and Manipulating Dynamic Content with AJAX and JSON*.

The console output for the preceding example is as follows:

```
Loop: 1
Loop: 2
Loop: 3
```

 You can access the JavaScript console in various ways depending on your choice of browser:

- **Chrome**: *Ctrl + Shift + J* (**Mac**: *command + option + J*)
- **Internet Explorer**: *F12*
- **Firefox**: *Ctrl + Shift + K*

There's more...

It is also possible to select elements based on other properties such as their `rel` or `disabled` attributes.

The following code shows us how we can select an anchor element that has a `rel` attribute of `nofollow`:

```
$(function(){
    var nofollow = $('a[rel="nofollow"]');
});
```

See also

> ▸ *Finding and selecting sibling elements*

Finding and selecting sibling elements

You may not always know the specific element that you need to select. You may only know its parent, and therefore, you will need to search through the elements within the parent in order to find the specific element that you are looking for. This recipe will show you how to find elements through their parents in various ways.

Getting ready

Open your text editor or IDE with the latest version of jQuery, ready to be included into the HTML page that you will create as part of this recipe.

How to do it...

To learn the various ways in which jQuery can help you to search for DOM elements based on a parent element, perform each of the following steps:

1. Create a web page with the following HTML and JavaScript code:

```
<!DOCTYPE html>
<html>
<head>
    <title>Finding and selecting sibling elements</title>
    <script src="jquery.min.js"></script>
    <script>
        $(function(){
            var element1 = $('#content .top .top-left'); //Select the
top left division element
```

```
            var element2 = $('.parent').find('a'); //Select the
    anchor element
            var element3 = $('.parent').find('.grandchild');
                //Select the grandchild element
        });
    </script>
</head>
<body>
<div class="division-container">Some text <span>within</span> a
div <span>which</span> has a many <span>span</span> elements.</
div>
<div id="content">
    <div class="top">
        <div class="top-left">Left</div>
        <div class="top-right">Right</div>
    </div>
</div>
<ul class="info-list">
    <li>List Item 1</li>
    <li>List Item 2</li>
    <li>List Item 3</li>
</ul>
<ul class="second-info-list">
    <li>Second List Item 1</li>
    <li>Second List Item 2</li>
    <li>Second List Item 3</li>
</ul>
<div class="parent">
    <div class="child">
        <div class="grandchild">
            <a href="#">A Link</a>
        </div>
    </div>
</div>
</body>
</html>
```

2. This code uses multiple class names in the same way as you would use them with CSS to select child elements from HTML. Alternatively, you can use jQuery's `find()` function on a parent element to search within.

How it works...

The simplest way to select a child element based on its parent is by using the same selectors as you would in CSS (that is, `.classname .anotherclass`). Having said this, you do not always know the exact location of the sibling element you are looking for. If this is the case, we can use the useful jQuery's `find()` function. jQuery's `find()` function will search within the specified parent element for the sibling element that you are looking for.

Based on the HTML within the *How to do it...* section, the following JavaScript illustrates how you can access a child element directly in the same manner as you would in CSS:

```
$(function(){
    var element1 = $('#content .top .top-left');
});
```

This would make the DOM element available within the `content` variable. More on what this means is covered later in the chapter.

To find a child element without knowing its exact location, we can use the following JavaScript to locate the anchor within the `<div class="grandchild">` element:

```
$(function(){
    var element2 = $('.parent').find('a');
});
```

Note that you only need to specify the parent selector and the element you are looking for. The `find()` method simply traverses the DOM based on the specified parent element until it either finds the element you are looking for or runs out of elements to check against. You can use ID and class names within the `find()` method as well as HTML notations.

There's more...

You can also use CSS3 selectors such as `:first-child` and `:last-child` within `$()` to help you select the required DOM element.

See also

- ▶ *Selecting elements*

Creating DOM elements

To create rich and interactive user interfaces, we need to be able to dynamically add DOM elements to a web page. Elements may need to be added to a web page based on user interaction or another event such as page load.

Getting ready

For this recipe, you are going to need another blank HTML file. Create a new HTML file named `recipe-3.html` within the same directory as the one used for the previous recipe's files.

How to do it...

Learn how to create DOM elements with jQuery by performing the following steps:

1. Add the following HTML code to your `recipe-3.html` file in order to create a basic HTML page with an unordered list and include the jQuery library:

```
<!DOCTYPE html>
<html>
<head>
    <title>Creating DOM elements</title>
    <script src="jquery.min.js"></script>
    <script></script>
</head>
<body>
<div id="container">
    <ul id="myList">
        <li>List Item 1</li>
        <li>List Item 2</li>
        <li>List Item 3</li>
    </ul>
</div>
</body>
</html>
```

2. Add the following JavaScript within the script tags in the head of the HTML document. The following JavaScript code will add two buttons to the DOM after the `#myList` element utilizes jQuery's `after()` and `insertAfter()` functions:

```
$(function(){
    $('#myList').after("<button>Button 1</button>");
    $('<button>Button 2</button>').insertAfter("#myList");
});
```

How it works...

To dynamically add DOM elements to any part of the document, we can use the `append()`, `addAfter()`, `after()`, `addBefore()`, and `before()` functions of jQuery. The functions `after()` and `insertAfter()` essentially perform the same action; the difference lies in the order in which the expressions are specified. This is the same for `insertBefore()` and `before()`.

Based on the HTML file in the *How to do it...* section, the following JavaScript will add two button elements after the unordered list element:

```
$(function(){
    $('#myList').after("<button>Button 1</button>");
    $('<button>Button 2</button>').insertAfter("#myList");
});
```

Once the preceding JavaScript has been executed, the HTML rendered in the browser should be modified as follows:

```
<!DOCTYPE html>
<html>
<head>
    <title> Creating DOM elements</title>
    </head>
<body>
<div id="container">
    <ul id="myList">
        <li>List Item 1</li>
        <li>List Item 2</li>
        <li>List Item 3</li>
    </ul>
        <button>Button 2</button>
        <button>Button 1</button>
</div>
</body>
</html>
```

Note that even though the second button was added last, it is first in the HTML. This is because we have specified that the button should be inserted after the unordered list element. Both `.before()` and `.insertBefore()` jQuery methods work exactly in the same way, except that the button elements would be above the unordered list element.

A common requirement of dynamic web pages and web applications is to be able to add new items to a list. This is best achieved using the `.append()` function:

```
$(function(){
    $('#myList').append("<li>List Item 4</li>");
});
```

This JavaScript will add the new list item with the text `List Item 4` to the bottom of the `#myList` unordered list element. Alternatively, the `prepend()` function could be used to insert the list item at the top of the list.

There's more...

jQuery provides developers with many ways to add, append, insert, and update elements into the DOM that could not be demonstrated within a single recipe. Ensure that you are aware of the alternatives by reading the jQuery documentation.

See also

 ▸ *Inserting content into an element*
 ▸ *Removing DOM elements*
 ▸ *Re-using DOM elements*

Inserting content into an element

Interactive and dynamic web applications and websites not only require the web developer to be able to create DOM elements but also require the developer to be able to add dynamic content. This is easily achievable with another set of jQuery functions.

Getting ready

Create a blank HTML document named `recipe-4.html`, and ensure that you have the latest version of jQuery available to be included within this HTML document.

How to do it...

Learn how to dynamically add content into the DOM by performing each of the following steps:

1. Add the following code to your newly created HTML document, which will create a simple HTML web page:

```
<!DOCTYPE html>
<html>
```

```
<head>
    <title>Insert content into an element</title>
    <script src="jquery.min.js"></script>
    <script>

    </script>
</head>
<body>
<div id="container">
    <p>Here is some current HTML content</p>
</div>
<textarea id="myTextarea"></textarea>
</body>
</html>
```

2. Insert the following JavaScript code within the script tags in the document head. This code will inject different HTML content and elements into the DOM at various points.

```
$(function(){
    //Remove the container elements current HTML
    $('#container').html("<p>I have replaced the all the HTML
within the #container element</p>");

    //Add some more HTML to the beginning of the container element
    $('#container').prepend("<p>Another paragraph that has been
prepended.</p>");

    //Add a button to the end of the container element after all
other HTML content
    $('#container').append("<button>A Button Appended</button>");

    //Add some text into the text area element
    $('#myTextarea').val("Added some text using .text()");
});
```

How it works...

The quickest way to add content to an element is to use the `html()` function. By providing this function with a string as an argument, it will replace the selected element's current DOM contents with the provided string. If no string is provided, this function will return the element's DOM contents formatted as an HTML string.

Besides replacing the content of an element, we can also use `append()` and `prepend()` to add additional content at the end and at the beginning of the current content, respectively. Additionally, we have other functions available such as `text()`, which will decode any HTML before it inserts the string within the element. The `text()` function is typically used for text areas for this reason.

Based on the HTML provided in the previous section, we can alter the content of the `#container` element using the jQuery functions previously discussed as follows:

```
$(function(){
$('#container').html("<p>I have replaced the all the HTML within
    the #container element</p>");

$('#container').prepend("<p>Another paragraph that has been
    prepended.</p>");

$('#container').append("<button>A Button Appended</button>");

$('#myTextarea').val("Added some text using .text()");
});
```

After each of these functions has been executed, the HTML file rendered by the browser will be transformed, which is illustrated as follows:

```
<!DOCTYPE html>
<html>
<head>
    <title>Insert content into an element</title>
</head>
<body>
<div id="container">
    <p>Another paragraph that has been prepended.</p><p>I have
        replaced the all the HTML within the #container element</p>
    <button>A Button Appended</button>
</div>
<textarea id="myTextarea">Added some text using .text()</textarea>
</body>
</html>
```

See also

▸ *Creating DOM elements*

Modifying the DOM element properties

We can use jQuery to dynamically modify element properties such as class, style, and disabled, which means that it is possible to visually alter and change the function of a range of HTML elements.

Getting ready

Once again, this recipe requires an additional blank HTML document. Create a file named `recipe-5.html`, and have it open and ready for editing.

How to do it...

Learn how to alter the properties of the DOM element by performing each of the following steps:

1. Add the following HTML code to your blank `recipe-5.html` file in order to create a basic HTML page with two types of inputs:

```
<!DOCTYPE html>
<html>
<head>
    <title>Modifying DOM element attributes and properties</title>
    <script src="jquery.min.js"></script>
    <script>

    </script>
</head>
<body>
<input type="checkbox" />
<input type="text" />
</body>
</html>
```

2. Within the preceding HTML code, add the following JavaScript code inside the script tags to disable the input, modify its value, and check the checkbox:

```
$(function(){
    //Set the checkbox to be checked
    $('input[type="checkbox"]').prop('checked', true);
    //Disable any text inputs
    $('input[type="text"]').prop('disabled', true);
    //Change the value of any text inputs
    $('input[type="text"]').val("This is a new Value!");
});
```

How it works...

jQuery provides us with a `prop()` function that will either retrieve the specified property if no value is specified, or if a value is provided, it will alter the specified property on the selected element. This can be used to change property values such as `checked` on a checkbox or the `disabled` property on a text input. We could use the `prop()` function to alter the value of a text input; however, it is preferable to use the `val()` function that is available specifically for this task.

Typically, this would be done based on a user-triggered event, but to illustrate this as simply as possible, the following JavaScript does so on page load:

```
$(function(){
    $('input[type="checkbox"]').prop('checked', true);
});
```

This JavaScript will check each input within the page that is of the type `checkbox`. Similarly, we can alter the disabled state of a text input with only a few modifications:

```
$(function(){
    $('input[type="text"]').prop('disabled', true);
});
```

We can also use the `val()` function to add some text to each of these text inputs using the following JavaScript:

```
$(function(){
    $('input[type="text"]').val("This is a new Value!");
});
```

Often, you can chain functions with jQuery. You can achieve the previous two actions by using both the functions inline (that is, `$('input[type="text"]').prop('disabled', true).val("This is a new Value!");`), and they will be executed in turn.

See also

> ▸ *Enabling and disabling buttons by changing their properties*
> ▸ *Adding and removing CSS classes to dynamically change their style*

Adding and removing CSS classes to dynamically change their style

jQuery comes bundled with class manipulation functions in order to allow developers to easily alter the style of any HTML element.

Getting ready

For element style changes to be of any use, we first need to declare some styles within an HTML document. The following HTML code has a range of styles and elements that we can work with to illustrate this functionality of jQuery:

```html
<!DOCTYPE html>
<html>
<head>
    <title>Add and remove CSS classes to dynamically change their
        style</title>
    <script src="jquery.min.js"></script>
    <script></script>
    <style type="text/css">
        .green {
            background-color: #008000;
            color: #FFFFFF;
        }
        .red {
            background-color: #FF0000;
            color: #FFFFFF;
        }
        .yellow {
            background-color: #FFFF00;
            color: #000000;
        }
    </style>
</head>
<body>
    <p id="sometext">
        Here is some text that can have different styles applied to
            it dynamically</p>
    <button id="green-btn">Green</button>
    <button id="red-btn">Red</button>
    <button id="yellow-btn">Yellow</button>
</body>
</html>
```

Within this HTML code, we have three buttons with their own unique IDs. We also have a paragraph with an ID. There are three CSS classes defined: green, red, and yellow. With jQuery, we can listen for the click of either of these buttons and then dynamically apply one of these classes to the paragraph element.

If you save this HTML file and open it within a browser, you should have the following web page:

Here is some text that can have different styles applied to it dynamically

| Green | Red | Yellow |

How to do it...

1. Add the following JavaScript code within the script tags in the HTML page you have just created:

```
$(function(){
    //Listen for a click event on the green button
$('#green-btn').click(function(){
    //When the green button has been clicked
    //Remove all classes current on the #sometext paragraph
    $('#sometext').removeClass();
    //Add the .green class to the #sometext paragraph
    $('#sometext').addClass('green');
});
    //Listen for a click on the red button
$('#red-btn').click(function(){
    //When the red button has been clicked
    //Remove all classes from the #sometext paragraph
    $('#sometext').removeClass();
    //Add the .red class to the #sometext paragraph
    $('#sometext').addClass('red');
    });
    //Listen for a click on the yellow button
$('#yellow-btn').click(function(){
        //When the yellow button has been clicked
        //Remove all classes from the #sometext paragraph
    $('#sometext').removeClass();
    //Add the .yellow class to the #sometext paragraph
    $('#sometext').addClass('yellow');
    });
});
```

2. Opening the HTML document in your browser will now allow you to change the #sometext paragraph style by selecting either of the three available buttons.

How it works...

jQuery allows us to attach a click event handler to any element by using the `click()` function. We can then execute a set of code of our choice by passing a function as an argument to the `click()` method. To add a class to an element, we can use the `addClass()` function and provide the class name as a string argument. This function will add the specified class name to the selected element.

jQuery also provides us with a `removeClass()` function. This allows us to either remove a specific class from an element by providing `removeClass()` with a string, or when a string is not provided, it will remove all the classes from the selected element. We will need to use this in order to prevent multiple classes being added to the paragraph element when either of the buttons has been clicked more than once.

The following screenshot illustrates this web page after the **Yellow** button has been clicked:

Here is some text that can have different styles applied to it dynamically

Green   Red   Yellow

See also

▸ *Modifying the DOM element properties*

▸ *Enabling and disabling buttons by changing their properties*

Enabling and disabling buttons by changing their properties

The ability to dynamically enable and disable buttons is particularly useful for situations such as saving data to a web server. In order to prevent a user from making multiple save requests while the request is being made and the client is waiting for a response, you can dynamically disable the save button. Once the client has received a response from the web server, you can re-enable the save button.

This functionality can also be very effective in simple situations, such as enabling the search button when the user has inputted a search term. This makes it clear to the user that they cannot search unless a term has been entered.

Getting ready

Create a blank HTML document named `recipe-7.html`, and have it open and ready for editing.

How to do it...

1. The following HTML code creates a web page with a search input and a search button, which is disabled by default. Add the following code to `recipe-7.html`:

    ```html
    <!DOCTYPE html>
    <html>
    <head>
        <title>Enable and disable buttons by changing their
            properties </title>
        <script src="jquery.min.js"></script>
        <script>

        </script>
    </head>
    <body>
        <input type="text" id="search-input" />
        <button id="search-btn" disabled>Search</button>
    </body>
    </html>
    ```

2. Saving and opening this HTML in a browser should provide you with a very simple web page having a single input and a disabled button as illustrated in the following screenshot:

3. Add the following JavaScript within the script tags in the head section of the HTML document created previously:

    ```javascript
    $(function(){
        //Listen for a key up event on the search input
        $('#search-input').keyup(function(){
            //When a user presses and releases a key
            //Check to see if the length of the inputted
            //data is greater than 2
            if ($(this).val().length > 2) {
                //If the input length is greater than
    ```

```
            //two then we enable the search button
            $('#search-btn').prop("disabled", false);
    } else {
            //If the input length is equal to 2 or less we
                disable the search button
            $('#search-btn').prop("disabled", true);
    }
});
});
```

4. Opening this page within a web browser will provide you with an input and a disabled search button until you enter some text into the search input. When text is entered into the search input and the length of the text is greater than two characters, the search button will become available.

How it works...

Our aim is to enable the search button once there has been some text inputted into the search input by the user. To do this, we need to attach a `.keyup()` event handler to the search input. This will allow us to execute some code while the user is inputting some text. By providing a function as an argument to the `keyup()` function, we can then check the inputted data. If the input data has a length of two or more characters (as a search less than three characters would be a little ambiguous), we can enable the search button.

Using the following JavaScript, we are able to listen for data input, check the input length, and depending on this, enable or disable the search button:

```
$(function(){
$('#search-input').keyup(function(){
    if ($(this).val().length > 2) {
        $('#search-btn').prop("disabled", false);
    } else {
    $('#search-btn').prop("disabled", true);
    }
});
});
```

First of all, we attach the `keyup` event to the search input using `$('#search-input').keyup();`, referencing its ID. Then, within the callback function, we are able to check the length of the currently inputted text using `$(this)`, which refers to the element to which we have attached the `keyup` event. The `val()` function then gets the inputted text, and we can use the `length` property to find its length. Using an `if/else` statement, we can decide if the search button needs to be enabled or disabled.

To enable or disable the search button, we use jQuery's `prop()` function and set the disabled property to either `true` or `false`.

See also

▸ *Modifying the DOM element properties*

▸ *Adding and removing CSS classes to dynamically change their style*

Updating an image within a page

jQuery allows the developer to dynamically change images on a web page. This recipe will show you how to do this and also show you how to use a timestamp in order to prevent the browser from using a cached image, which can often be a problem when swapping images dynamically in this way.

Getting ready

For this recipe, you are going to need four different images. Ensure that you have four small images named black.png, red.png, blue.png, and green.png available.

How to do it...

To understand how jQuery can be used to change an image, complete each of the following steps:

1. Create a file named recipe-8.html within an easily accessible directory, and add the following HTML code to this file:

```html
<!DOCTYPE html>
<html>
<head>
    <title>Change an image source and tackle browser caching
        to ensure it is always updated</title>
    <script src="jquery.min.js"></script>
    <script>

    </script>
</head>
<body>
    <img src="images/black.png" id="square" />
    <div>
        <button id="red-btn">Red</button>
        <button id="green-btn">Green</button>
        <button id="blue-btn">Blue</button>
    </div>
</body>
</html>
```

2. Within the directory where the `recipe-8.html` file is created, create another directory called `images` and within this, add four images given as follows:

   ❑ `black.png`

   ❑ `red.png`

   ❑ `blue.png`

   ❑ `green.png`

3. Add the following JavaScript within the `<script></script>` tags of `recipe-8.html`:

```
$(function(){
    //Listen for a click on the red button
$('#red-btn').click(function(){
    //When the red button has been clicked, change the source of
the #square image to be the red PNG
    $('#square').prop("src", "images/red.png");
});
    //Listen for a click on the green button
$('#green-btn').click(function(){
    //When the green button has been clicked, change the source of
the #square image to be the green PNG
    $('#square').prop("src", "images/green.png");
});
//Listen for a click on the blue button
$('#blue-btn').click(function(){
    //When the blue button has been clicked, change the source of
the #square image to be the blue PNG
    $('#square').prop("src", "images/blue.png");
});
});
```

4. Opening this web page within a browser will allow you to change the source of the displayed image from the default `black.png` to another source depending on which button is clicked.

How it works...

To change the source of an image, we can use jQuery's `prop()` function and specify the new image name for the `src` property. To do this, when either of the buttons created using our HTML code are clicked, a click event handler is attached for each button using `.click()`, referencing the buttons' IDs, and then within the `click()` callback function, `.prop()` is executed with the appropriate image source specified, shown as follows:

```
$(function(){
$('#red-btn').click(function(){
```

```
    $('#square').prop("src", "images/red.png");
});

$('#green-btn').click(function(){
    $('#square').prop("src", "images/green.png");
});

$('#blue-btn').click(function(){
    $('#square').prop("src", "images/blue.png");
});
});
```

There's more...

This recipe illustrates the way a jQuery developer can easily change an image's source using a very simple example. A more realistic situation where this implementation will be used is within a web application where an image can be uploaded, for example, when a user chooses their avatar.

Traditionally, a user will be presented with a preview of their current avatar and then be able to choose an image from their computer to upload. Using AJAX, the web page can send this new image to the server; the server can then process and save this image and respond to the client web page. The web page, using jQuery's prop() method, can then update the current preview with the newly uploaded image and create a seamless transition without the need for the page to be refreshed in order to display the new image.

A problem occurs when the server uses the same filename for the new image as the old one. This is often the case when a user can only have one avatar; for the sake of simplicity, the avatar image is then saved using the user's unique ID (for example, 123.png).

When the server responds to the client with the new image filename, as the filename is the same, the browser will think that it is the same image. This may cause the browser to use the cached version of the avatar image, which will be the old image. To prevent this from happening, we can prepend a timestamp onto the image's filename. This will make the browser treat the image as new and force it to load the new image. We can modify the previous JavaScript to achieve the following:

```
$(function(){
$('#red-btn').click(function(){
    $('#square').prop("src", "images/red.png?t=" + new Date().
getTime());
});

$('#green-btn').click(function(){
    $('#square').prop("src", "images/green.png?t=" + new Date().
getTime());
```

```
    });

    $('#blue-btn').click(function(){
        $('#square').prop("src", "images/blue.png?t=" + new Date().
    getTime());
    });
});
```

Using JavaScript's `new Date()` method, we create a new date that will be equal to the current date and time equal to the current time in milliseconds. We then use `.getTime()` to return a timestamp in milliseconds. When the source is updated, it will look as follows:

```
<img src="images/red.png?t=1371992012690" id="square">
```

This code will force the browser to reload the image using the newly specified source, provided the user does not update their image within the same millisecond (practically impossible).

Populating list elements

List elements are commonly used around the Web; they can be used to display search results, menus, and navigational items to name a few. Thanks to CSS, they no longer need to be boring, and it is possible to style list elements to make your data beautiful.

With jQuery, it is possible to populate a list element dynamically. This can be done directly from a JavaScript array via an AJAX response, with data from a web server or some other source.

Getting ready

Create a blank HTML document named `recipe-9.html`, and ensure that it is saved to a location where the latest version of jQuery can be included.

How to do it...

Learn how to dynamically populate a list with jQuery by performing each of the following recipes:

1. In order to demonstrate how you can use jQuery to populate a list element, we will create a JavaScript array of objects. Add the following HTML and JavaScript code to `recipe-9.html`, which you have just created:

```
<!DOCTYPE html>
<html>
<head>
    <title>Populating list elements</title>
    <script src="jquery.min.js"></script>
```

```
<script type="text/javascript">
    var names = [
        {
            id: 1,
            firstname: 'Leon',
            lastname: 'Revill'
        },
        {
            id: 2,
            firstname: 'Allyce',
            lastname: 'Wolverson'
        },
        {
            id: 3,
            firstname: 'Harry',
            lastname: 'Round'
        },
        {
            id: 4,
            firstname: 'Chris',
            lastname: 'Wilshaw'
        }
    ];
    $(function(){

    });
</script>
</head>
<body>
    <ul id="namelist"></ul>
</body>
</html>
```

 At the top of our JavaScript code, we have created an array of objects which includes a set of names. We are going to use this array to populate the list element #namelist within the HTML code.

2. Add the following JavaScript within `$(function(){});`, just under the JavaScript array. This JavaScript will use the objects within the JavaScript array we created in the *Getting ready* section to populate the list element on our page.

```
$.each(names, function(index, obj){
$('#namelist').append("<li>#" + obj.id + " " +
    obj.firstname + " " + obj.lastname + "</li>");
});
```

How it works...

We use jQuery's `$.each()` function to loop through each of the JavaScript objects within the `names` array. Then, for each of these objects, we can create a `<li>` element and insert the values of the `id`, `firstname`, and `lastname` variables. Finally, we can use the jQuery `append()` function to append the list element to the end of the unordered list.

Within the `$.each()` function, the first parameter is the array we wish to iterate through and the second parameter is the function we wish to execute for each of the objects within the `names` array. The specified function also has two arguments: `index` and `obj`. The `index` argument will contain the current array index of the JavaScript object, and the `obj` variable will contain the actual JavaScript object. Both these variables are available within the specified callback function.

We are then able to reference `obj.propertyName` (replace `propertyName` with a property of the object) in order to access specific parts of the object we wish to use. By doing this, we construct a string and pass it to the `append()` function, which then appends it to the specified `#nameslist` unordered list.

Open the HTML page within the browser, and you should see the list populated with the names from the JavaScript array, illustrated as follows:

- #1 Leon Revill
- #2 Allyce Wolverson
- #3 Harry Round
- #4 Chris Wilshaw

See also

- ▶ *Creating DOM elements*
- ▶ *Re-using DOM elements*

Understanding pagination

Pagination is the act of collating large amounts of data and presenting it to the user in small, easy-to-read sections or pages.

With a combination of jQuery, JavaScript functions, and event handlers, we are able to easily collate and present data to the user in pages.

Getting ready

To create a paginated set of data, we first need some data to paginate and then a location to place the paginated data. Use the following code to create an HTML page:

```
<!DOCTYPE html>
<html>
<head>
    <title>Chapter 1 :: DOM Manipulation</title>
    <script src="jquery.min.js"></script>
    <script>
        var animals = [
            {
                id: 1,
                name: 'Dog',
                type: 'Mammal'
            },
            {
                id: 2,
                name: 'Cat',
                type: 'Mammal'
            },
            {
                id: 3,
                name: 'Goat',
                type: 'Mammal'
            },
            {
                id: 4,
                name: 'Lizard',
                type: 'Reptile'
            },
            {
                id: 5,
                name: 'Frog',
                type: 'Amphibian'
            },
            {
                id: 6,
                name: 'Spider',
                type: 'Arachnid'
            },
            {
                id: 7,
```

```
                name: 'Crocodile',
                type: 'Reptile'
            },
            {
                id: 8,
                name: 'Tortoise',
                type: 'Reptile'
                },
                {
                    id: 9,
                    name: 'Barracuda',
                    type: 'Fish'
                },
                {
                    id: 10,
                    name: 'Sheep',
                    type: 'Mammal'
                },
                {
                    id: 11,
                    name: 'Lion',
                    type: 'Mammal'
                },
                {
                    id: 12,
                    name: 'Seal',
                    type: 'Mammal'
                }
            ];
        var pageSize = 4;
        var currentPage = 1;
        var pagedResults = [];
        var totalResults = animals.length;
        $(function(){
    });
    </script>
</head>
<body>
    <ul id="list"></ul>
    <button class="previous"><< Previous</button>
    <button class="next">Next >></button>
</body>
</html>
```

Within the JavaScript in this page, we have declared a large array of objects named `animals`, which represents a set of animals. Below this array, we have declared four more variables, which we will require in order to paginate the `animals` array:

- ▶ `pageSize`: This indicates the amount of results we wish to be held on a single page
- ▶ `currentPage`: This indicates the current page that is being displayed
- ▶ `pagedResults`: This indicates an array that contains a section of the `animals` array, which represents the page
- ▶ `totalResults`: This indicates the number of objects within the `animals` array; in this case, `12`

How to do it...

To create a dynamic list with pages, perform each of the following steps:

1. Directly after `$(function(){})`; but still within the `<script></script>` tags, add the following JavaScript function:

```
function updateList() {
//Grab the required section of results from the animals
    list
var end = (currentPage * pageSize);
var start = (end - pageSize);
pagedResults = animals.slice(start, end);
//Empty the list element before repopulation
$('#list').empty();

//Disable the previous button if we are on the first page
if (currentPage <= 1) {
    $('.previous').prop("disabled", true);
}
//Enable the previous button if we are not on the first
    page
else {
    $('.previous').prop("disabled", false);
}

//Disable the next button if there are no more pages
if ((currentPage * pageSize) >= totalResults) {
    $('.next').prop("disabled", true);
}
//Enable the next button if there are results left to page
else {
```

```
    $('.next').prop("disabled", false);
}

//Loop through the pages results and add them to the list
$.each(pagedResults, function(index, obj){
    $('#list').append("<li><strong>" + obj.name + "</strong> (" +
obj.type + ")</li>");
});
}
```

2. Add the following JavaScript within $(function(){}); in the preceding HTML page:

```
//Populate the list on load
updateList();
$('.next').click(function(){
//Only increase the current page if there are enough results
if ((currentPage * pageSize) <= totalResults) currentPage++;
updateList();
});

$('.previous').click(function(){
//Only decrease the current page if it is currently greater than 1
if (currentPage > 1) currentPage--;
updateList();
});
```

How it works...

Although pagination can seem quite complicated, in principle, it is simple. We will need to use jQuery's click() function to listen for click events on the next and previous buttons. When these buttons are pressed, the currentPage variable is either incremented or decremented based on which button is clicked. After this, the updateList() function takes the currentPage value, works out which section of data it needs to use from the animals array, populates the pagedResults array with this data, and then loads these results into the HTML list element, #list.

Additionally, we will need to disable the next or previous buttons depending on which page the user is currently viewing. If they are currently viewing the first page, the previous button can be disabled using jQuery's prop() function to set its disabled property to true. If the user is viewing the last page (which our function can work out using the totalResults, currentPage, and pageSize variables), we need to disable the next button.

```
//Populate the list on load
updateList();
$('.next').click(function(){
```

```
//Only increase the current page if there are enough results
if ((currentPage * pageSize) <= totalResults) currentPage++;
updateList();
});

$('.previous').click(function(){
//Only decrease the current page if it is currently greater than 1
if (currentPage > 1) currentPage--;
updateList();
});
```

To expand on the well-commented code, the first thing we do is call a function named `updateList()`, which we will look at a little later in this recipe.

 Remember that any code within `$(function(){});` is executed on page load.

Next, we attach a click event handler to the next button by passing a callback function as an argument. For this event function, we are able to specify some code to be executed every time the next button is clicked. The code we specify increments the `currentPage` variable by 1. If there is another page of data available, it works this out by forming the `((currentPage * pageSize) <= totalResults)` condition as part of the `if` statement.

Finally, as a part of this click function, we call the previously mentioned `updateList()` function.

We apply the same logic to the previous button also, except that we are decrementing the `currentPage` value if the current page is greater than one; hence, there is a page to go back to.

Below `$(function(){});` but still within the `<script></script>` tags, add the following JavaScript function to your HTML page:

```
function updateList() {
//Grab the required section of results from the animals list
var end = (currentPage * pageSize);
var start = (end - pageSize);
pagedResults = animals.slice(start, end);
//Empty the list element before repopulation
$('#list').empty();

//Disable the previous button if we are on the first page
if (currentPage <= 1) {
    $('.previous').prop("disabled", true);
}
```

```
//Enable the previous button if we are not on the first page
else {
    $('.previous').prop("disabled", false);
}

//Disable the next button if there are no more pages
if ((currentPage * pageSize) >= totalResults) {
    $('.next').prop("disabled", true);
}
//Enable the next button if there are results left to page
else {
    $('.next').prop("disabled", false);
}

//Loop through the pages results and add them to the list
$.each(pagedResults, function(index, obj){
    $('#list').append("<li><strong>" + obj.name + "</strong> (" + obj.
type + ")</li>");
});
}
```

To maintain good practices, the code is well-commented once again. The first action that this function performs is calculating which section of the animals array it needs to use. Once it has calculated the start and end values, which are index values for the animals array (for example, 0 to 4 for page one), it uses JavaScript's slice() function to copy this data from the animals array to the pagedResults array.

Be careful to not use the similar, JavaScript's .splice() function as this will actually remove the data from the animals array as well as copy it to the pagedResults array. Additionally, slice() takes two arguments: the first is a zero-indexed number stating the start location of the array (that is, 0 is the beginning), and the second argument is not the location within the array but the number of elements from the starting point.

With the required results stored in the pagedResults array, it uses jQuery's empty() function to empty the unordered list, #list, of any data. This is to prepare the list for repopulation. Otherwise, when the next or previous button is clicked and the updateList() function is run, the results will just get appended to the end of the current list and not replaced.

The next section of code is to determine if the next and previous buttons need to be either disabled or enabled. We can work out whether the previous buttons need to be disabled by putting the condition (`currentPage <= 1`), which simply checks to see if the current page is less than or equal to one; if it is, we need to disable the previous button; otherwise, we need to enable it. This is done using jQuery's `prop()` function, which allows us to manipulate the properties on selected elements; here, we change the `disabled` property to either `true` or `false`. We can determine whether we need to disable the next button using ((`currentPage * pageSize`) `>=` `totalResults`), which calculates whether there are enough objects within the `animals` array to create the next page; if there are not, we disable the button, but if there are, we enable it.

Finally, we use jQuery's `$.each()` function to iterate through each of the objects within the `pagedResults` array and append a list element with the data from each object to the unordered list on the page.

If you open the HTML page within the browser, you should see a similar page to the one illustrated as follows:

- **Dog** (Mammal)
- **Cat** (Mammal)
- **Goat** (Mammal)
- **Lizard** (Reptile)

On page load, the list is populated with the first page of results, as `currentPage` is set to `1` and the `updateList()` function is also set to run on page load, which disables the previous button.

Removing DOM elements

jQuery makes it easy for the developer to completely remove DOM elements, which is often useful when creating rich user interfaces. Having the ability to remove elements is useful in situations where your interface represents some information from a database, and it provides a way for the user to delete database items. If this UI is using AJAX to send the delete request to the web server, you will need to reflect the delete action on the client side and remove the element representing the database item.

Getting ready

Create a blank HTML document, and save it as `recipe-11.html` to an easily accessible location on your computer.

How to do it...

Understand how to remove DOM elements using jQuery by performing each of the following steps:

1. Add the following HTML code to the `recipe-11.html` page you have just created:

```
<!DOCTYPE html>
<html>
<head>
    <title>Removing DOM elements</title>
    <script src="jquery.min.js"></script>
    <script>

    </script>
</head>
<body>
    <ul id="list">
        <li>Item 1 <button class="remove-btn">X</button></li>
        <li>Item 2 <button class="remove-btn">X</button></li>
        <li>Item 3 <button class="remove-btn">X</button></li>
        <li>Item 4 <button class="remove-btn">X</button></li>
    </ul>
</body>
</html>
```

2. Within the `<script></script>` tags of the previous HTML document, add the following JavaScript code:

```
$(function(){
//Listen for a click on any of the remove buttons
$('.remove-btn').click(function(){
    //When a remove button has been clicked
    //Select this buttons parent (the li element) and remove
        it
    $(this).parent().remove();
});
});
```

3. Open the HTML document in a browser and click on the remove button to remove the selected list item.

How it works...

jQuery provides us with a `remove()` function, which will remove the selected element from the DOM. In a situation as the one mentioned previously, you would have a list of items that represent the records within the database. Each of these list items would provide a remove button, allowing the user to delete the selected item.

In a real-world situation, this delete button would make an AJAX request to a web server, wait for the response, and then remove the selected element on the client side. To keep this recipe simple, we will just be looking at the JavaScript code to remove the element on the client side and will not be working with AJAX.

 Chapter 3, Loading and Manipulating Dynamic Content with AJAX and JSON, contains a wealth of AJAX recipes.

We can use jQuery's `click()` function to listen for a click event on one of the delete buttons. Then, we can use `$(this).parent()` to select the `<li>` element we wish to delete, because the delete button is a sibling of this list element. We can then use the `remove()` method with no arguments to remove the selected list element.

See also

- *Creating DOM elements*
- *Re-using DOM elements*

Re-using DOM elements

When using jQuery to dynamically create elements such as list items, divisions, and input, it can be useful to be able to re-use these elements without having to rewrite them within JavaScript. Instead, it may be beneficial to copy the elements and just modify the sections you wish to change.

Getting ready

Using the text editor of your choice, create a blank HTML document named `recipe-12.html`, which is within a location that has easy access to the latest version of jQuery.

How to do it...

Learn how to re-use DOM elements by performing each of the following recipe steps:

1. Within the `recipe-12.html` page you have just created, add the following HTML, CSS, and JavaScript code:

```
<!DOCTYPE html>
<html>
<head>
    <title>Reusing DOM elements</title>
    <style type="text/css">
        .one {
            background-color: #CCC;
            color: #333;
        }
        .two {
            background-color: lawngreen;
            color: white;
        }
        .three {
            background-color: darkgreen;
            color: white;
        }
        .four {
            background-color: black;
            color: #666;
        }
        .dinosaur {
            background-color: darkred;
            color: red;
        }
    </style>
    <script src="jquery.min.js"></script>
    <script>
        var animals = [
            {
                id: 1,
                name: 'Dog',
                type: 'Mammal',
                class: 'one'
            },
            {
                id: 2,
                name: 'Cat',
```

```
                  type: 'Mammal',
                  class: 'one'
               },
               {
                  id: 3,
                  name: 'Goat',
                  type: 'Mammal',
                  class: 'one'
               },
               {
                  id: 4,
                  name: 'Lizard',
                  type: 'Reptile',
                  class: 'two'
               },
               {
                  id: 5,
                  name: 'Frog',
                  type: 'Amphibian',
                  class: 'three'
               },
               {
                  id: 6,
                  name: 'Spider',
                  type: 'Arachnid',
                  class: 'four'
               }
          ];
          $(function(){

          });
      </script>
  </head>
  <body>
  <ul id="animal-list">
      <li class='dinosaur'><strong><span class='name'>T-
         Rex</span></strong> <span
         class='type'>Dinosaur</span></li>
  </ul>
  </body>
  </html>
```

2. Within the HTML page you created from the preceding code, add the following JavaScript within `$(function(){});`:

```
$.each(animals, function(index, obj){
//Clone the first element in the animal list
var listTemplate = $('#animal-list li').first().clone();
//Change its name to match this objects name
listTemplate.find('.name').html(obj.name);
//Changes its type to match this objects type
listTemplate.find('.type').html(obj.type);
//Remove all its current classes
listTemplate.removeClass();
//Add the class from this object
listTemplate.addClass(obj.class);
//Append the modified element to the end of the list
$('#animal-list').append(listTemplate);
});
```

3. If you open your newly created web page within a browser, you should be provided with a populated list element that matches the objects within the JavaScript array `animals`.

How it works...

By using jQuery's `$.each()` method, we are able to iterate through each of the objects within the JavaScript `animals` array. Then, for each of the JavaScript objects, we clone the first element in the unordered list using `$('#animal-list li').first().clone();` and store it within the `listTemplate` variable. This variable now holds a copy of the first list element within the unordered list `#animal-list`. We can now manipulate this element as we would do with any other DOM element. We are able to use jQuery's `find()` function to locate the span elements with the `.name` and `.type` class names. We can then alter their content to match the current object's name and type values. Next, we remove the previous styles on the cloned element with `removeClass()` (not providing an argument will remove all current classes without having to specify each one of them), and add the style that is specified within the JavaScript object using the `addClass()` function that jQuery provides us with. Finally, we can append the modified HTML element to the end of the list using `append()`.

See also

▶ *Removing DOM elements*
▶ *Creating DOM elements*

2
Interacting with the User by Making Use of jQuery Events

In this chapter, we will cover:

- ▶ Detecting button clicks
- ▶ Detecting element clicks
- ▶ Detecting change
- ▶ Updating content based on user input
- ▶ Detecting key press events on inputs
- ▶ Restricting input character length
- ▶ Changing page elements on mouse hover
- ▶ Triggering events manually
- ▶ Preventing event triggers
- ▶ Creating a custom event

Introduction

This chapter looks at how you can make use of jQuery's many events to allow your interface to respond to different user interactions, such as button clicks, and also how jQuery events can help you with form validation.

Detecting button clicks

Clicking on website elements is a primary user interaction; therefore, detecting these clicks is a very fundamental aspect in creating interactive web applications. There are various ways in which jQuery developers can listen for certain button presses within their web page.

Getting ready

Using your favorite text editor or IDE, create a blank HTML page named `recipe-1.html` in an easily accessible location.

How to do it...

Create two buttons with click event handlers by performing the following steps:

1. Add the following HTML code to `recipe-1.html`. Be sure to change the location of the jQuery library in the JavaScript file, pointing it to where the latest version of jQuery is downloaded on your computer.

```
<!DOCTYPE html>
<html>
<head>
    <title>Chapter 2 :: jQuery Events</title>
    <script src="jquery.min.js"></script>
    <script>

    </script>
</head>
<body>
    <button class="button1">Button 1</button>
    <button class="button2">Button 2</button>
</body>
</html>
```

2. Within the script tags, add the following JavaScript code, which attaches click event handlers to both of the button elements:

```
$(function() {
    $('.button1').click(function(){
    alert("Button 1 clicked");
    });
    $('body').on("click", ".button2", function(){
    alert("Button 2 clicked");
    });
});
```

3. Open `recipe-1.html` within a web page and click on either of the buttons. You will be presented with a different JavaScript alert for each button, demonstrating that the event handlers have been executed.

How it works...

We can use various selectors to select button elements and then attach event handlers to these elements. In the preceding example, we select the first button using its class name, `.button1`, and the second button using the class name `.button2`.

With each button selected via the `$()` method, we can choose a method for attaching a click event to our buttons. The `.click()` method, as shown in the following code snippet, is dedicated for this purpose. By passing a callback function as an argument, we can specify a set of commands to be executed once the buttons have been clicked.

```
$('.button1').click(function(){
    alert("Button 1 clicked");
});
```

The preceding code will display the specified alert once the first button has been clicked. The following code uses an alternative function, `.on()`, which also handles other event types:

```
$('body').on("click", ".button2", function(){
    alert("Button 2 clicked");
});
```

This method is a little different as we first select the container of our buttons and then specify the button identifier (that is, `.button2`).

There's more...

The `.on()` method has some additional benefits over `.click()` alongside the previously mentioned memory benefit. If any elements are added to the DOM dynamically after the `.click()` function has been called, they will not have a click event attached. If the `.on()` method is used, provided that the dynamically added elements are added within the specified container, they will be caught by the click event handler. Consider the following code as an example of this situation:

```
<!DOCTYPE html>
<html>
<head>
    <title>Chapter 2 :: jQuery Events</title>
    <script src="jquery.min.js"></script>
    <script>
        $(function(){
            $('.button1').click(function(){
```

```
                    alert("Button 1 clicked");
                });
                $('body').on("click", ".button2", function(){
                    alert("Button 2 clicked");
                });
                setTimeout(function(){
                    $('.additional').append("<button
class='button1'>Button 1 again</button>");
                    $('.additional').append("<button
class='button2'>Button 2 again</button>");
                }, 2000);
            });
        </script>
    </head>
    <body>
    <button class="button1">Button 1</button>
    <button class="button2">Button 2</button>
    <div class="additional"></div>
    </body>
    </html>
```

This code will attach an event handler to each of the buttons on page load using the
`.click()` and `.on()` methods, respectively. Then, using the `setTimeout()` function, it
will dynamically add two more buttons to the DOM; one button with the `.button1` class and
the other with the `.button2` class. If you open this web page in a browser and wait for the
second set of buttons to be created and then click on the additional **Button 1** button, no click
event will be fired. Click on the additional **Button 2** button, and you will see the alert box being
fired as desired.

See also

▸ *Detecting element clicks*

▸ *Detecting key press events on inputs*

Detecting element clicks

Having the ability to detect if a user has clicked on elements other than buttons can provide
additional flexibility to your web application. You can attach click events to any HTML
elements, just as we did with the buttons in the previous recipe.

Getting ready

To work through this recipe, we are first going to need a blank HTML page named `recipe-2.html`, the same as in the other recipes. Remember that you need to have the latest version of jQuery downloaded and easily accessible on your computer so that it can be included in `recipe-2.html`.

How to do it...

To understand how you can detect user clicks on elements other than buttons, perform the following steps:

1. Add the following HTML to the `recipe-2.html` page you have just created. This HTML creates a very basic web page with an input, an anchor, and a division element.

```
<!DOCTYPE html>
<html>
<head>
    <title>Chapter 2 :: jQuery Events</title>
    <script src="jquery.min.js"></script>
    <script>

    </script>
</head>
<body>
<a href="#">Link 1</a>
<input type="text" name="input1" />
<div class="clickme">Click Me!</div>
</body>
</html>
```

2. Within the script tags in the head tag of the HTML page we just created, add the following JavaScript code. This JavaScript code uses two different methods of attaching click event handlers to three DOM elements.

```
$(function() {
    $('a').click(function(){
    alert("You have clicked a link!");
    });
    $('body').on('click', 'input[type="text"]', function(){
    alert("You have clicked a text input!");
    });
    $('.clickme').click(function(){
    alert("You have clicked a division element");
    });
});
```

3. Ensure that all the changes have been saved and then open `recipe-2.html` in a browser. When you click on any of the elements, you will be presented with a different JavaScript alert, demonstrating that each of these click events are being caught by the event handlers we created earlier in the recipe.

How it works...

We can select DOM elements using their tag names, such as `a` to select a link, and then use the `.click()` or `.on()` functions to attach a click event handler, as shown in the following code snippet. We can also use the CSS selector `input[type="text"]` to select all text inputs on the page.

```
$('.clickme').click(function(){
  alert("You have clicked a division element");
});
```

The preceding jQuery code attaches a click event to each DOM element with the `.clickme` class. These elements can be any DOM elements such as divs, buttons, links, inputs, and text areas. This gives the jQuery developer the flexibility to be able to interpret user interactions across all page elements.

 See the *Detecting button clicks* recipe of this chapter to understand the difference between `.click()` and `.on()` and why `.on()` is the preferred implementation.

See also

- ► *Detecting button clicks*
- ► *Detecting key press events on inputs*

Detecting change

While creating dynamic and interactive websites and web applications, it is useful to know when a user has changed something on the page, such as the value of a selected input, a text input, or any other element that has a modifiable value.

Getting ready

Once more, create a new blank HTML document named `recipe-3.html`. Ensure that you have the latest version of jQuery downloaded, which can be included into this HTML file.

How to do it...

To learn how to attach change event handlers to various element types, perform the following steps:

1. Add the following HTML code to the HTML document you have just created, and update the reference to the jQuery library in order to ensure that the latest version of jQuery is being included into the page:

```html
<!DOCTYPE html>
<html>
<head>
    <title>Chapter 2 :: jQuery Events</title>
    <script src="jquery.min.js"></script>
    <script>

    </script>
</head>
<body>
<select id="names">
    <option value="Leon">Leon</option>
    <option value="Allyce">Allyce</option>
    <option value="Jane">Jane</option>
</select>
<input type="text" value="The large cat sat on the mat" id="cat"
/>
</body>
</html>
```

2. Within the script tags, add the following JavaScript code to attach change event handlers on the different elements:

```javascript
$(function(){
    $('#names').change(function(){
     var newValue = $(this).val();
     alert("Input value changed to: " + newValue);
    });
    $('#cat').change(function(){
     var newValue = $(this).val();
     alert("Input value changed to: " + newValue);
    });
});
```

3. Ensure that all the changes have been saved. Now, open `recipe-3.html` in a web browser; if you change the value of one of the elements on the page, you will be presented with an alert informing you of the change.

How it works...

Selecting each input element using `$()` and then using the `.change()` function to attach a change event handler allows us to specify the code to be executed once the user has changed the value of each input.

Within the callback function, which is provided to the `.change()` function as an argument, we can get the new value. Using `this`, which refers to the selected element, we can use `$(this).val()` to retrieve the newly chosen value and display it within an alert.

If you open the web page within a browser and change the selected input value to `Allyce`, an alert will be displayed similar to the one shown in the following screenshot:

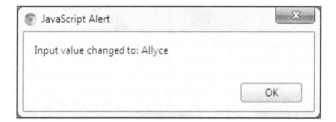

This is done using `.val()` to return the `value="Allyce"` property on the selected option in the drop-down input which has the change event handler attached.

When using the `.change()` event handler on a text input, this change event will not be fired until the input box has lost focus, that is, the user has clicked on another part of the web page. As it is often desirable to detect an immediate change, you should consider using a key press event to catch these changes instead.

There's more...

The *Detecting button clicks* recipe discussed the benefits of using the `.on()` method over using `.click()`. These benefits also apply in this situation as the `.on()` method can also be used with the change event. Consider the following code:

```
$('body').on("change", "#names", function(){
    var newValue = $(this).val();
    alert("Input value changed to: " + newValue);
});
```

- ▸ *Detecting button clicks*
- ▸ *Detecting key press events on inputs*
- ▸ *Updating content based on user input*

Updating content based on user input

jQuery allows developers to easily process user input and then update the page to reflect this input. The previous recipes of this chapter have looked at detecting changes on input values and clicks on various page elements. This recipe will help you to create a web page that will update a header element based on the title that has been selected from a drop-down menu.

Getting ready

Create a blank HTML document named `recipe-4.html`, with the latest version of the jQuery library downloaded and ready for use.

How to do it...

Using techniques similar to those you have learned in the previous recipes, perform the following steps to make changes to the DOM based on user interaction:

1. Add the following HTML code to `recipe-4.html`, which you have just created; don't forget to update the reference to the jQuery library. This HTML creates a basic HTML web page with a drop-down menu element, allowing the user to choose a number of titles. There is also a header element that we can manipulate with jQuery based on user selection.

```
<!DOCTYPE html>
<html>
<head>
    <title>Chapter 2 :: jQuery Events</title>
    <script src="jquery.min.js"></script>
    <script>

    </script>
</head>
<body>
<select id="title">
<option value="#">Select your title...</option>
    <option value="1">Title 1</option>
    <option value="2">Title 2</option>
```

```
            <option value="3">Title 3</option>
        </select>
        <h1 id="main-title">No Title</h1>
    </body>
</html>
```

2. Add the following JavaScript code within the script tags to attach a change event handler to the select input #title:

```
$(function(){
        $('#title').change(function(){
        var titleText = "";
        switch ($(this).val()) {
            case "1":
                    titleText = "This is the text for title 1";
                break;
            case "2":
                titleText = "This is the text for title 2";
                    break;
                case "3":
                    titleText = "This is the text for title 3";
                    break;
            default:
                titleText = "No Title";
        }
            $('#main-title').html(titleText);
        });
    });
```

3. Running this web page in a browser and selecting a new option from the drop-down menu will update the text of the header accordingly.

How it works...

First, we instruct jQuery to attach a change event handler to the #title select input using the following code:

```
$(function() {
    $('#title').change(function(){

    });
}
```

When the user changes the selected option in the drop-down input, the change event handler is executed.

In the `function` argument, we can use `$(this)` to refer to the `#title` select input and then use `$(this).val();` to get its selected value. Once we have this value, we can perform any action we require using JavaScript. In this example, we determine which title has been selected using a JavaScript `switch` statement, as shown in the following code snippet:

```
var titleText = "";
switch ($(this).val()) {
    case "1":
        titleText = "This is the text for title 1";
        break;
    case "2":
        titleText = "This is the text for title 2";
        break;
    case "3":
        titleText = "This is the text for title 3";
        break;
    default:
        titleText = "No Title";
}
```

Depending on the selected title value, we create some text which we then provide to `$('#main-title').html();`. This will update the `#main-title` header element's HTML to be the provided text.

This illustrates a very simple task of how a jQuery developer can process user input and perform an action to alter the page.

See also

▸ *Detecting change*

▸ *Changing page elements on mouse hover*

Detecting key press events on inputs

jQuery provides three event functions that allow the jQuery developer to determine what key a user is pressing, and when and how the user is pressing it. The `.keyup()` function is an event handler that can be attached to an input and will be fired once the pressed key has been fully released; likewise, `.keydown()` will be fired once the key has been fully pressed. The third available event handler is `.keypress()`, which is fired instantly when a key is pressed.

These methods allow the developer to provide powerful client-side validation or to provide the user with simple features such as triggering a form submission when the *Enter* key is pressed.

Getting ready

Create a blank HTML file named `recipe-5.html` which we can use for this recipe.

How to do it...

Use a variety of event handlers to detect user key press events by performing the following steps:

1. Add the following HTML code to the web page you have just created. Update the reference to the jQuery library to ensure that the latest version is being referenced into the web page. This HTML creates a simple page that has an input and an unordered list element, which we can use to output some event information in order to illustrate what each part of our jQuery code is achieving.

    ```html
    <!DOCTYPE html>
    <html>
    <head>
        <title>Chapter 2 :: jQuery Events</title>
        <script src="jquery.min.js"></script>
        <script>

        </script>
    </head>
    <body>
    <input type="text" class="myInput" />
    <ul id="myList"></ul>
    </body>
    </html>
    ```

2. Within the script tags, add the following JavaScript code to attach both the `keyup` and `keydown` event handlers:

    ```javascript
    $(function(){
        $('.myInput').keyup(function(){
          $('#myList').append("<li>Key up!</li>");
        });
        $('.myInput').keydown(function(event){
          $('#myList').append("<li>Key down!</li>");
          if (event.which == 13) {
            $('#myList').append("<li>Enter key pressed!</li>");
          }
        });
    });
    ```

How it works...

We can attach both the `keyup` and `keydown` event handlers by first selecting our `.myInput` element and then specifying one of the event handler functions as shown in the following code:

```
$('.myInput').keydown();
```

We have added an `event` variable as an argument to the callback function on the `keydown` event. From this `event` variable, we can detect which key has been pressed using `event.which`. This is often useful as we can determine whether the key that the user has just pressed down is the *Enter* key, which we would be likely to want to perform a specific action on, such as for form submission or when we want to trigger an AJAX call. In this example, we simply append a list item to our `#myList` unordered list to illustrate the concept.

We replicate this procedure within our `keyup` event handler and use the `.append()` function to append a new DOM element into the list.

Once you load this web page in a browser and enter text in the input box, you will be able to see the events trigger as the list element updates on every key press. You will be able to see something similar to the following screenshot:

There's more...

This recipe provides two examples with `keydown` and `keyup`. Try experimenting with the code, and use the alternative `keypress()` function in the same way to see how it works.

 ▸   *Detecting button clicks*

 ▸   *Detecting element clicks*

 ▸   *Restricting input character length*

 ▸   *Detecting change*

Restricting input character length

It is possible to limit the characters a user is able to input into a text field by utilizing jQuery's `keypress` events. In some situations, this can be a powerful user experience feature, as the user is visually aware of the characters that they cannot provide instead of having to wait for a response from the server informing them of this error.

Getting ready

Once again, we are going to need a blank HTML document with the latest version of jQuery to work through this recipe. Create `recipe-6.html` and ensure that you have jQuery downloaded and ready to go.

How to do it...

Learn how to restrict a user from entering certain characters into a text input using jQuery by performing the following steps:

1. Add the following HTML code to your newly created `recipe-6.html` file that creates a basic HTML web page with a single input element:

```
<!DOCTYPE html>
<html>
<head>
    <title>Chapter 2 :: jQuery Events</title>
    <script src="jquery.min.js"></script>
    <script>

    </script>
</head>
<body>
<input type="text" class="myInput" />
</body>
</html>
```

2. Within the script tags of the HTML page, add the following JavaScript code, which binds a `keypress` event handler to the input and prevents any nonalphanumeric character input in the selected text input:

```
$(function() {
    $('.myInput').keypress(function (event) {
        var regex = new RegExp("^[a-zA-Z0-9]+$");
        var key = String.fromCharCode(event.which);
        if (!regex.test(key)) {
            return false;
        }
    });
});
```

3. Open `recipe-6.html` in a browser and attempt to type a nonalphanumeric character into the input textbox; you will see that it is not possible to do so.

How it works...

We attach the `keypress` event handler to the `.myInput` element and specify the `event` variable as an argument as shown in the following code snippet:

```
$('.myInput').keypress(function (event) {

});
```

This allows us to specify commands to be executed on `keypress` when the `.myInput` field has focus.

We declare a regular expression variable which we can use to evaluate whether the entered character is alphanumeric.

```
var regex = new RegExp("^[a-zA-Z0-9]+$");
```

Each key on the keyboard has a unique numeric code that can be accessed using `event.which`. Then, to determine if the key pressed is alphanumeric, we need to retrieve its string value (for example, alphanumeric value for f is 102), which can be done with the following code:

```
var key = String.fromCharCode(event.which);
```

This now allows us to apply the regular expression and determine if it meets our alphanumeric requirements. If it does not, we prevent such key value from being entered by returning `false` as follows:

```
if (!regex.test(key)) {
    return false;
}
```

We allow the character to be displayed in the textbox if the pressed key was a valid alphanumeric character.

There's more...

It is important to understand that client-side validation such as this is a powerful user experience feature, but it should never be solely relied upon. Any validation done on the client side should always be mirrored on the server. This is because it is extremely easy for a user to bypass client-side validation. It is often as easy as turning off JavaScript from the browser settings. Remember that any client-side language such as JavaScript is completely open to manipulation by the end user. For this reason, client-side validation should only be used as a user experience enhancement and never a form of explicit validation of data input.

See also

▸   *Detecting key press events on inputs*

Changing page elements on mouse hover

jQuery provides many ways to bind mouse event handlers that can give the jQuery developer more control and flexibility than CSS pseudo classes such as `:hover`. These event handlers make it possible to create a rich and interactive user experience based on user actions.

 With the release of jQuery 2.0, jQuery no longer officially supports earlier browsers such as IE6, IE7, and IE8. However, methods such as `.hover()` can still provide benefits that will allow you to support earlier versions of browsers. Be wary, however, that some parts of the jQuery library may no longer work.

Getting ready

To demonstrate the mouse hover event, we need to firstly create a blank HTML document. Create `recipe-7.html` in an easily accessible location on your computer.

How to do it...

The following are the steps to understand how jQuery can be used to detect when a user is performing a hover action:

1.   With your newly created HTML document, add the following HTML and CSS code to create a web page with some basic form elements:

```
<!DOCTYPE html>
```

```
<html>
<head>
    <title>Chapter 2 :: jQuery Events</title>
    <style type="text/css">
        .info {
            width: 530px;
            border: solid 2px yellow;
            padding: 10px;
            text-align: center;
            margin-top: 10px;
            display: none;
        }
    </style>
    <script src="jquery.min.js"></script>
    <script>

    </script>
</head>
<body>
<label>Your Name:</label>
<input type="text" name="name" class="hoverinfo"
  rel="Please provide us with your name." />
<label>Your Email:</label>
<input type="text" name="email" class="hoverinfo"
  rel="Please provide us with your email address" />
<button class="hoverinfo" rel="Click here to submit your
  information to us">Submit</button>
<div class="info"></div>
</body>
</html>
```

2. Now we have a web page with three simple form elements and a div tag in which we can display information about the hovered item. Use the following JavaScript code and place it within the script tags to attach the `mouseover` and `mouseleave` event handlers to each of the elements with the `.hoverinfo` class:

```
$(function(){
    $('.hoverinfo').mouseover(function(){
        $('.info').html($(this).attr("rel"));
        $('.info').fadeIn();
    }).mouseleave(function(){
        $('.info').hide();
    });
});
```

3. Open the web page in a browser and hover over the different form elements; you will see the appropriate message displayed.

How it works...

We use the following CSS code to add some basic styles to our `.info` div element so that it will stand out on the page once displayed:

```
.info {
  width: 530px;
  border: solid 2px yellow;
  padding: 10px;
  text-align: center;
  margin-top: 10px;
  display: none;
}
```

We have added `display: none;` to prevent the `.info` element from being displayed on the screen, leaving this to the jQuery code.

We add the `.hoverinfo` class to each HTML element that includes extra information, so we can identify them within our jQuery code. We then use the following code to attach both a `mouseover` and `mouseleave` event handler to each of the `.hoverinfo` elements:

```
$('.hoverinfo').mouseover(function(){

}).mouseleave(function(){

});
```

The `mouseover` event handler will be executed when the users move their mouse over any of the `.hoverinfo` elements. Similarly, the `mouseleave` event will be executed once the user's mouse pointer has left any of the HTML elements with the `.hoverinfo` class.

Inside the `mouseover` event handler, we can use `$(this).attr("rel");` to get the text of the `rel` attribute (or the value of any HTML attribute) that we have added to each of the `.hoverinfo` elements. This can then be used with the following code:

```
$('.info').html($(this).attr("rel"));
$('.info').fadeIn();
```

We pass the text from the `rel` attribute to the `.html()` function, which will replace the existing HTML code inside the `.info` div element. We then use jQuery's `.fadeIn()` function to provide an animation and show the `.info` element with the value from the `rel` attribute.

Finally, the `mouseleave` event handler uses `$('.info').hide();` to again hide the element from view, allowing the process to be repeated once another of the `.hoverinfo` element's `mouseover` events has been triggered.

There's more...

jQuery includes many additional mouse event handlers that can be used for a variety of user interactions. Ensure that you choose the one most suitable for your situation. Visit the jQuery documentation (`http://api.jquery.com/category/events/mouse-events/`) to learn more.

See also

▸ *Updating content based on user input*

Triggering events manually

There may be parts of your web application where reacting to events fired by user interaction is not enough. jQuery allows us to manually trigger events from within our code.

Getting ready

When creating a web application, there may be times when you require a form that is handled solely by your jQuery code and is not submitted as a typical HTML form, perhaps to make an AJAX request instead. This is what we will demonstrate in this recipe. To get started, once again create another blank HTML document named `recipe-8.html`. Ensure that it is placed in an easily accessible location on your computer.

How to do it...

Learn how to manually trigger events from within JavaScript by performing the following steps:

1. Add the following HTML code to `recipe-8.html` in order to create a very basic web page with a set of form elements and a submit button:

```
<!DOCTYPE html>
<html>
<head>
    <title>Chapter 2 :: jQuery Events</title>
    <script src="jquery.min.js"></script>
    <script>

    </script>
```

```
</head>
<body>
<label>First Name:</label>
<input type="text" name="firstname" />
<label>Last Name:</label>
<input type="text" name="lastname" />
<label>Your Email:</label>
<input type="text" name="email" />
<button class="submit-btn">Submit</button>
</body>
</html>
```

2. Add the following jQuery code within the script tags to create an event handler for the **Submit** button and to manually trigger the submit button click event when the user presses *Enter* inside any of the text inputs:

```
$(function() {
    $('.submit-btn').on("click", function(){
      alert("Submit the form!");
    });
    $('input[type="text"]').keypress(function(event){
      if (event.which == 13) {
        $('.submit-btn').trigger("click");
      }
    });
});
```

How it works...

We often want to mimic typical behavior such as form submission when the *Enter* key is pressed inside one of our form inputs. We can use the following code to listen for a key press event on all of our text inputs:

```
$('input[type="text"]').keypress(function(event){
  if (event.which == 13) {
    $('.submit-btn').trigger("click");
  }
});
```

This code will be executed once the user has pressed a key inside a text input. When they do so, we use `event.which == 13` to check if the *Enter* key is pressed (that is, the character code of *Enter* is 13). If it has been pressed, we use the jQuery function `.trigger()` and pass the string `click` to manually trigger the click event on the selected element, which in this case is `.submit-btn`.

Using the following code, a click event handler can be attached to `.submit-btn`:

```
$('.submit-btn').on("click", function(){
  alert("Submit the form!");
});
```

The code within the `function` argument is executed and the alert is displayed.

There's more...

There are many other jQuery event handler functions that can be used to manually trigger an event if no callback function is provided as an argument. For example, consider the following code:

```
$('input[type="text"]').keypress(function(event){
  if (event.which == 13) {
    $('.submit-btn').click();
  }
});
```

This code uses the `.click()` function to manually trigger a click event, as opposed to using the `.trigger()` function. There is no noticeable difference between the two methods, but note that both are available.

Preventing event triggers

There are many situations where a jQuery developer will want to prevent the default browser actions of events of normal HTML elements such as forms, buttons, or even their own event handlers. jQuery provides the ability to stop these events. This allows the developer to prevent situations such as multiple button clicks, multiple form submissions, and accidental submissions, or generally allow the developer to change the normal behavior of typical events.

Getting ready

Create a blank HTML file named `recipe-9.html` and ensure that the latest version of the jQuery library is available.

How to do it...

Understand how to prevent default browser actions by performing the following steps:

1. Add the following HTML code to `recipe-9.html`; ensure that you update the reference to the jQuery library to the correct location on your computer:

```
<!DOCTYPE html>
<html>
<head>
    <title>Chapter 2 :: jQuery Events</title>
    <script src="jquery.min.js"></script>
    <script>

    </script>
</head>
<body>
<form method="POST" id="myForm">
    <label>First Name:</label>
    <input type="text" name="firstname" />
    <label>Last Name:</label>
    <input type="text" name="lastname" />
    <label>Your Email:</label>
    <input type="text" name="email" />
    <button class="submit-btn">Submit</button>
</form>
</body>
</html>
```

2. Use the following jQuery code and place it within the script tags to catch the button click of the **Submit** button and prevent the form from being submitted:

```
$(function() {
  $('.submit-btn').on("click", function(event){
    event.preventDefault();
    event.stopPropagation();
    var response = confirm("Are you sure you want to submit
      this form?");
    if (response) {
      $('#myForm').submit();
    }
  });
});
```

3. Opening `recipe-9.html` in a browser and clicking on the **Submit** button will present you with a JavaScript confirmation message, which will catch your response and then submit the HTML form, depending on your choice. The form will not be submitted until you have responded to this message box, thanks to the `event.preventDefault();` and `event.stopPropagation();` methods.

How it works...

The following jQuery code allows us to click on the **Submit** button and create a click event handler using the `.on()` function. We provide `click` as the first argument to specify that we require the click event handler, and the `.on()` function provides an interface for many other types of events.

```
$('.submit-btn').on("click", function(event){

});
```

We provide the `event` variable as an argument in the `.on()` callback function. We can then use the following jQuery functions to create our desired effect:

```
event.preventDefault();
event.stopPropagation();
```

The `event.prevenDefault();` function prevents the default action of the current event; in this case, the form submission. This allows us to handle the event in our own way, such as providing extra functionality or resulting in a different action entirely. The `event.stopPropagation();` function will prevent the event from bubbling up through the parent and ancestor DOM elements. When an event is fired on an element, the event is also fired on the parent and all ancestor elements within the DOM, and as a result, we can still fire the event we are trying to initially prevent.

As we have used these methods to prevent the form submission, we can ask the user if they are sure they would like to submit the form. We use the native JavaScript `confirm()` function to do this as follows:

```
var response = confirm("Are you sure you want to submit this
    form?");
    if (response) {
        $('#myForm').submit();
}
```

We store the user's response in a variable which we can then evaluate. If they click on **OK** to confirm the form submission, we can go ahead and submit the form using `$('#myForm').submit();`. Otherwise, we do nothing and the form is not submitted.

See also

► *Triggering events manually*

Creating a custom event

jQuery provides the developer with ways to handle built-in JavaScript events with functions such as `.click()`, `.hover()`, and others. jQuery also allows developers to create their own event types for additional functionality. With the creation of custom events, developers are also able to pass data around their application more easily.

Getting ready

Create another blank HTML document named `recipe-10.html` in an easily accessible location.

How to do it...

Learn how to create a custom event using jQuery by performing the following steps:

1. Add the following HTML code to this newly created HTML document. Remember to update the reference to the jQuery library to point to its local location on your computer.

```
<!DOCTYPE html>
<html>
<head>
    <title>Chapter 2 :: jQuery Events</title>
    <script src="jquery.min.js"></script>
    <script>

    </script>
</head>
<body>
    <button rel="green">Green</button>
    <button rel="blue">Blue</button>
    <p class="colourme"></p>
</body>
</html>
```

2. We can now bind a custom event handler to our paragraph and trigger it when one of our button elements is clicked. Add the following JavaScript code within the script tags:

```
$(function() {
    $('.colourme').on("switchColour", function(event, colour,
      text){
        $(this).html(text);
        $(this).css("color", colour);
    });
    $("button").click(function(){
        var colour = $(this).attr("rel");
        $('.colourme').trigger("switchColour", colour, colour +
          ' button pressed... ']);
    });
});
```

3. Open your newly created web page, and by clicking on either of the two buttons, you should see the paragraph text change along with its color, corresponding to the button that was clicked.

How it works...

jQuery provides us with a `.on()` function that allows us to specify the name of the event we wish to bind to the selected element. We can specify a built-in jQuery event or we can provide the name of our own event. We do this using the following JavaScript code:

```
$('.colourme').bind("switchColour", function(event, colour, text){
    $(this).html(text);
    $(this).css("color", colour);
});
```

This code binds an event handler for our custom `switchColour` event to the paragraph element with the `colourme` class. The second argument we provide to the `.on()` function is a callback method that has its own three arguments: `Event`, which holds the event information, and then `colour` and `text`, which are our own custom properties that we can use later.

Within the function, we use `$(this).html(text);` in order to change the content of the currently selected `.colourme` paragraph element to be the text provided within the `text` variable. We also apply some CSS using `$(this).css("color", colour);` (use the spelling `color` not colour) that changes the color of the text to that of the value provided as the `colour` variable.

Now that our custom event has been created, we need to be able to trigger this event, which can be done using the following code:

```
$("button").click(function(){
   var colour = $(this).attr("rel");
   $('.colourme').trigger("switchColour", [colour, colour + '
     button pressed... ']);
});
```

In the preceding JavaScript code, we use the jQuery provided `.click()` function to execute a set of code once either of the button elements have been clicked. Within the click event handler, we first retrieve the `rel` attribute of the element, which we specified as a variable `colour` in the HTML.

We then use the `.trigger()` function and specify our custom event to be triggered. We provide a second parameter as an array, containing both the variables we specified in our custom event using `.on()`, `colour`, and `text`.

The `.trigger()` function will fire our custom event and provide any bound elements with the information we provide. The .colourme paragraph that is bound to this event will have its inner HTML changed and its CSS color property modified to become the specified color.

3
Loading and Manipulating Dynamic Content with AJAX and JSON

In this chapter, we will cover:

- ▶ Loading HTML from a web server into a page
- ▶ Using AJAX and handling server errors
- ▶ Processing JSON data
- ▶ Searching JavaScript objects
- ▶ Sorting JavaScript objects
- ▶ Caching JSON and AJAX requests
- ▶ Creating a search feature
- ▶ Creating an autosuggest feature
- ▶ Waiting for an AJAX response

Introduction

jQuery allows the developer to make AJAX calls that will update website content without the need for refreshing a complete web page. jQuery's AJAX functionality adds an additional dimension to a website that allows it to become more of a web application. This chapter looks at how a developer can make these AJAX requests, receive data, and process it. In addition to processing and utilizing data received from an AJAX request, this chapter also looks at some of the other major features of AJAX including search and suggestion.

For most of the recipes in this chapter, you will either need to run a web server on your local machine or have access to an online web server. Some basic knowledge of PHP and MySQL will be useful as the required web server will make use of these technologies. To learn more about these technologies, you can refer to the following resources:

 ▶   To learn more on PHP, refer to `http://www.php.net`

 ▶   To learn more on MySQL, refer to `http://www.mysql.com`

Loading HTML from a web server into a page

At the most basic level, AJAX allows us to update a single page element with new content from a web server. This recipe looks at how we can set up some data to be received from a web server with PHP and how we can then receive this data and apply it to our web page.

Getting ready

Ensure that you have a web server running and have access to its web root.

How to do it...

Perform the following steps to create the required PHP, MySQL, and HTML in order to understand how to use jQuery with AJAX:

1. Before we can request for any data from the web server to be displayed within our web page, we need to be able to serve this data from a web server. Create a PHP file named `request-1.php`. Add the following PHP code and save it within the web root of your web server:

```php
<?php
  $num = rand(1, 5);
  switch ($num) {
    case 1:
      $quote = "Learn from yesterday, live for today, hope
        for tomorrow. The important thing is not to stop
        questioning.";
```

```
      break;
   case 2:
      $quote = "Only two things are infinite, the universe
         and human stupidity, and I'm not sure about the
         former.";
      break;
   case 3:
      $quote = "The difference between stupidity and genius
         is that genius has its limits.";
      break;
   case 4:
      $quote = "Try not to become a man of success, but
         rather try to become a man of value.";
      break;
   case 5:
      $quote = "Any man who can drive safely while kissing
         a pretty girl is simply not giving the kiss the
         attention it deserves.";
      break;
}
echo $quote;
```

2. The second step is to create a jQuery-powered HTML page that can request data from our PHP script. Within the web root of your web server, create an HTML file named `recipe-1.html` and add the following HTML code to it:

```html
<!DOCTYPE html>
<html>
<head>
   <title>Chapter 3 :: AJAX & JSON</title>
   <script src="jquery.min.js"></script>
   <style type="text/css">

   </style>
   <script>

   </script>
</head>
<body>
   <div class="left">
     Famous <br />Einstein Quotes
   </div>
   <div class="right">
     <p class="quote"></p>
     <button class="refresh">Get Quote</button>
```

```
    </div>
  </body>
</html>
```

3. We are now going to use CSS in order to add styles to our HTML page. Add the following CSS code within the `<style type="text/css"></style>` tags in the `recipe-1.html` file:

```css
.left {
  width: 200px;
  background-color: #CCC;
  float: left;
  height: 100px;
  text-align: center;
  font-size: 25px;
  padding: 40px 10px 10px 10px;
}
.right {
  width: 300px;
  float: left;
  margin-left: 10px;
  background-color: #333;
  color: #FFF;
  height: 120px;
  font-size: 20px;
  position: relative;
  padding: 20px 10px 10px 10px;
}
.refresh {
  position: absolute;
  right: 5px;
  top: 5px;

}
```

4. The final step is to add some jQuery code in order to request data from the PHP script and load it into our web page. Within the script tags in the header of the `recipe-1.html` file, add the following jQuery code:

```javascript
$(function() {
  $('.refresh').click(function() {
    $.ajax({
      url: '/request-1.php',
      type: 'GET'
    }).done(function(data){
```

```
        $('.quote').html(data);
      });
    });
  });
```

How it works...

Now, let us understand the steps performed previously in detail.

PHP

The aim of using the PHP script is to provide a random quote by Albert Einstein as a string. To be able to do this at random, we first need to generate a random number. This is done using the PHP `rand()` function as follows:

```
$num = rand(1, 5);
```

This will create a variable with a random integer value between 1 to 5. We can then use this random number to determine which quote to output. We use a switch statement based on the $num variable to create a $quote variable with a random Einstein quote:

```
switch ($num) {
    case 1:
        $quote = "Learn from yesterday, live for today, hope for
            tomorrow. The important thing is not to stop
            questioning.";
        break;
    case 2:
        $quote = "Only two things are infinite, the universe and
            human stupidity, and I'm not sure about the former.";
        break;
    case 3:
        $quote = "The difference between stupidity and genius is
            that genius has its limits.";
        break;
    case 4:
        $quote = "Try not to become a man of success, but rather try
            to become a man of value.";
        break;
    case 5:
        $quote = "Any man who can drive safely while kissing a
            pretty girl is simply not giving the kiss the attention it
            deserves.";
        break;
}
```

Finally, we echo the value of `$quote`:

```
echo $quote;
```

If you were to visit this file served from a web server (that is, `http://localhost/request.php`) in your browser, you will be presented with a random quote every time you refresh the page, as shown in the following screenshot:

Only two things are infinite, the universe and human stupidity, and I'm not sure about the former.

HTML

We need an HTML page to load our PHP-generated quote. Within the HTML, we define a simple HTML layout. We create a division element with the class `left`. This box simply holds the title **Famous Einstein Quotes**. We define a second div element with the class `right` and two child elements, a paragraph and a button.

In the preceding screenshot, the box on the right-hand side made up of the paragraph element with a `quote` class is where we will load our dynamic content using jQuery. We will use the button to allow the user to trigger the dynamic load of the quote. Note that you could also load the quote on page load without the need of user interaction.

CSS

To make the web page containing our dynamic quotes, we use some very basic CSS to style and align the various elements we have created in our HTML as follows:

```
.left {
    width: 200px;
    background-color: #CCC;
    float: left;
    height: 100px;
    text-align: center;
    font-size: 25px;
    padding: 10px;
    padding-top: 40px;
}
```

We make the div element with the `left` class have a static width and height and then force it to float on the left-hand side of the browser window. A static height is set to ensure that both the left and right div elements are of equal height. We also add some basic text formatting including `line-height`, `text-align`, and `font-size`, which are self-explanatory. We also change the background color of the div element and add some padding for further text alignment.

```
.right {
    width: 300px;
    float: left;
    margin-left: 10px;
    background-color: #333;
    color: #FFF;
    height: 120px;
    font-size: 20px;
    position: relative;
    padding: 10px;
    padding-top: 20px;
}
```

We add very similar styles to the right-hand side division element with the addition of `position: relative;`, which allows us to prevent sibling elements with an absolute position from floating outside this div element.

```
.refresh {
    position: absolute;
    right: 5px;
    top: 5px;
}
```

As the parent `.right` division element has a relative position, we can make the position of the `.refresh` button absolute and set the top and right position values as static, forcing the button to float to the top-right corner of our `.right` division box.

jQuery

Using jQuery, we can make a request to the `request.php` page we created earlier, which is on our web server. First, we create an event handler and attach it to the refresh button, so we can make a request when the user clicks on this button.

```
$('.refresh').click(function() {

});
```

Any code within `function(){}` will be executed when the user clicks on the `.refresh` button. Within this callback function, we can make the AJAX request using `$ajax`, which is provided by jQuery:

```
$.ajax({
    url: '/request.php',
```

```
    type: 'GET'
}).done(function(data){
    $('.quote').html(data);
});
```

We provide `$.ajax()` with an object, which allows us to specify a set of parameters required to make the AJAX call. In this example, we provide the `url` and `type` parameters that tell jQuery where to make the request and what kind of request it should be.

 Read the documentation on `$.ajax()` to learn more about other parameters that can be provided. The API documentation can be found at `http://api.jquery.com/jQuery.ajax/`.

Additionally, we append a `.done()` function after the AJAX request method and provide it with a callback function that accepts the argument `data`. This `data` argument will hold the response from the server. Within the callback function, we use `$('.quote').html(data);` to replace the HTML in the `.quote` paragraph with the response from our PHP script. If a user visits this HTML page and clicks on the **Get Quote** button, they will be presented with a result as shown in the following screenshot:

> Famous
> Einstein Quotes
>
> Get Quote
>
> The difference between stupidity and genius is that genius has its limits.

See also

- ► *Creating a search feature*
- ► *Creating an autosuggest feature*
- ► *Waiting for an AJAX response*

Using AJAX and handling server errors

In an ideal world, your web application would never go wrong. Unfortunately, this is not the case, and web developers need to gracefully handle errors and provide the user with useful feedback.

For example, system errors occur when a server cannot be reached or a file/web page is missing. System errors are typically unavoidable and out of the user's control. They differ from application errors such as invalid data input, which a user can correct.

Getting ready

Since this recipe deals with AJAX errors and we will be calling a PHP script that does not exist, we only require HTML and JavaScript for this recipe. Create a blank HTML document named `recipe-2.html` and ensure that you have the latest version of jQuery downloaded and ready for use.

How to do it...

Learn how to handle AJAX errors by carefully performing the following steps:

1. Add the following HTML code to create a simple web page with a single button that will trigger an AJAX request:

```
<!DOCTYPE html>
<html>
<head>
  <title>Chapter 3 :: AJAX & JSON</title>
  <script src="jquery.min.js"></script>
  <script>

  </script>
</head>
<body>
  <button id="makeRequest">Make AJAX request</button>
</body>
</html>
```

2. Within the script tags, add the following jQuery code that will make an AJAX request to a nonexistent file when the #makeRequest button has been clicked:

```
$(function() {
  $('#makeRequest').click(function() {
  $.ajax({
    url: 'i-do-not-exist.html',
    type: 'GET'
  }).done(function(data){
    //Will not succeed as no file exists
  });
  });
});
```

3. Under the AJAX request (but still within `$(function(){});`), add the following code, which will create a global AJAX error event handler that is fired every time an AJAX request fails:

```
$(document).ajaxError(function(event, request, settings) {
  alert("Error trying to reach '" + settings.url + "'.
    ERROR CODE: " + request.status + " ERROR MESSAGE: " +
    request.statusText);
});
```

How it works...

The HTML page we created is self-explanatory. We create a button that can trigger the AJAX request. This is obviously the simplest example to illustrate the error handling concept, which can then be applied to any AJAX request situation using jQuery.

We create an event handler for the `#makeRequest` button and provide a callback function to be executed on-click as follows:

```
$('#makeRequest').click(function() {
  $.ajax({
    url: 'i-do-not-exist.html',
    type: 'GET'
  }).done(function(data){
  //Will not succeed as no file exists
  });
});
```

We add the AJAX request within the callback function using the `$.ajax()` function provided by jQuery. We then pass a JavaScript object to this method, where we specify the URL of a nonexistent file and the type of the request; in this case, `GET`. Note that the `.done()` function chained onto the `$.ajax()` function will never be executed if the AJAX request fails.

We create a global AJAX error handler and attach it to the document so that it will catch all AJAX errors within our page:

```
$(document).ajaxError(function(event, request, settings) {
  alert("Error trying to reach '" + settings.url + "'. ERROR CODE:
    " + request.status + " ERROR MESSAGE: " + request.statusText);
});
```

There are three arguments provided to the callback function of the `.ajaxError` method that we can use to learn more about the error. In this example, we extract the target URL from the `settings` variable and the status information from the `request` object.

If you open this HTML file in a web browser and click on the `#makeRequest` button, you will be presented with a JavaScript alert box that provides you information about the error, as shown in the following screenshot:

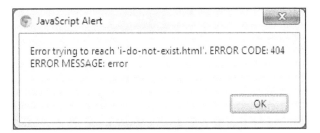

There's more...

In this example, we created a global AJAX error handler to catch all the AJAX request errors within our page. A global AJAX error handler is ideal for request errors such as file missing or host unreachable. In these cases, errors can be handled in the same way for all AJAX requests, and more specific information about an individual request is not required.

There might be instances in your application where you may need to handle one or more AJAX request errors differently. For this, you can use the `.fail()` function, which is used in the same way as `.done()`. The following jQuery code provides an example usage of `.fail()` to achieve the same result for a simple AJAX request as our global error handler:

```
$.ajax({
    url: 'i-do-not-exist.html',
    type: 'GET'
}).done(function(data){
    //Will not succeed as now file exists
}).fail(function(event){
    alert("An error occurred. Error Code: " + event.status);
});
```

Note that there is less information directly available about the error.

Processing JSON data

JavaScript Object Notation (**JSON**) provides web developers with a clean and efficient way to encode data. JSON is a widely adopted format. It simplifies data processing and manipulation. To read more about why you should use JSON, visit `http://www.revillweb.com/why-use-json/`.

Getting ready

Ensure that your web server is running and you have access to the web root where you can save/upload the files that you will create as part of this recipe.

How to do it...

Learn how to use JSON-formatted data with JavaScript by performing the following steps:

1. Create a PHP file named `request-3.php` and save it to the web root of your web server. Use the following PHP code to create and output a list of names as JSON data:

```php
<?php
  //Create an array of people
  $people = array(
    1 => array(
      "firstname" => "Luke",
      "lastname" => "Skywalker"
    ),
    2 => array(
      "firstname" => "Darth",
      "lastname" => "Vader"
    ),
    3 => array(
      "firstname" => "Mace",
      "lastname" => "Windu"
    )
  );
  //Ensure the browser is expecting the correct content
  //type format and charset
  header("Content-Type: application/json; charset=UTF-8");
  //Encode the array of people into JSON data
  echo json_encode($people);
?>
```

2. Create an HTML page named `recipe-3.html` within the web root of your web server. Add the following HTML to this page, which creates an unordered list element that can be populated with our JSON data once processed:

```html
<!DOCTYPE html>
<html>
<head>
  <title>Chapter 3 :: AJAX & JSON</title>
  <script src="jquery.min.js"></script>
  <script>
```

```
    </script>
  </head>
  <body>
    <ul id="peopleList"></ul>
  </body>
</html>
```

3. Within the script tags in the head tag of the HTML page, add the following jQuery code to perform an AJAX request to the `request-3.php` page created earlier:

```
$(function(){
  $.ajax({
    url: '/request-3.php',
    type: 'GET'
  }).done(function(data){
  });
});
```

4. Within the `.done()` callback function, use the jQuery `$.each()` function to process the JSON data returned from our PHP page and add a new list item for each person to the list within our HTML page:

```
$.each(data, function(key, value) {
  $('#peopleList').append("<li>#" + key + " " +
  value.firstname + " " + value.lastname + "</li>");
});
```

How it works...

Now, let us understand the steps performed previously in detail.

PHP

In a real-world application, you would typically be retrieving data from a database. In this recipe, we are creating a simple, two-dimensional array of names that will act as our database, allowing us to concentrate on the jQuery code.

```
$people = array(
  1 => array(
    "firstname" => "Luke",
    "lastname" => "Skywalker"
  ),
  2 => array(
    "firstname" => "Darth",
    "lastname" => "Vader"
  ),
  3 => array(
    "firstname" => "Mace",
    "lastname" => "Windu"
  )
);
```

Next, we manually specify the response content type and character set. The content type and character set of the response should be specified so that the web browser and jQuery code know the format in which to expect the data. Most web browsers will work this out without an issue. However, Internet Explorer 9 and lower versions are particularly problematic in this area, and it is always good practice to manually specify the content type and charset using the PHP's `header()` function:

```
header("Content-Type: application/json; charset=UTF-8");
```

Note that we have set the charset as `UTF-8`, not `utf8` or `utf-8`. Once again, most browsers will be fine with either, but some earlier Internet Explorer versions will produce undesirable effects if the character set is not formatted correctly.

 The browser-related issues mentioned in this recipe are not likely to occur within this example with such simple data. This is a best practice and will provide a greater benefit to larger and more complex web applications that use AJAX and JSON.

Finally, we encode our PHP array in the JSON format using the PHP provided `json_encode()` function and output the results using `echo` as follows:

```
echo json_encode($people);
```

If you visit the `request-3.php` page directly, you will see the output of the `people` array within the browser window in the following format:

```
{"1":{"firstname":"Luke","lastname":"Skywalker"},"2":{"firstname":
"Darth","lastname":"Vader"},"3":{"firstname":"Mace",
"lastname":"Windu"}}
```

Alternatively, using the browser developer tools and selecting the network tab, you can view the response in a more readable manner.

HTML

Our HTML page does nothing more than include the jQuery library and creates an HTML unordered list element, which we can populate with the JSON data once processed by jQuery.

jQuery

Putting our code within `$(function(){});` will lead to its execution on page load. We use jQuery's `$.ajax()` functionality to make the AJAX request to our previously created PHP file as follows:

```
$.ajax({
  url: '/request.php',
  type: 'GET'
}).done(function(data){
});
```

By providing the `url` and `type` parameters within an object to this method, we tell a method to make a `GET` request to the `request-3.php` file present in the web root of our web server. We then append a `.done()` function onto the `$.ajax();` method, which will be executed when the request has been made successfully. The `.done()` method takes a callback function as an argument with the `data` variable that contains all the response data from the request—the JSON data from the PHP file.

Now that we have the response data available within the `data` variable, we can process the JSON data and populate our HTML list element using the following code:

```
$.each(data, function(key, value) {
    $('#peopleList').append("<li>#" + key + " " + value.firstname +
        " " + value.lastname + "</li>");
});
```

`$.each();` is another function provided by jQuery which allows us to loop through a set of data that is specified as the first argument in this example (that is, `data`). The second argument is the callback function to execute for each of the items found within the `data` variable. This callback function also takes two arguments, `key` and `value`. Using these variables, we can get all the information from the JSON data including the array key (for example, 1, 2, 3, and so on) and the values; the first and last names for each object.

Finally, we select the `#peopleList` element, and we use the `append()` function to append an HTML list item to the unordered list with the data from each of the `people` JSON objects.

See also

▸ *Searching JavaScript objects*
▸ *Sorting JavaScript objects*

Searching JavaScript objects

With objects being the main method of holding data within your application, it can be very useful to be able to find objects matching a certain criteria. jQuery does not provide a direct method for us to search through objects and arrays of objects; however, we can easily create this functionality.

Getting ready

Using your favorite text editor, create a blank HTML document named `recipe-4.html`, and ensure that you have the latest version of jQuery installed. Add the following HTML code to this HTML file:

```
<!DOCTYPE html>
<html>
```

```
<head>
  <title>Chapter 3 :: AJAX & JSON</title>
  <script src="jquery.min.js"></script>
  <script>

  </script>
</head>
<body></body>
</html>
```

Ensure that you update the reference to the jQuery library to point out the location where it is saved on your computer. This HTML page provides us with a web page where we can execute JavaScript for this recipe.

How to do it...

Create a JavaScript function that will make searching through an object easy by performing the following steps:

1. Within the script tags of the newly created `recipe-4.html` page, create an array of objects on which we can perform searches:

    ```
    var people = [
    {
      title: "Mr",
      firstname: "John",
      lastname: "Doe"
    },
    {
      title: "Mrs",
      firstname: "Jane",
      lastname: "Doe"
    },
    {
      title: "Sir",
      firstname: "Johnathan",
      lastname: "Williams"
    },
    {
      title: "Sir",
      firstname: "Edward",
      lastname: "Tailor"
    }
    ];
    ```

2. Below this array of objects, add the following recursive function that we can use to iterate through the preceding objects and find matches based on the provided arguments:

```
function findObjects(parameter, value, object) {
  var matches = [];
  for (var i in object) {
    if (typeof object[i] == 'object') {
      matches = matches.concat(findObjects(parameter,
        value, object[i]));
    } else if (i == parameter && object[parameter] ==
      value) {
      matches.push(object);
    }
  }
  return matches;
}
```

3. Call the function by specifying the parameter you would like to look for, the value you would like to match, and then the object/objects you would like to search through:

```
var results = findObjects("title", "Sir", people);
console.log(results);
```

4. Open `recipe-4.html` in a browser and then the JavaScript console (*Ctrl + Shift + J* in Chrome); you will be presented with the results of the search.

How it works...

First of all, an array of objects representing people is created. This does not need to be a static set of data and could have been loaded from an AJAX request as seen in the previous recipes.

Our `findObjects()` function will allow us to search through an object or an array of objects. This function takes three arguments. The first argument is `parameter`, which is the object we want to search within; in this example, `title`. The second argument is the actual value we want to find matches against; the above example uses `Sir`. The final argument is the array of objects we created.

We first create an empty array within the function, which will hold each of the objects that match our specified criteria:

```
var matches = [];
```

Using the native JavaScript `for` loop, we can iterate through the object/objects.

```
for (var i in object) {
}
```

If we provide an array of objects, `object[i]` will represent a different object within the array on each iteration. If we provided a single object, then `i` will be a different property within the provided object on each iteration.

Since JavaScript objects can also hold other objects or arrays, we need to allow for recursion so that we can search through an infinite depth of objects. To do this, we first check to see if `object[i]` (the currently iterated object or property value) is an object. If it is, we call our `findObjects()` function from within itself and provide the current object as the last argument:

```
if (typeof object[i] == 'object') {
  matches = matches.concat(findObjects(parameter, value,
    object[i]));
}
```

As the `findObjects()` function will return an array of matches, we use `matches = matches.concat()` to add the array of returned results to the current array of matches. We add an `else if` statement to filter instances where the value is not an object.

```
if (typeof object[i] == 'object') {
  matches = matches.concat(findObjects(parameter, value,
    object[i]));
} else if (i == parameter && object[parameter] == value) {
  matches.push(object);
}
```

Within the `else if` statement, we check to see if the current property (represented by `i`) matches the parameter we provided as an argument. If this is true, we check whether the value for this property matches the value we provided as an argument. If this is also true, we use `matches.push(object)` to add the current object to the `matches` array. Finally, once we have iterated through all the objects and properties, we return the `matches` array.

In the preceding example, we then simply use `console.log();` to output the array of matching objects to the browser's JavaScript console. This array can be used in any manner, such as to populate an HTML list element.

There's more...

Searching through JavaScript objects will often become a common part of your application. Be sure to make functions such as this as universal as possible, and do not code them for a single operation. You will then be able to make this function globally available within your application and re-use it throughout. Also, be careful when writing recursive functions, as it is easy to create infinite loops and complex, unreadable code.

See also

  ▸   *Processing JSON data*

  ▸   *Sorting JavaScript objects*

Sorting JavaScript objects

Along with the ability to efficiently find objects that match a criteria, you will often require your objects to be in a certain order for outputting.

Getting ready

As with the previous recipe, create an HTML page named `recipe-5.html` where we can add and execute JavaScript code for this recipe using the following code:

```html
<!DOCTYPE html>
<html>
<head>
  <title>Chapter 3 :: AJAX & JSON</title>
  <script src="jquery.min.js"></script>
  <script >

  </script>
</head>
<body></body>
</html>
```

Update the reference to the jQuery library in order to ensure that it includes the correct file on your computer.

How to do it...

Create a reusable function to sort a JavaScript object by performing the following step-by-step instructions:

  1. Within the script tags in the `recipe-5.html` file you have just created, add the following JavaScript code:

```javascript
var people = [
  {
    title: "Mrs",
    firstname: "Jane",
    lastname: "Doe"
  },
```

```
    {
      title: "Sir",
      firstname: "Johnathan",
      lastname: "Williams"
    },
    {
      title: "Mr",
      firstname: "John",
      lastname: "Andrews"
    },
    {
      title: "Sir",

      firstname: "Edward",
      lastname: "Tailor"
    }
  ];
```

2. Below this array, add the following function that can be used to sort JavaScript objects within an array:

```
function sortObjectsByParam(param) {
  return function(a, b) {
    if (a[param] == b[param]) { return 0; }
    if (a[param] > b[param]) { return 1; }
    else { return -1; }
  }
}
```

3. Use this function with the native JavaScript .sort() function as follows:

```
people.sort(sortObjectsByParam("lastname"));
console.log(people);
```

4. Opening this web page in a browser and looking at the JavaScript console will provide you with a list of the objects we created in the JavaScript array in step 1. The difference is that they will be ordered by the last name as opposed to their original order.

How it works...

We must have an array of objects to successfully use our .sort() function to reorder them. This array of objects can be static, as in the example, or can be loaded from a server via an AJAX request.

JavaScript provides a `.sort()` function, which takes a function as an argument and provides two arguments to this callback function. The typical usage of `.sort()` would be as follows:

```
people.sort(function(a, b){
  //Compare objects here
});
```

The `a` and `b` arguments are two objects from the array. We can compare these two objects and determine which object needs to be placed before the other.

In our example, we require some additional functionality; we need to be able to specify which parameter on which we want to sort the objects. As we cannot provide the `.sort()` callback function with an additional argument, we wrap the callback in another function as follows:

```
function sortObjectsByParam(param) {
  return function(a, b) {

  }
}
```

We can then specify a property on which to sort the objects, which can then be used within the callback function. The callback function must return either 0 or a positive or negative number. In our example, 0 means that no sorting is required and that both objects are equal. 1 means that a should be placed before b and -1 means that b should be placed before a. We can do this evaluation within the callback function as follows:

```
function sortObjectsByParam(param) {
  return function(a, b) {
    if (a[param] == b[param]) { return 0; }
    if (a[param] > b[param]) { return 1; }
    else { return -1; }
  }
}
```

We use `a[param]` and `b[param]` to check only the specified parameter of the objects. We can now use this function in conjunction with the native JavaScript `.sort()` function to reorder our objects based on the specified parameter as follows:

```
$(function(){
  people.sort(sortObjectsByParam("lastname"));
  console.log(people);
});
```

This would alphabetically reorder the array of objects we created earlier by their last name. So, the object `Mr John Andrews` would be the first in the array and so on.

There's more...

Similar to the function used for searching objects, this function should not be coded for a single operation so that it can be used throughout your application. Reusable code will make your application more manageable and easier to debug.

See also

▸ *Processing JSON data*

▸ *Searching JavaScript objects*

Caching JSON and AJAX requests

One way by which a web developer can increase the speed of his/her web application is by limiting the number of requests made to the web server. It is very important to ensure that you are making data calls only when you need to. We can use caching to ensure that requests are made only when a new set of data is required.

Getting ready

Ensure that your web server is up and running and you have permission to add files to the server's web root directory.

How to do it...

Learn how to speed up your JavaScript applications using simple caching methods by performing the following instructions:

1. Create a PHP file named `request-6.php` in the web root of your web server. Use the following PHP code to create and output a list of names as JSON data:

```php
<?php
  //Create an array of people
  $people = array(
    1 => array(
      "firstname" => "Luke",
      "lastname" => "Skywalker"
    ),
    2 => array(
      "firstname" => "Darth",
      "lastname" => "Vader"
    ),
    3 => array(
```

```php
        "firstname" => "Mace",
        "lastname" => "Windu"
    )
);
//Ensure the browser is expecting the correct content
//type format and charset
header("Content-Type: application/json; charset=UTF-8");
//Encode the array of people into JSON data
echo json_encode($people);
```

2. Use the following HTML code to create a page named `recipe-6.html` within the web root of your web server so that you can make AJAX requests to your PHP file:

```html
<!DOCTYPE html>
<html>
<head>
  <title>Chapter 3 :: AJAX & JSON</title>
  <script src="jquery.min.js"></script>
  <script>

  </script>
</head>
<body>
  <ul id="peopleList"></ul>
  <button class="getPeople">Get People</button>
</body>
</html>
```

3. Within the script tags in the head tag of the HTML page, add the following jQuery code to make an AJAX request to retrieve the `people` array created in the PHP file and then cache the results:

```javascript
var cache = [];
$(function(){
    $('.getPeople').click(function(){
      if (cache.length == 0) {
        $.ajax({
            url: '/request-6.php',
            type: 'GET',
            async: false
        }).done(function(data){
            cache = data;
        });
      }
      $('#peopleList').empty();
      $.each(cache, function(key, value){
```

```
        $('#peopleList').append("<li>#" + key + " " +
           value.firstname + " " + value.lastname  + "</li>");
      });
    });
  });
```

How it works...

Now, let us understand the steps performed previously in detail.

PHP

Please refer to the previous recipe, *Processing JSON data*, of this chapter for a detailed look at how this PHP code works.

HTML

The HTML page we created is very basic and does not require a great deal of explanation. We simply create an unordered list element, which we can populate with jQuery, and a button, which the user can click on to trigger the AJAX request to load the JSON data from the PHP file.

jQuery

First, we create an empty JavaScript array that we can use to cache the data received from AJAX requests as follows:

```
var cache = [];
```

Then, within `$(function(){});`, which will be executed on page load, we attach a click event handler to the `.getPeople` button.

```
$(function(){
  $('.getPeople').click(function(){
  });
});
```

Within the callback function for this event handler, we check to see if there is currently anything within the `cache` array by evaluating its length:

```
if  (cache.length == 0) {

}
```

If there is nothing in the `cache` array, we do not have any cached data. We need to make an AJAX request to our PHP file in order to get the JSON data as shown in the following code snippet. This will ensure that an AJAX request is made only when data is required, and a request will not be made every time the button is clicked.

```
if  (cache.length == 0) {
  $.ajax({
    url: '/request.php',
```

```
      type: 'GET',
      async: false
  }).success(function(data){
      cache = data;
  });
}
```

On the success of the AJAX request, we store the results within our `cache` array. Note that we have set the `async` property to `false`, meaning that any JavaScript code below the AJAX request will not be executed until there has been a response. This is to prevent the HTML list being populated before the `cache` array has been populated with data. This would not be the ideal solution for large applications because this can cause the browser to hang or crash if the AJAX request takes a long time to respond. Read the *Waiting for an AJAX response* recipe of this chapter to learn the preferred method of waiting for AJAX request completion.

With the `cache` array populated, we can use it to add items to our HTML unordered list. We use the jQuery `$.each()` function, which allows us to iterate through each of the objects within the `cache` array. For each of these objects, we use `.append()` to add a list item along with the data from the object to the #peopleList list.

```
$('#peopleList').empty();
$.each(cache, function(key, value){
  $('#peopleList').append("<li>#" + key + " " + value.firstname +
    " " + value.lastname  + "</li>");
});
```

Before we populate the list, we first use `$('#peopleList').empty();` to empty the list in the DOM. This is to prevent additional button clicks from adding duplicate items.

There's more...

This method of caching data can speed up your web application. This method, however, will not be suitable for situations where the requested data is changing frequently, as the user will only get updated data when they refresh or revisit the page.

AJAX requests in jQuery have their own form of caching, which is essentially the same as the browser cache. Through the settings provided to the `$.ajax()` function, you can control how this type of cache works. Although this cache can be useful, it does not offer the same level of control as the manual caching method we implemented in this recipe.

Creating a search feature

Allowing your users to search through data within your web application is a basic principle. This recipe will show you how to create a fast and efficient search feature that uses jQuery and AJAX with a PHP and MySQL backend.

Getting ready

This recipe not only requires that you have a running web server that has PHP5, but you will also need a MySQL server that is ready to accept connections from PHP scripts.

How to do it...

Learn how to create a search feature from scratch, which will show you valuable jQuery principles in action, by performing the following steps:

1. We need to create a database and a table to store the data that the users will be able to search. Create a database named `jquerycookbook` on your database server, and use the following SQL code to create and populate a table with some data:

    ```
    USE `jquerycookbook`;

    CREATE TABLE IF NOT EXISTS `stationary` (
      `id` bigint(20) unsigned NOT NULL AUTO_INCREMENT,
      `title` varchar(128) NOT NULL,
      PRIMARY KEY (`id`)
    ) ENGINE=InnoDB  DEFAULT CHARSET=latin1 AUTO_INCREMENT=6 ;

    INSERT INTO `stationary` (`id`, `title`) VALUES
    (1, 'Ruler'),
    (2, 'Pencil'),
    (3, 'Pen'),
    (4, 'Rubber'),
    (5, 'Sharpener');
    ```

2. In order to allow the users to search the data present in our database from their browser (the client), we need to be able to extract the information from the database based on their search. We can do this using PHP to query the MySQL database for data based on the search term, which will be provided by the user via the client. Before we can do this, we need to be able to connect to the database we just created. Create a PHP file named `db.inc.php` within the web root of your web server and add the following code:

    ```php
    <?php
        $dbhost = 'localhost'; //hostname
        $dbuser = 'root'; //database username
        $dbpass = ''; //database password
        $dbname = 'jquerycookbook'; //database name

        $db = new mysqli($dbhost, $dbuser, $dbpass);

        $db->select_db($dbname);
    ```

```php
if($db->connect_errno > 0){
    die('ERROR! - COULD NOT CONNECT TO mySQL
    DATABASE: ' . $db->connect_error);
}
```

3. Be sure to change the `$dbhost`, `$dbuser`, and `$dbpass` values to match your configuration.

4. Create a PHP file named `search.php` in the web root of your web server and add the following code:

```php
<?php
    //Prepare an object to hold data we are going to send
    //back to the jQuery
    $data = new stdClass;
    $data->success = false;
    $data->results = array();
    $data->error = NULL;
    //Has the text been posted?
    if (isset($_POST['text'])) {
        //Connect to the database
        require_once('db.inc.php');
        //Escape the text to prevent SQL injection
        $text = $db->real_escape_string($_POST['text']);
        //Run a LIKE query to search for titles that are like
        //the entered text
        $q = "SELECT * FROM `stationary` WHERE `title`
            LIKE '%{$text}%'";
        $result = $db->query($q);
        //Did the query complete successfully?
        if (!$result) {
            //If not add an error to the data array
            $data->error = "Could not query database for search
                results, MYSQL ERROR: " . $db->error;
        } else {
            //Loop through the results and add to the results
            //array
            while ($row = $result->fetch_assoc()) {
                $data->results[] = array(
                    'id' => $row['id'],
                    'title' => $row['title']
                );
            }
            //Everything went to plan so set success to true
            $data->success = true;
        }
```

```
    }
    //Set the content type for a json object and ensure
    //charset is UTF-8. Not utf8 otherwise it will not work in IE
    header("Content-Type: application/json; charset=UTF-8");
    //json encode the data
    echo json_encode($data);
```

5. Create an HTML file named `recipe-7.html` in the web root of your web server using the following HTML code:

```html
<!DOCTYPE html>
<html>
<head>
  <title>Chapter 3 :: AJAX & JSON</title>
  <script src="jquery.min.js"></script>
  <script src='script-7.js'></script>
  <link href='style-7.css' rel="stylesheet" />
</head>
<body>
  <div id='frame'>
    <div class='search'>
      <div class='header'>
        <h1>Chapter 3 :: Search Feature</h1>
        <input type='text' id='text' />
        <button id='search'>Search</button>
      </div>
      <div id='results-holder'>
        <div class="loading-holder">
          <div class="loading">Loading...</div>
        </div>
        <ul id='results-list'></ul>
      </div>
    </div>
  </div>
</body>
</html>
```

6. To make our search feature more attractive, we can use CSS to style the HTML page we have just created. You may have noticed that within the HTML page header, we included a CSS file named `style-7.css`. Create the `style-7.css` file, save it to the web root of your web server, and add the following CSS code:

```css
/* Include a web font from Google  */
@import url(http://fonts.googleapis.com/css?family=Denk+One);
/* Basic CSS for positioning etc */
```

```css
body {
  font-family: 'Denk One', sans-serif;
}
#frame {
  width: 500px;
  margin: 125px auto auto auto;
  border: solid 1px #CCC;
  /* SOME CSS3 DIV SHADOW */
  -webkit-box-shadow: 0 0 10px #CCC;
  -moz-box-shadow: 0 0 10px #CCC;
  box-shadow: 0 0 10px #CCC;
  /* CSS3 ROUNDED CORNERS */
  -moz-border-radius: 5px;
  -webkit-border-radius: 5px;
  -khtml-border-radius: 5px;
  border-radius: 5px;
  background-color: #FFF;
}
.search .header {
  margin: 25px;
}
.search .header {
  text-align: center;
}
.search .header input {
  width: 350px;
}
#results-holder {
  min-height: 200px;
}
.loading {
  text-align: center;
  line-height: 30px;
  display: none; /* DONT DISPLAY BY DEFAULT */
}
.loading-holder {
  height: 30px;
}
/* Styling for the results list */
#results-list {
  margin: 0;
  padding: 0;
  list-style: none; /* REMOVE THE BULLET POINTS */
}
```

```css
#results-list li {
  line-height: 30px;
  border-bottom: solid 1px #CCC;
  padding: 5px 5px 5px 10px;
    color: #333;
}
/* REMOVE THE BORDER FROM THE LAST LIST ELEMENT SO IT DOESN'T
CLASS WITH THE FRAME BORDER */
#results-list li:last-child {
        border: none;
}


/* STYLE THE NO RESULTS LIST ITEM */
#results-list .no-results {
  text-align: center;
  font-weight: bold;
  font-size: 14px;
}
```

7. Using jQuery, we will be able to accept the user's search query and send the request to our PHP script. Create a JavaScript file named `script-7.js` within the web root of your web server. Note that this was also included within the header of the HTML file. Add the following jQuery code to this file:

```javascript
$(function(){
  //Hide the result list on load
  $('#results-list').hide();
  //Click event when search button is pressed
  $('#search').click(function(){
    doSearch();
  });
    //Keypress event to see if enter was pressed in text
    //input
  $('#text').keydown(function(e){
  if(e.keyCode == 13){
    doSearch();
  }
  });
});

function doSearch() {
  var searchText = $('#text').val();
  //Rehide the search results
  $('#results-list').hide();
  $.ajax({
```

```
      url: '/search.php',
      type: 'POST',
      data: {
        'text': searchText
      },
      beforeSend: function(){
        $('.loading').fadeIn();
      },
      success: function(data) {
        $('.loading').fadeOut();
        //Was everything successful, no errors in the PHP
        //script
        if (data.success) {
          $('#results-list').empty();
          if(data.results.length > 0) {
            $.each(data.results, function(){
              $('#results-list').append("<li>" + this.title +
              "</li>");
            });
          } else {
            $('#results-list').append("<li class=
            'no-results'>Your search did not return any
            results</li>");
          }
          //Show the results list
          $('#results-list').fadeIn();
        } else {
          //Display the error message
          alert(data.error);
        }
      }
    });
}
```

8. Visiting the `recipe-7.html` file on your web server will present you with a simply-styled search input, allowing you to perform a search on the stationary items we added to our MySQL database. The following screenshot is similar to the one you will see after a search is completed:

How it works...

Now, let us understand the steps performed previously in detail.

SQL

With the SQL code, we simply tell the SQL script to use the `jquerycookbook` database that we created; we create a table named `stationary` and then insert five stationary items into the table.

PHP

The first PHP script we created, `db.inc.php`, was simply to connect to the database we created, which will then allow us to query the data within it. We created four variables to hold the hostname of the database server (typically localhost), the username, the password, and finally the name of the database to which we wish to connect.

```
$dbhost = 'localhost'; //hostname
$dbuser = 'root'; //database username
$dbpass = ''; //database password
$dbname = 'jquerycookbook'; //database name
```

After we have this information available within our PHP script, we create a new `mysqli` connection and select the `jquerycookbook` database for use.

```
$db = new mysqli($dbhost, $dbuser, $dbpass);
$db->select_db($dbname);
```

Finally, we add some basic error handling code that would stop any further execution if the connection to the database server failed. We also provide some information about the error for debugging.

```
if ($db->connect_errno > 0){
   die('ERROR! - COULD NOT CONNECT TO mySQL
   DATABASE: ' . $db->connect_error);
}
```

Now that we have a script that we can call in order to connect to our database, it is possible for us to write the PHP script that will take information from the client and perform queries on the database.

First, we create an object named $data to hold the results and any errors from the script. We create this object using PHP's stdClass as follows:

```
$data = new stdClass;
$data->success = false;
$data->results = array();
$data->error = NULL;
```

Next, we check to see if the request from the client included some POST information with text as the key. This prevents the script from running needlessly if we have no query text.

```
if (isset($_POST['text'])) {
```

PHP's isset() function simply checks to see if the provided argument is set and available for use. If there has been some data posted to the script with the key text, we can continue to connect to the database by including our database connection script using require_once();. There are various ways by which you can include additional PHP files. We use require_once() because we cannot continue with the execution without the database connection. If the specified file is not found when using require_once(), the script provides a fatal error and ceases the execution.

```
if (isset($_POST['text'])) {
   //Connect to the database
   require_once('db.inc.php');
   //Escape the text to prevent SQL injection
   $text = $db->real_escape_string($_POST['text']);
}
```

After including the database connection file and connecting to the database, we can refer to the $db connection variable that is instantiated within that file. We then use the real_escape_string() function that will remove any harmful characters from the provided text string with the aim to prevent a security breach, such as MySQL injection (read more on this at http://dev.mysql.com/tech-resources/articles/guide-to-php-security-ch3.pdf). We put $_POST['text'] through this function and store the result in a $text variable, which we can now safely use within MySQL queries.

```
$q = "SELECT * FROM `stationary` WHERE `title` LIKE '%{$text}%'";
$result = $db->query($q);
if (!$result) {
   $data->error = "Could not query database for search results,
   MYSQL ERROR: " . $db->error;
} else {

}
```

We construct a MySQL LIKE query using the $text string and then use $result = $db->query($q); to execute the query on the database. We first evaluate the $result variable for a false value to determine if the query was executed successfully. If the query isn't executed successfully, we store an error within the $data object.

If the query is executed successfully, we can prepare the results to send back to the client as follows:

```
if (!$result) {
   $data->error = "Could not query database for search results,
   MYSQL ERROR: " . $db->error;
} else {
   while ($row = $result->fetch_assoc()) {
      $data->results[] = array(
         'id' => $row['id'],
         'title' => $row['title']
      );
   }
   $data->success = true;
}
```

By using a while loop with $result->fetch_assoc(), we are able to iterate through each of the results returned from the database query. We can then extract the information we require and store each item within the results array in the $data object. Once this is complete, we set the success variable of the $data object to true, which will tell the jQuery within the client that everything went according to plan.

Finally, we set the headers in order to force the jQuery to expect JSON data, encode our $data object into JSON, and output the encoded data as follows:

```
header("Content-Type: application/json; charset=UTF-8");
echo json_encode($data);
```

HTML

The HTML page we created provides the user with an input where they can type in their search query and a button to submit the search. It provides us with an unordered list element to display the results to the user. We also create a div element showing a **Loading...** message with the help of jQuery, which will be displayed when the AJAX request is made.

CSS

The CSS we created positions our HTML elements on the page and styles each item to provide a greater user experience. Note that we are using Google Fonts to add additional aesthetics to our search feature; you can read more about this at `http://www.google.com/fonts/`.

jQuery

Within the `script-7.js` file, we perform three actions on page load as shown in the following code snippet:

```
$(function(){
  $('#results-list').hide();
  $('#search').click(function(){
    doSearch();
  });
  $('#text').keydown(function(e){
    if(e.keyCode == 13){
      doSearch();
    }
  });
});
```

Firstly, we hide the results list using `$('#results-list').hide();` so that it will be hidden by default. We then attach a click event handler to the search button which will perform the search when this button is clicked. Within the callback function for this event handler, we call the `doSearch();` function, which is declared later in our JavaScript file. The final action that we perform on page load is adding a `keydown` event handler to the search input which allows us to detect if the *Enter* key has been pressed. If it has, we can call the `doSearch();` function to trigger the search.

The `doSearch()` function performs the AJAX request, sending the search query text to the PHP script. It also processes the response and updates the HTML page appropriately. The function gets the inputted text from the search input using `$('#text').val();` and stores it in the `searchText` variable for use. It also hides `#results-list` to ensure that it is always hidden before the AJAX request is made, providing room to display the loading text.

```
function doSearch() {
  var searchText = $('#text').val();
  $('#results-list').hide();
}
```

This function uses the jQuery-provided `$.ajax()` method to set up and make an AJAX request to our `search.php` script:

```
$.ajax({
  url: '/search.php',
  type: 'POST',
  data: {
    'text': searchText
  },
  beforeSend: function(){
    $('.loading').fadeIn();
  },
  success: function(data) {
    $('.loading').fadeOut();
  }
});
```

The initial parameters we provide to the AJAX function are the URLs in which we wish to make the request, the type of request we would like to make, and the data we would like to send with the request. We specify the request target as the `search.php` file and the request type as `POST`, so we can send data to the PHP file without needing it to be within the URL. Within the data object, we put the `searchText` variable with a key of `text`, which will be picked up by our PHP script that we created earlier, allowing it to use the user-inputted text.

We include `beforeSend` after these initial parameters, which allows us to specify a callback function to be executed just before the AJAX request is made. We are able to add some animation and show the `.loading` div element within this function using `$('.loading').fadeIn();`. This will display the **Loading...** text, informing the user that the request is in progress. Within the `success` callback function, which is executed once the request is successful and a response has been received, we are able to hide the **Loading...** div element with some additional animation using `$('.loading').fadeOut();`.

The `success` callback function has the data argument which will hold all of the response data from the PHP file. Looking back at the PHP script, you will remember the `$data` object we created to store information about the response. We check to see if the `success` property of this object is set to `true`, meaning that the query was successful.

```
success: function(data) {
  $('.loading').fadeOut();
  if (data.success) {

  } else {
    alert(data.error);
  }
}
```

If the `success` property is not set to `true` and something does go wrong, we then use `alert(data.error);` to alert the user with the error message created by the `search.php` script.

If `data.success` is set to `true`, we can process the search results and update the HTML page as follows:

```
success: function(data) {
  $('.loading').fadeOut();
  if (data.success) {
    $('#results-list').empty();
    if(data.results.length > 0) {
      $.each(data.results, function(){
        $('#results-list').append("<li>" + this.title + "</li>");
      });
    } else {
      $('#results-list').append("<li class='no-results'>Your
      search did not return any results</li>");
    }
    $('#results-list').fadeIn();
  } else {
    alert(data.error);
  }
}
```

Within the `if` statement, we empty the results list of any data to prevent multiple searches from duplicating results. We do this using `$('#results-list').empty();`. Then, we check the length of `results`. If there are results, we need to process them; otherwise, we display a message to the users informing them that their search did not return any results. This is done with the following code:

```
$('#results-list').append("<li class='no-results'>Your search did
  not return any results</li>");
```

If the `data.results.length > 0` condition is evaluated as `true`, it means that there are results to display, and hence, we use the jQuery `$.each()` function to iterate through each of the results in the response and append them to the results list as follows:

```
$.each(data.results, function(){
  $('#results-list').append("<li>" + this.title + "</li>");
});
```

Now, the users' search results will be visible within the list.

See also

▸ *Creating an autosuggest feature*

Creating an autosuggest feature

Autosuggest features are in abundance on the Internet. There are many plugins available for jQuery and jQuery UI which will allow you to add the autosuggest feature to your site quickly and easily. This recipe will show you how to create one from scratch which you can customize and add your own unique features to.

Getting ready

The server-side code for this recipe mirrors that of the previous one. Ensure that you have a web server and a MySQL database server running and ready to use.

How to do it...

The following are the steps to create an autosuggest feature:

1. Please refer to the previous recipe of this chapter, *Creating a search feature*, to create and set up a stationary database and the `search.php` script. We will be using the exact same code for the autosuggest feature.

2. Within the web root of your web server, create an HTML file named `recipe-8.html`. Add the following HTML code to create the basics of the autosuggest user interface:

```
<!DOCTYPE html>
<html>
<head>
  <title>Chapter 3 :: AJAX & JSON</title>
  <script src="jquery.min.js"></script>
  <script src='script-8.js'></script>
  <link href='style-8.css' rel="stylesheet" />
</head>
<body>
  <div id='frame'>
    <div class='search'>
      <div class='header'>
        <h1>Chapter 3 :: Auto-Suggest</h1>
      </div>
      <div class="suggest-input">
        <input type='text' id='text' />
        <ul class="suggest-list"></ul>
```

```
        </div>
      </div>
    </div>
  </body>
</html>
```

3. You may have noticed that within the header of our `recipe-8.html` file, we have included a cascading stylesheet named `style-8.css`. Create this file and save it within the web root of your web server. Add the following CSS code, which will style and position the HTML elements within `recipe-8.html`:

```css
/* Include a web font from Google  */
@import url(http://fonts.googleapis.com/css?family=Denk+One);
/* Basic CSS for positioning etc */
body {
   font-family: 'Denk One', sans-serif;
}
#frame {
   width: 500px;
   margin: 125px auto auto auto;
   border: solid 1px #CCC;
   /* SOME CSS3 DIV SHADOW */
   -webkit-box-shadow: 0 0 10px #CCC;
   -moz-box-shadow: 0 0 10px #CCC;
   box-shadow: 0 0 10px #CCC;
   /* CSS3 ROUNDED CORNERS */
   -moz-border-radius: 5px;
   -webkit-border-radius: 5px;
   -khtml-border-radius: 5px;
   border-radius: 5px;
   background-color: #FFF;
}
.search .header {
   margin: 25px;
}
.search .header {
   text-align: center;
}
.suggest-input input {
   width: 440px;
}
.suggest-input {
   position: relative;
   padding: 25px;
}
```

```css
/* SUGGESTION LIST STYLES */
.suggest-list {
  position: absolute;
  width: 424px;
  background-color: #f1f1f1;
  margin: 0;
  left: 25px;
  top: 50px;
  z-index: 100;
  display: none;
  list-style: none;
  padding: 10px;
}
```

4. Along with the CSS file, we are also including `script-8.js` into our HTML page. Create this JavaScript file and add the following code:

```javascript
$(function(){
  $('#text').keyup(function(e){
    if ($('#text').val().length > 2) {
      $('.suggest-list').show();
      makeSuggestion();
    } else {
      $('.suggest-list').hide();
    }
  });
  $('.search').on("click", ".suggestion", function(){
    $('#text').val($(this).html());
  });
});

function makeSuggestion() {
  var searchText = $('#text').val();
  $('.suggest-list').empty();
  $.ajax({
    url: '/search.php',
    type: 'POST',
    data: {
      'text': searchText
    },
    beforeSend: function(){
      $('.suggest-list').append("<li class=
        'loading'>Loading...</li>");
    },
    success: function(data) {
```

```
    if (data.success) {
      $('.suggest-list').empty();
      if(data.results.length > 0) {
        $.each(data.results, function(){
          $('.suggest-list').append("<li><a href='#'
            class='suggestion'>" + this.title +
            "</a></li>");
        });
      } else {
        $('.suggest-list').append("<li class=
          'no-results'>Nothing to suggest...</li>");
      }
    } else {
      alert(data.error);
    }
  }
});
}
```

5. Visiting `recipe-8.html` served by a web server will present you with the
    autosuggest feature. It will suggest items based on the text inputted into the textbox
    as you type. There will be no suggestions until the user inputs more than two
    characters. This is shown in the following screenshot:

How it works...

Now, let us understand the steps performed previously in detail.

SQL and PHP

Please refer to the previous recipe of this chapter, *Creating a search feature*, which will
explain in detail how the SQL and PHP code is created.

HTML

The HTML file we created is very simple. We create an input box which allows the user to input text, and we create an unordered list element which we can populate with suggestions using jQuery.

CSS

The CSS code we created adds basic styling to our feature, which includes the positioning of the main text input area.

The main task of this CSS code is to position the suggestion list such that suggestions are displayed directly below the input box. For this to be possible, we first need to set the position of the `.suggest-input` div element to `relative`. This will allow us to have sibling elements which are absolutely positioned, without them floating off to other areas of the page.

```css
.suggest-input {
    position: relative;
    padding: 25px;
}
```

With this positioning set, we can go ahead and add the required styles to our `.suggest-list` element, which will hold the suggestions. We need to position the element directly below the input box. This means that we will need to make the `.suggest-list` element the same width as the input box. We also need to ensure that the left and top positions of the `.suggest-list` element are specified, taking into account the size and padding of the input textbox.

```css
.suggest-list {
    position: absolute;
    width: 424px;
    background-color: #f1f1f1;
    margin: 0px;
    padding: 0px;
    left: 25px;
    top: 50px;
    z-index: 100;
    display: none;
    list-style: none;
    padding: 10px;
}
```

In this section of CSS, we remove any default padding and margins from the list element and set its position to absolute. Any element with absolute positioning will not be affected by other elements on the page, apart from their parents if they have a relative position. This leaves us to be able to set its left and top positional values to control exactly where it will sit in relation to the text input. We also set the `z-index` value of this element to `100` to ensure that it will always float above the other elements on the page. Finally, we use `display: none;`, which will make this element hidden by default as we want to display this dynamically with jQuery.

jQuery

Within our `script-8.js` file, we perform two actions when the page is loaded as follows:

```
$(function(){
  $('#text').keyup(function(e){
    if ($('#text').val().length > 2) {
      $('.suggest-list').show();
      makeSuggestion();
    } else {
      $('.suggest-list').hide();
    }
  });
  $('.search').on("click", ".suggestion", function(){
    $('#text').val($(this).html());
  });
});
```

The former action is to attach a `keyup` event handler to the text input. This event handler will execute when the user enters a character into the input box and releases a key. Within the callback function, we check the current length of the text input using `$('#text').val();`. If this value is greater than 2, we need to look for some suggestions; so, we call the `makeSuggestion()` function, which is declared further down in the JavaScript file. We also show the `.suggest-list` element using `$('.suggest-list').show();` so that it is visible to the user. If the inputted text is less than two characters in length, all we do is ensure that the `.suggest-list` is hidden with `$('.suggest-list').hide();`.

The latter action we perform on page load is to attach another event handler. This event handler will listen for clicks on any element with the `.suggestion` class. We use the `.on()` function provided by jQuery so that we can listen for click events on elements that have been dynamically added to the DOM, which is not possible using the `.click()` function. Please refer to the *Detecting button clicks* recipe in *Chapter 2, Interacting with the User by Making Use of jQuery Events*, to learn more about these event handler functions. Within the callback function of this event handler, we get the HTML code of the clicked element using `$(this).html()`. Provide this to the `$('#text').val();` function, which will update the value of the text input. This will be used to allow the user to click on a suggestion and update the text input with its value.

Our `makeSuggestion()` function takes the text from the input element and sends an AJAX request to our `search.php` file to query the database and look for anything similar to what the user has inputted. This function then takes the results and populates the `.suggest-list` list for the user to select.

The first part of the function gets the current value of the text input and empties the `.suggest-list` unordered list element.

```
var searchText = $('#text').val();
$('.suggest-list').empty();
```

Next, we use the `$.ajax()` function to set up the AJAX request. We specify the `search.php` file as the target, using the `url` parameter, the request type as `POST`, and provide the inputted text as data to be sent to the PHP file. Please refer to the *Creating a search feature* recipe for greater detail on this.

```
$.ajax({
    url: 'search.php',
    type: 'POST',
    data: {
        'text': searchText
    },
    beforeSend: function(){
        $('.suggest-list').append("<li
            class='loading'>Loading...</li>");
    },
    success: function(data) {


    }
});
```

We use the `beforeSend` parameter and provide a callback function that appends a list item with the `.suggest-list` element with the text **Loading...**. This callback function will be executed just before the AJAX request is made, allowing us to inform the user that the request is loading, as shown in the following screenshot:

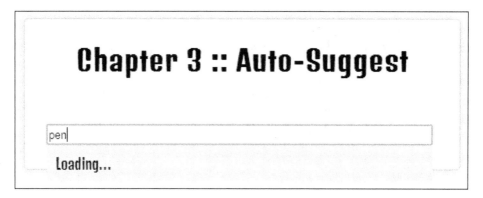

Chapter 3 :: Auto-Suggest

pen

Loading...

The `success` callback function, which is executed when the request has been successful, is the function where we check to see if the database query has returned the desired results; if there are any suggestions to populate the list with.

```
success: function(data) {
    if (data.success) {
        $('.suggest-list').empty();
        if (data.results.length > 0) {
```

```
    $.each(data.results, function(){
      $('.suggest-list').append("<li><a href=
        '#' class='suggestion'>" + this.title + "</a></li>");
    });
  } else {
    $('.suggest-list').append("<li class='no-results'>
      Nothing to suggest...</li>");
  }
} else {
  alert(data.error);
}
}
```

The `data` argument within the `success` callback function holds all the data sent from the PHP file. The object we created to send back to the client in the PHP has a `success` parameter, which we can use to check if everything went according to plan.

```
if (data.success) {

} else {
  alert(data.error);
}
```

If something went wrong, we display the error message as an alert, which is provided by the PHP within the `error` parameter.

If the query is executed successfully, we first empty the suggestion list once more to remove the loading item that was added in the `beforeSend()` callback function. We then check the length of the results using `data.results.length` to see if there are any suggestions with which we can populate our list element. If there are, we use the jQuery `$.each()` function to iterate through each item and append it to our `.suggest-list` element. We also wrap the suggestion in the `<a></a>` tags with the `.suggestion` class. Clicking on these suggestions will fire the event handler we created earlier and then update the text input with the suggested text.

There's more...

Since the autosuggest feature is such a common implementation on modern websites and web applications, there are many jQuery plugins available to help you add this feature to your application. jQuery UI, which is jQuery's own user interface framework, has an autosuggest module readily available. You should investigate this further to see if your application can benefit from this ready-built solution. *Chapter 9, jQuery UI*, is dedicated to jQuery UI, as the name suggests, and you will also find an entire recipe on implementing the autocomplete feature.

See also

▸   *Creating a search feature*

Waiting for an AJAX response

The default behavior of jQuery AJAX requests is that they run asynchronously, which means that you can run many AJAX requests or other JavaScript processes at the same time. If you call the $.ajax() function with the default settings, any JavaScript code after this AJAX request will be executed without waiting for a response. In most cases, this is the desired behavior, but there are some situations where you will want to prevent further execution until there has been a response to the AJAX call. This may be because you require some information from the first AJAX call to make a second, or just that your application requires data from the first call before it can run the second. There are a few ways to achieve this; refer to the *Caching JSON and AJAX requests* recipe of this chapter to see a very basic implementation where you simply turn off the asynchronous behavior. The preferred implementation though uses jQuery's .when() and .done() functions.

Getting ready

Ensure that your web server is up and running and you have access to add files to the web root.

How to do it...

Understand the correct way to wait for an AJAX response with jQuery by performing the following steps:

1. Create an HTML file named recipe-9.html in the web root of your web server. Add the following code, which has a button that can trigger a series of AJAX requests and an element that can be updated with information about the responses:

```
<!DOCTYPE html>
<html>
<head>
  <title>Chapter 3 :: AJAX & JSON</title>
  <script src="jquery.min.js"></script>
    <script src="script-9.js"></script>
</head>
<body>
  <button class="load">Load</button>
  <div class="info"></div>
</body>
</html>
```

2. To be able to wait for a set of AJAX requests, we need to be able to make successful calls to the web server. Create a PHP file named `loading1.php` in the web root of your web server and add the following code to simulate a working PHP script. In your application, this could be any PHP script.

```php
<?php
for ($i = 1; $i <= 2; $i++) {
   sleep(1);
}
echo "Call 1 complete.";
```

3. Create another PHP file named `loading2.php` within the web root of your web server and add the following code:

```php
<?php
for ($i = 1; $i <= 5; $i++) {
   sleep(1);
}
echo "Call 2 complete.";
```

4. You may have noticed that within the header of the HTML page, we included `script-9.js`. Create this file and save it in the web root of your web server, adding the following code:

```javascript
$(function(){
   $('.load').click(function(){
      $.when(call1(), call2()).done(function(c1, c2){
         $('.info').append("Both AJAX requests complete!");
      });
   });
});
function call1() {
   return $.ajax({
      url: '/loading1.php',
      type: 'GET'
   }).success(function(data){
      $('.info').append(data);
   });
}
function call2() {
   return $.ajax({
      url: '/loading2.php',
      type: 'GET'
   }).success(function(data){
      $('.info').append(data);
   });
}
```

5. Opening `recipe-9.html` within a web browser and clicking on the **Load** button will give you the output from each of the AJAX calls. Finally, you will see the output from the `.done()` function, which is only executed once both the AJAX requests have been completed.

How it works...

Now, let us understand the steps performed previously in detail.

HTML

Our very basic HTML page simply creates a button that will trigger the AJAX requests and provides an HTML element for us to update with data from the responses.

PHP

The two PHP scripts we created are just to simulate the end points for the AJAX calls. Both scripts are nearly identical, with two subtle differences. The `loading1.php` script loops twice, calls the PHP `sleep()` method, and provides 1 as an argument. This will pause the script for 1 second on each iteration of the `for` loop.

```php
<?php
  for ($i = 1; $i <= 2; $i++) {
    sleep(1);
  }
  echo "Call 1 complete.";
?>
```

After the execution of the `for` loop, the script outputs the `Call 1 complete` message, which can then be displayed in the web browser using jQuery. The second script, `loading2.php`, is the same, except that its `for` loop iterates five times and we provide a different output to differentiate between the two scripts.

The two scripts loop a different number of times to make sure that the former script will complete first, allowing us to demonstrate that we can wait for both scripts to complete within our jQuery code.

jQuery

In our JavaScript file, we attach a click event handler to the `.load` button that will be created on page load. Within the callback function for this event, we use the jQuery `$.when()` function and provide the results of the `call1()` and `call2()` functions as arguments. We then chain `.done()` at the end of the `$.when()` function, which will be executed once the `when()` function is complete. Within the `.done()` function, we provide a callback, which allows us to provide an argument for each of the functions we provided to `$.when()`. As the functions we provided to `$.when()` are AJAX requests, the arguments provided within the callback of the `.done()` function will all contain the response, status, and the `jqXHR` object from each of the AJAX requests.

The `jqXHR` object is the return value of the jQuery `$.ajax()` function, which holds a lot of information regarding the AJAX request. The `.done()` function will not be executed until `call1()` and `call2()` have received a complete response from their respective AJAX requests and have finished executing.

```
$(function(){
  $('.load').click(function(){
    $.when(call1(), call2()).done(function(c1, c2){
      $('.info').append("Both AJAX requests complete!");
    });
  });
});
```

Within the callback for the `.done()` function, we append some text to the `.info` HTML element showing that both the AJAX calls within `$.when()` are complete.

The two call functions we created simply return `$.ajax()`, which both make a GET request to the PHP files we created. For each of these AJAX requests, we append the `.success()` function that will be executed once the respective AJAX call has been successful. Within the callback function for `.success()`, we append the response of the call to the `.info` HTML element using `$('.info').append();`.

If you visit the root of your web server with a browser and select the load button, you will first see the response from the `loading1.php` script added to the `.info` div element. Shortly after, you will see the response from the `loading2.php` script and the text from the `.done()` callback added.

See also

▶ *Caching JSON and AJAX requests*

4
Adding Attractive Visuals with jQuery Effects

In this chapter, we will cover:

- ▶ Sliding page elements
- ▶ Hiding and showing elements
- ▶ Fading elements
- ▶ Toggling effects
- ▶ Stopping effects
- ▶ Chaining effects
- ▶ Creating a basic photo gallery
- ▶ Creating a blinking button
- ▶ Removing elements with effects

Introduction

This chapter will show you how to add simple effects to your interfaces to increase the overall aesthetics and user experience of your website. Adding basic effects to elements can have a huge impact on user's impressions. jQuery provides functions that allow the developer to quickly add effects such as slide, fade, hide, and more.

Sliding page elements

The ability to slide page elements allows the developer to create an array of interfaces such as the accordion. This recipe will show you how to apply the slide effect to a range of elements.

Getting ready

Using your favorite text editor or IDE, create a blank HTML page in an easily accessible location and save this file as `recipe-1.html`. Ensure that you have the latest version of jQuery downloaded at the same location as this HTML file.

How to do it...

Learn how to use jQuery to slide page elements by performing the following steps:

1. Add the following HTML code to `recipe-1.html`. Be sure to change the source location of the jQuery library, pointing it to where the latest version of jQuery is downloaded and placed on your computer.

```
<!DOCTYPE html>
<html>
<head>
  <script src="jquery.min.js"></script>
  <script src="recipe-1.js"></script>
  <title>Chapter 4 :: JQuery Effects</title>
  <link type="text/css" media="screen" rel="stylesheet"
    href="recipe-1.css" />
</head>
<body>
  <div class="frame">
    <div class="actions">
      <button id="down">Slide Down</button>
      <button id="up">Slide Up</button>
    </div>
    <div class="box one"></div>
    <div class="box two"></div>
    <div class="box three"></div>
    <div class="box four"></div>
  </div>
</body>
</html>
```

2. You may have noticed that, in addition to the jQuery library file, we also included a second JavaScript file named `recipe-1.js`. Create this JavaScript file and save it in the same directory as the HTML file. Add the following JavaScript code to the `recipe-1.js` file:

```
$(function(){
  $('#up').click(function(){
    $('.one').slideUp(4000);
    $('.two').slideUp(3000);
    $('.three').slideUp(2000);
    $('.four').slideUp(1000);
  });
  $('#down').click(function(){
    $('.one').slideDown(4000);
    $('.two').slideDown(3000);
    $('.three').slideDown(2000);
    $('.four').slideDown(1000);
  });
});
```

3. Along with these two JavaScript files, we have also included a CSS file to add some style to our HTML elements. Create `recipe-1.css` within the same directory and add the following code:

```
.frame {
  width: 530px;
  height: 190px;
  margin: 50px auto auto auto;
  background-color: #E1E1E1;
  padding: 10px;
}
.frame .box {
  width: 125px;
  height: 125px;
  float: left;
  margin-right: 10px;
}
.frame .box:last-child {
  margin-right: 0;
}
.frame .actions {
  background-color: #333333;
  margin-bottom: 10px;
  text-align: center;
  padding: 10px;
}
```

```
.frame .actions button {
  height: 35px;
}
.one {
  background-color: red;
}
.two {
  background-color: green;
}
.three {
  background-color: blue;
}
.four {
  background-color: orange;
}
```

4. Open `recipe-1.html` in a web browser and you should see a web page similar to the following screenshot:

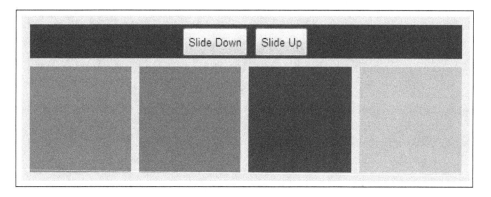

5. Click on the **Slide Up** button to see the slide up effect applied to each of the colored box elements at different speeds; then click on **Slide Down** to see the reverse.

How it works...

Now, let's understand the steps performed previously in detail.

HTML

The HTML file that we created for this recipe simply creates four boxes using div elements and then provides two buttons that can be used in conjunction with jQuery to trigger the element effects.

jQuery

We wrap all our JavaScript code within `$(function(){});`. This will ensure our code is executed on page load. Inside the function, we attach a click event to each of the buttons as demonstrated in the following code snippet:

```
$('#up').click(function(){
    $('.one').slideUp(4000);
    $('.two').slideUp(3000);
    $('.three').slideUp(2000);
    $('.four').slideUp(1000);
});
$('#down').click(function(){
    $('.one').slideDown(4000);
    $('.two').slideDown(3000);
    $('.three').slideDown(2000);
    $('.four').slideDown(1000);
});
```

The `.click()` function allows us to provide a set of code to be executed when the corresponding button has been clicked by the user. Inside the callback function for each of the `.click()` methods, we select the div element of each box and use the jQuery `.slideUp()` and `.slideDown()` functions, depending on which button has been clicked.

The jQuery slide functions allow you to specify a range of parameters. In the preceding example, we have specified the effect duration in milliseconds. This allows us to control the time taken for each of the box elements to slide up or down, providing a waterfall effect.

CSS

The CSS file we created adds style and positions each of the HTML elements, allowing us to best showcase the jQuery slide functionality. It allows us to change the background color of each of the boxes and allows us to center-align the interface.

There's more...

In the previous example, if you click on both the **Slide Up** and **Slide Down** buttons multiple times, you may notice some flicker between the different box elements. This flicker occurs because when the slide up effect is complete, the CSS `display` property of the box element is set to `none`. This means that not only will the element be invisible but it also will not affect any neighboring elements in terms of position.

Therefore, the element that is set to float left will have room to move further left as the box element that has completed its slide up effect is no longer in the way. This is shown in the following screenshot:

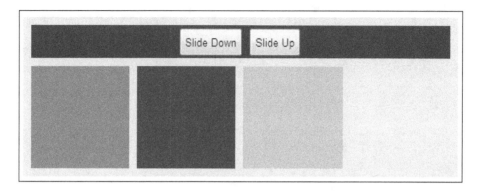

Here you can see the second, green box element has its display value set to none, causing the other box elements to float further to the left. The display may flicker more when the slide animations have been triggered multiple times and elements have to shift to the left as additional elements become invisible. Issues such as this can be prevented by not allowing the trigger to trigger the effects multiple times. A simple solution to this has been explained in the *Creating a basic photo gallery* recipe later on in this chapter.

See also

- ▸ *Fading elements*
- ▸ *Hiding and showing elements*
- ▸ *Creating a basic photo gallery*

Hiding and showing elements

jQuery includes functions that will allow you to simply hide and show elements, although you can use these functions in conjunction with other effects.

Getting ready

Create a new HTML file named `recipe-2.html` and save it to the same folder as your jQuery library.

How to do it...

Understand how you can use jQuery to easily hide and show elements in the DOM by performing the following steps:

1. In `recipe-2.html`, add the following HTML code. Ensure that the reference to the jQuery library is pointing to the correct location and filename of your downloaded version.

```
<!DOCTYPE html>
<html>
<head>
  <title>Chapter 4 :: JQuery Effects :: Recipe 2</title>
  <script src="jquery.min.js"></script>
  <script src="recipe-2.js"></script>
</head>
<body>
<button class="show">Show</button>
<button class="hide">Hide</button>
<p class="text">Hiding and showing HTML elements with
  jQuery is so easy!</p>
</body>
</html>
```

2. Create a JavaScript file named `recipe-2.js` and save it within the same directory as the HTML file you have just created. Add the following JavaScript code to this file:

```
$(function(){
  $('#show').click(function(){
      $('.text').show();
  });
  $('#hide').click(function(){
      $('.text').hide();
  });
});
```

3. Opening `recipe-2.html` in a web browser will present you with a very basic web page that has two buttons and some text. Clicking on the **Show** and **Hide** buttons will perform the associated effect on the text, demonstrating how simple it is to show and hide elements with jQuery.

How it works...

Now, let's understand the steps performed previously in detail.

HTML

The HTML code used in this recipe is very basic and needs little explanation. The HTML code creates a web page with two buttons. Each has its own ID—show and hide. There is also a single paragraph element with a text class. The IDs will be used by jQuery to listen a click event and perform effects on the paragraph element.

jQuery

Similar to the previous recipe, we attach a click event handler to each of the buttons. This allows us to perform the effects based on which button has been clicked. To do this, we use the following code:

```
$('#show').click(function(){
  $('.text').show();
});
$('#hide').click(function(){
  $('.text').hide();
});
```

To perform the show and hide effects, we use the corresponding jQuery functions, show() and hide(). These jQuery functions simply toggle the display property of the selected element (in this case, the paragraph element is of the text class). The display property is set to none to hide the element; it is set to block to show the element.

There's more...

There are additional benefits to using jQuery's show() and hide() functions. Using jQuery, you can show and hide elements based on their inner HTML code. You can also use the show() and hide() functions in conjunction with other jQuery effects or animations.

See also

- ▶ *Fading elements*
- ▶ *Sliding page elements*

Fading elements

If showing or hiding elements is not enough, jQuery provides the ability to fade HTML elements in and out. This recipe utilizes the jQuery's fade-in and fade-out functionalities to add more effect when choosing to display or hide elements.

Getting ready

Create a blank HTML file named `recipe-3.html` and save it in the same directory as the latest version of jQuery.

How to do it...

Use jQuery to fade DOM elements in and out by performing the following steps:

1. Add the following HTML code to `recipe-3.html`, ensuring the reference to the jQuery library is correct:

```
<!DOCTYPE html>
<html>
<head>
  <title>Chapter 4 :: JQuery Effects :: Recipe 3</title>
  <script src="jquery.min.js"></script>
  <script src="recipe-3.js"></script>
  <link type="text/css" media="screen" rel="stylesheet"
    href="recipe-3.css" />
</head>
<body>
  <div class="frame">
    <div class="top">
      <label>Add Item:</label>
      <input type="text" id="new-item" />
      <button id="add-new-item">Add</button>
    </div>
    <ol class="list"></ol>
  </div>
</body>
</html>
```

2. Create a CSS file in the same directory. Save it as `recipe-3.css` and add the following code to style the HTML page:

```
.frame {
  width: 500px;
  min-height: 200px;
  margin: 50px auto auto auto;
  background-color: #E1E1E1;
  padding: 10px;
}
.top {
  background-color: #333333;
  padding: 10px;
```

```
  text-align: center;
  color: #FFF;
}
.list li {
  line-height: 30px;
}
```

3. Create a JavaScript file named `recipe-3.js` and add the following jQuery code:

```
$(function(){
  $('#add-new-item').click(function(){
    var item = $('#new-item').val();
    if (item.length > 0) {
      var newItem = $("<li>" + item + "</li>").fadeIn();
      $('.list').append(newItem);
      $('#new-item').val("");
    }
  });
});
```

4. Open `recipe-3.html` in a web browser and you will be presented with a web page similar to the following screenshot:

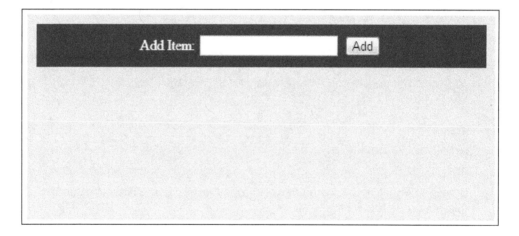

5. Entering some text into the **Add Item** textbox and clicking on the **Add** button will append the inputted text to a list using the jQuery fade effect.

How it works...

Now, let's understand the steps performed previously in detail.

HTML

The HTML code creates a simple interface that includes the text input with a button and an empty ordered list element, which can then be populated with jQuery.

CSS

A CSS file was added to position and style the simple user interface so we could better demonstrate the fade effect with jQuery.

jQuery

First of all, the jQuery code attaches a click event to the **Add** button using the following code:

```
$(function(){
    $('#add-new-item').click(function(){

    });
});
```

We add the following code to this callback function to provide the desired effect of adding the input text to the list using the `fadeIn()` function:

```
var item = $('#new-item').val();
if (item.length > 0) {
var newItem = $("<li>" + item + "</li>");
$('.list').append(newItem).fadeIn();
$('#new-item').val("");
}
```

This code creates the `item` variable and assigns the value of the input box to it using `$('#new-item').val()`. We then check to see if the length of this value is greater than zero, as we do not want to add blank items to the list. We are able to check the length of a string with JavaScript by simply using `variablename.length` (in this example, `item.length`).

Within this `if` statement, we create another variable named `newItem`. We assign to it a newly created HTML list item element with the value from the input box using the `item` variable. We wrap the list item within jQuery's selector (`$()`), allowing us to use the `fadeIn()` function on this DOM element.

Now that we have a list item, we can append it to the ordered list element with the class name `list` by using the jQuery-provided `append()` function. This will add the newly created DOM element as the last child of the ordered list. Because we used the `fadeIn()` function on this DOM element, it will firstly appear hidden and then fade in, giving us our desired effect.

There's more...

Within this recipe, we used the `fadeIn()` function, which allows us to take an element from invisible to visible with the fade effect. jQuery also provides us with a `fadeOut()` function that offers the reverse functionality. Both of these functions take a range of parameters, allowing the developer to adjust the behavior. The primary parameter is duration, which allows us to specify how long it takes the element to fade in or out in milliseconds. Read about the available options for these functions at `http://api.jquery.com/fadeIn/`.

Additionally, jQuery provides a `fadeTo()` function, allowing you to adjust the opacity of an element if you do not want to completely hide or show it once the effect has completed. Read more about this functionality at `http://api.jquery.com/fadeTo/`.

See also

- ► *Removing elements with effects*
- ► *Creating a basic photo gallery*
- ► *Creating a blinking button*

Toggling effects

Many of the jQuery effects have opposing functions, such as `hide()` and `show()` and `fadeIn()` and `fadeOut()`. So far, the recipes in this chapter have handled each of these functions separately; for example, one button to show and another to hide. For some of these functions, jQuery provides us with the ability to be able to toggle these opposing effects. This is beneficial because we do not need to deal with each case separately or decide which of the two we need to use. This recipe will look at the toggle functions and show you how they can be used.

Getting ready

In your favorite text editor or IDE, create a blank HTML file named `recipe-4.html` and save it in the same directory as your jQuery library.

How to do it...

1. Add the following HTML code to `recipe-4.html` to create a basic web page:

```
<!DOCTYPE html>
<html>
<head>
  <script src="jquery.min.js"></script>
  <script src="recipe-4.js"></script>
```

```
    <title>Chapter 4 :: JQuery Effects :: Recipe 4</title>
  </head>
  <body>
    <div>
      <button class="fadeToggle">Toggle Fade!</button>
      <button class="slideToggle">Toggle Slide!</button>
      <button class="hideToggle">Toggle Hide!</button>
    </div>
    <p class="text">Here is some text that can be faded in
      and out! Here is some text that can be faded in and
      out! Here is some text that can be faded in and out!
      Here is some text that can be faded in and out! Here is
      some text that can be faded in and out! Here is some
      text that can be faded in and out! Here is some text
      that can be faded in and out! Here is some text that
      can be faded in and out! Here is some text that can be
      faded in and out! Here is some text that can be faded
      in and out! Here is some text that can be faded in and
      out! Here is some text that can be faded in and
      out!</p>
  </body>
</html>
```

2. You may have noticed that we are including a JavaScript file in this HTML page. Create this JavaScript file in the same directory as `recipe-4.html` and save it as `recipe-4.js`. Add the following jQuery code to this file to attach click event handlers to the button elements within the HTML:

```
$(function(){
  $('.fadeToggle').click(function(){
    $('.text').fadeToggle();
  });
  $('.slideToggle').click(function(){
    $('.text').slideToggle();
  });
  $('.hideToggle').click(function(){
    $('.text').toggle();
  });
});
```

3. Open `recipe-4.html` in a web browser and you should see a web page similar to the following screenshot:

> Toggle Fade! Toggle Slide! Toggle Hide!
>
> Here is some text that can be faded in and out! Here is some text that can be faded in and out! Here is some text that can be faded in and out! Here is some text that can be faded in and out! Here is some text that can be faded in and out! Here is some text that can be faded in and out! Here is some text that can be faded in and out! Here is some text that can be faded in and out! Here is some text that can be faded in and out! Here is some text that can be faded in and out! Here is some text that can be faded in and out! Here is some text that can be faded in and out!

4. Clicking on one of the buttons will toggle the associated effect and apply it to the paragraph element.

How it works...

Now, let's understand the steps performed previously in detail.

HTML

The HTML code in this recipe creates a paragraph element with some text. This element has the class name of `text`, which allows us to select this element and perform a range of effects. In addition to this paragraph element, the HTML provides three different buttons. Each button has a different class name, allowing us to detect each individual click with jQuery and perform different effects based on the clicked button.

jQuery

The jQuery code in this recipe is very basic. On page load, we attach a click event handler to each of the buttons. Each click event handler has a different toggle function inside its callback function.

jQuery's toggle functions determine the state of the selected element and then perform the opposing effect. This means that we do not need to program this logic into our application and can offload it to jQuery. By using the `toggleFade()` function, we can use one line of code to fade the paragraph element in or out without having to code for each scenario, as we have done in previous recipes. The same goes for the `slideToggle()` method, which performs the slide animation. Finally, we can use the `toggle` method, which simply hides or shows the selected element.

There's more...

Like other jQuery effect functions, the toggle functions take a set of optional parameters. The main parameter is the effect duration. The following code will force the slide effect to last for 1000 milliseconds:

```
$('.slideToggle').click(function(){
$('.text').slideToggle(1000);
});
```

You can read about the other available options as part of the jQuery API documentation, which can be found at `http://api.jquery.com/slideToggle/`.

Stopping effects

As your application grows and you begin to have more complex effects, you may want to be able to stop these effects and transitions. This could be due to a user action that negates the requirement for a current effect or some other form of event.

Getting ready

Create a blank HTML document named `recipe-5.html` and save it to the same directory as the latest version of the jQuery library.

How to do it...

Learn to stop jQuery effects by performing the following steps:

1. Add the following HTML code to `recipe-5.html` to create a basic web page that will allow us to demonstrate how to stop effects:

    ```
    <!DOCTYPE html>
    <html>
    <head>
      <script src="jquery.min.js"></script>
      <script src="recipe-5.js"></script>
      <title>Chapter 4 :: JQuery Effects :: Recipe 5 </title>
      <link type="text/css" media="screen" rel="stylesheet"
    href="recipe-5.css" />
    </head>
    <body>
    <div class="frame">
      <div class="actions">
        <button id="slide">Slide</button>
    ```

```
    <button id="stop">Stop</button>
    <button id="Finish">Finish</button>
  </div>
  <ul class="output"></ul>
  <div class="slideMe"></div>
</div>
</body>
</html>
```

2. To allow us to better demonstrate the jQuery effects, we need to add some CSS code to style and position the HTML elements in `recipe-5.html`. Create a CSS file named `recipe-5.css` in the same directory and add the following code:

```css
.frame {
  width: 600px;
  margin: auto;
  background-color: #CCC;
  padding: 10px;
}
.actions {
  padding: 10px;
  background-color: #333;
  text-align: center;
}
.slideMe {
  background-color: green;
  height: 150px;
  margin-top: 10px;
}
```

3. To start and stop the jQuery effects, create a JavaScript file named `recipe-5.js` and save it in the same directory as the HTML and CSS files. Add the following jQuery code:

```javascript
$(function(){
  $('#slide').click(function(){
    $('.slideMe').slideToggle(1000, function(){
      $('.output').append("<li>Slide effect completed.
        </li>");
    });
  });
  $('#stop').click(function(){
    $('.slideMe').stop();
  });
  $('#finish').click(function(){
```

```
    $('.slideMe').finish();
  });
});
```

4. Open `recipe-5.html` in a web browser and you will be presented with a web page similar to the following screenshot:

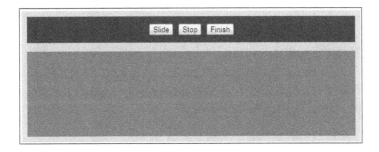

5. Clicking on the **Slide** button will begin the effect, and the green box division element will start to slide upward for 1000 milliseconds. Clicking on the **Stop** button will stop the effect at the point that you clicked it, and the **Finish** button will instantly complete the effect.

How it works...

Now, let's understand the steps performed previously in detail.

HTML

Our simple HTML for this recipe provides us with a division element to which jQuery can apply effects, some buttons that can be used to trigger jQuery code, and a list that we can use to output some information about the executed jQuery code.

CSS

The CSS code that was included into the HTML page allows us to position each of the HTML elements in a way that allows us to easily demonstrate the effects in this recipe.

jQuery

We attach three different click event handlers to the three buttons in our HTML page, selecting them by using their IDs: `slide`, `stop`, and `finish`. Within the callback functions to these event handlers, we start the slide effect using the following code:

```
$('#slide').click(function(){
$('.slideMe').slideToggle(1000, function(){
  $('.output').append("<li>Slide effect completed.</li>");
});
});
```

We have used the `slideToggle()` function to start either the slide down or slide up effect based on whether the `slideMe` division element is currently visible or not. We provide the `slideToggle()` function with two parameters. The first parameter is the duration in which we wish the slide effect to take effect. The second parameter is a callback function, which will be executed once the animation has been finished.

Inside this callback function, we append a list item to the unordered list element with the class name `output`. This means that when the slide effect has fully completed, a new list item will be visible within the `output` list. We have done this to demonstrate the difference between stopping an effect and finishing one, which is described later in this section.

The other two event handlers, described in the following code snippet, select the `slideMe` division element the same way as the previously mentioned event handler does, except these do not start an effect but stop the current one:

```
$('#stop').click(function(){
  $('.slideMe').stop();
});
$('#finish').click(function(){
  $('.slideMe').finish();
});
```

The `stop()` function will halt any currently running effects on the selected element. If the slide-up effect was half-way through completion and you clicked on **Stop**, you will see half of the green `slideMe` division element. The `stop()` function does not complete the slide effect, and therefore the `slideToggle()` callback function will not be executed and a list item will not be added to the output list. On the contrary, the `finish()` function instantly completes any effects being executed on the selected element. This means that if the slide-up effect was half-way through completion and you clicked on **Finish**, the `slideMe` division element will instantly become invisible and then a new item added to the output list, reading **Slide effect completed**. If there is code inside an effects callback function that is vital to your application, you can use `finish()` to ensure it is executed. Alternatively, you may not want to execute this code and/or want to visibly stop the effect; in this case, you would use `stop()`.

Chaining effects

jQuery allows us to chain the different effect functions onto a single selected element. This allows us to easily perform multiple effects in a sequential order.

How to do it...

Learn to use a powerful feature of jQuery to write better code by performing the following steps:

1. Create a blank HTML file named `recipe-6.html` and save it to an easily accessible location on your computer. Add the following HTML code to this file, ensuring to update the reference to the jQuery library:

```html
<!DOCTYPE html>
<html>
<head>
  <title>Chapter 4 :: JQuery Effects :: Recipe 6</title>
  <script src="jquery.min.js"></script>
  <script src="recipe-6.js"></script>
  <link type="text/css" media="screen" rel="stylesheet"
    href="recipe-6.css" />
</head>
<body>
  <button id="start">Start</button>
  <div class="box"></div>
</body>
</html>
```

2. Create a CSS file named `recipe-6.css` and add the following code:

```css
.box {
  width: 200px;
  height: 200px;
  background-color: red;
}
```

Create a JavaScript file and save it as recipe-6.js. Add the following JavaScript code.

```js
$(function(){
  $('#start').click(function(){
$('.box').fadeOut().fadeIn().slideUp().slideDown().fadeTo
  (1000, 0.1).fadeTo(1000, 1);
  });
});
```

3. Open the `recipe-6.html` file in a web page and click on the **Start** button. The red-colored box will perform a range of effects.

How it works...

This recipe provides a very simple example as to how you can chain the different effect functions that jQuery provides. In this example, we perform `fadeOut()`, `fadeIn`, `slideUp()`, `slideDown()`, and two `fadeTo()` effects on the box div element. Each of these effects will be executed in turn due to the following code, which is placed within the click event handler callback function for the `start` button:

```
$('.box').fadeOut().fadeIn().slideUp().slideDown()
  .fadeTo(1000, 0.1).fadeTo(1000, 1);
```

The `fadeTo()` functions, which animate and alter the selected elements' opacity, have been provided with two parameters. The first parameter is the duration of the effect in milliseconds and the second is the opacity the effect should finish on.

See also

▸ *Creating a basic photo gallery*

Creating a basic photo gallery

Most people are aware that there are many jQuery photo gallery implementations available on the Web; many as jQuery plugins, which allow for quick implementation. There are benefits to taking the time to learn how to create your own. You will gain a deep understanding of how some of these plugins work, making it easier for you to customize them to better suit your needs. You will also learn more great features of jQuery and how to implement some of the skills you have learned earlier in this book.

Getting ready

We will first need a blank HTML file named `recipe-7.html` saved in the same directory as the latest version of jQuery. To create an image gallery, we are also going to need some images. Find a variety of images freely available on the Internet for use in this recipe. Save at least eight images within a folder named `images` in the same directory as the `recipe-7.html` file.

How to do it...

Learn how to create an attractive photo gallery from scratch with jQuery by performing the following steps:

1. Add the following HTML code to `recipe-7.html` to create our web page and image gallery HTML template:

```
<!DOCTYPE html>
<html>
<head>
  <script src="jquery.min.js"></script>
  <script src="recipe-7.js"></script>
  <link rel="stylesheet" type="text/css" href=
    "recipe-7.css" media="screen" />
  <title>Chapter 4 :: JQuery Events :: Recipe 7 - jQuery
    image gallery</title>
</head>
<body>
  <div class="gallery" data-thumb-width="150">
    <div class="frame">
      <img src="images/Chrysanthemum.jpg" />
      <img src="images/Desert.jpg" />
      <img src="images/Hydrangeas.jpg" />
      <img src="images/Jellyfish.jpg" />
      <img src="images/Koala.jpg" />
      <img src="images/Lighthouse.jpg" />
      <img src="images/Penguins.jpg" />
      <img src="images/Tulips.jpg" />
    </div>
    <div class="bottom">
      <a href="#" class="arrow left-arrow" data-direction=
        "left"><i class="arrow-left"></i></a>
      <a href="#" class="arrow right-arrow" data-direction=
        "right"><i class="arrow-right"></i></a>
      <div class="thumbs"></div>
    </div>
  </div>
</body>
</html>
```

2. Update the source (src="") for each image inside the frame division element to point to the images you have just added.

3. Create a CSS file in the same directory as recipe-7.html named recipe-7.css and add the following CSS code to style our gallery:

```
body {
  margin: 0;
  padding: 0;
  background-color: #333;
}
.gallery {
  width: 600px;
```

```css
    margin: 50px auto auto auto;
    position: relative;
}
.gallery .frame {
  height: 450px;
  margin-bottom: 10px;
  position: relative;
}
.gallery .frame img {
  display: block;
  width: 100%;
  position: absolute;
  left: 0;
  top: 0;
}
.gallery .bottom {
  overflow: hidden;
}
.gallery .thumbs {
  height: 120px;
  white-space: nowrap;
  text-align: center;
}
.gallery .thumbs a {
  display: inline-block;
  opacity: 0.5;
  -webkit-transition: opacity 0.5s ease-in-out;
  -moz-transition: opacity 0.5s ease-in-out;
  -ms-transition: opacity 0.5s ease-in-out;
  -o-transition: opacity 0.5s ease-in-out;
  transition: opacity 0.5s ease-in-out;
}
.gallery .thumbs a:hover {
  opacity: 1.0;
}
.gallery .arrow {
  width: 50px;
  height: 50px;
  background-color: #000;
  position: absolute;
  -webkit-border-radius: 50px;
  -moz-border-radius: 50px;
  border-radius: 50px;
  bottom: 35px;
```

```css
}
.gallery .arrow.disabled {
  background-color: #252525;
}
.gallery .left-arrow {
  left: -60px;
}
.gallery .right-arrow {
  right: -60px;
}
.gallery .arrow-right {
  width: 0;
  height: 0;
  border-top: 12px solid transparent;
  border-bottom: 12px solid transparent;
  border-left: 12px solid #1a1a1a;
  position: absolute;
  right: 16px;
  top: 13px;
}
.gallery .arrow-left {
  width: 0;
  height: 0;
  border-top: 12px solid transparent;
  border-bottom: 12px solid transparent;
  border-right:12px solid #1a1a1a;
  position: absolute;
  right: 21px;
  top: 13px;
}
```

4. Create a JavaScript file named `recipe-7.js` and add the following JavaScript code to ignite our gallery into action:

```javascript
/** DECLARE SOME DEFAULT VARIABLES WHICH WILL BE USED
  THROUGHOUT **/
var images;
var imageWidth;
$(function(){
  imageWidth = $('.gallery').data("thumb-width");
  /** COLLECT ALL THE IMAGES FROM WITHIN THE .gallery DIV
    **/
  images = $('.gallery').find('img');
  /** FOR EACH OF THESE IMAGES, CREATE A THUMBNAIL AND ADD
    A CLASS TO IDENTIFY THE IMAGE AND THUMBNAIL
    RELATIONSHIP **/
```

```
$.each(images, function(index, value){
  $(value).addClass("img" + index);
  $('.gallery .thumbs').append("<a href='#' data-index=
    '" + index + "' class='thumb'><img src='" +
    $(this).prop("src") + "' width='" + imageWidth +
    "' height='120' border='0' /></a>");
});
/** UPDATE THE SCROLL BUTTONS **/
updateScrollButtons();
/** EVENT HANDLERS FOR SCROLL BUTTONS **/
$('.arrow').click(function(){
  var element = $(this);
  if (!element.hasClass('disabled')) {
    element.addClass('disabled');
    var scrollString = "-=";
    if ($(this).data("direction") == "left") {
      scrollString = "+=";
    }
    $('.thumbs').animate({
      marginLeft: scrollString + imageWidth + "px"
    }, "fast", function(){
      element.removeClass('disabled');
      updateScrollButtons();
    });
  }
});
/** EVENT HANDLERS FOR IMAGES **/
$('.gallery').on("click", ".thumb", function(){
  var thumb = $(this);
  var image = $('.img' + thumb.data('index'));
  $.each(images, function(index, value){
    if (!$(value).hasClass('img' + thumb.data('index')))
    {
      $(value).hide();
    }
  });
  if (image.css("display") != "block") {
    image.fadeIn();
  }
});
});
function updateScrollButtons() {
  var thumbs = $('.thumbs');
  var thumbsMarginLeft = parseInt(thumbs.css
    ("margin-left"));
```

```
    var thumbsMaxWidth = (images.length * imageWidth);
    if (thumbsMarginLeft >= 0) {
      $('.left-arrow').addClass('disabled');
    } else {
      $('.left-arrow').removeClass('disabled');
    }
    if ((thumbsMarginLeft * -1) >=
      (thumbsMaxWidth - thumbs.width() / 2)) {
      $('.right-arrow').addClass('disabled');
    } else {
      $('.right-arrow').removeClass('disabled');
    }
}
```

5. Open `recipe-7.html` in a web browser and you will be presented with a jQuery image gallery similar to the following screenshot:

6. Selecting the left and right arrows will allow you to scroll through the photos, and clicking on a photo will show the larger version in the main frame.

How it works...

Now, let us understand the steps performed previously in detail.

HTML

Thanks to jQuery, we are able to create an attractive and functional gallery with a minimal amount of HTML code. In addition to the basic HTML document structure, we define a division element with the class `gallery`. The following is the division element code that the jQuery will use to base most of its DOM interactions:

```
<div class="gallery" data-thumb-width="150"></div>
```

Additionally, we also use the HTML5 data attribute to define the thumbnail width. Our jQuery code will use this value to size the thumbnails.

Using the following HTML code, we also create a division element with the class name of `frame` whose siblings are the images that we want to display within our gallery:

```
<div class="frame">
<img src="images/Chrysanthemum.jpg" />
<img src="images/Desert.jpg" />
<img src="images/Hydrangeas.jpg" />
<img src="images/Jellyfish.jpg" />
<img src="images/Koala.jpg" />
<img src="images/Lighthouse.jpg" />
<img src="images/Penguins.jpg" />
<img src="images/Tulips.jpg" />
</div>
```

Finally, in our HTML, we create a left and right arrow, which will be used in conjunction with jQuery to scroll through the image thumbnails. We also create a div element with the class `thumbs`, which will be populated with the thumbnail images using the following jQuery code:

```
<div class="bottom">
<a href="#" class="arrow left-arrow" data-direction="left"><i
class="arrow-left"></i></a>
<a href="#" class="arrow right-arrow" data-direction="right"><i
class="arrow-right"></i></a>
<div class="thumbs"></div>
</div>
```

CSS

Most of the CSS code used in this recipe is very basic and simply places elements in the appropriate place on the page. The main gallery division element is set to 600 pixels in width and to be centered on the screen. To allow us to place the left and right arrows outside the gallery frame, we set their position to absolute and use negative margins to push them further left and right.

The main thumbnail scrolling section has its `overflow` value set to `hidden`, preventing the bulk of the thumbnails from being displayed. This allows us to scroll these elements into view using jQuery. The thumbnails themselves have their `display` value set to `inline-block`, allowing them to stack next to each other in a single line, left to right.

For additional effect, we have also used some basic CSS animations. The thumbnails have their opacity set to `0.5` so that they do not become the prominent focus of the application. CSS transitions are used to create a fade in effect when the user hovers over the thumbnails, as follows:

```
.gallery .thumbs a {
  display: inline-block;
  opacity: 0.5;
  -webkit-transition: opacity 0.5s ease-in-out;
  -moz-transition: opacity 0.5s ease-in-out;
  -ms-transition: opacity 0.5s ease-in-out;
  -o-transition: opacity 0.5s ease-in-out;
  transition: opacity 0.5s ease-in-out;
}
.gallery .thumbs a:hover {
  opacity: 1.0;
}
```

In addition to the official CSS3 `transition` property, we are also using the browser-specific alternatives to ensure the CSS animations work in all of the most popular browsers.

```
-webkit-transition: opacity 0.5s ease-in-out;
-moz-transition: opacity 0.5s ease-in-out;
-ms-transition: opacity 0.5s ease-in-out;
-o-transition: opacity 0.5s ease-in-out;
```

jQuery

Two variables are declared at the beginning of the JavaScript file so their values can be used throughout the application; these are known as global variables. The bulk of the application code is placed within the jQuery on-load function so that the code is executed once the page has been loaded, as follows:

```
var images;
var imageWidth;
$(function(){
  imageWidth = $('.gallery').data("thumb-width");
  /** COLLECT ALL THE IMAGES FROM WITHIN THE .gallery DIV **/
  images = $('.gallery').find('img');
  /** FOR EACH OF THESE IMAGES, CREATE A THUMBNAIL AND ADD A CLASS
      TO IDENTIFY THE IMAGE AND THUMBNAIL RELATIONSHIP **/
  $.each(images, function(index, value){
    $(value).addClass("img" + index);
```

```
$('.gallery .thumbs').append("<a href='#' data-index='" +
    index + "' class='thumb'><img src='" + $(this).prop("src") +
    "' width='" + imageWidth + "' height='120' border='0' />
    </a>");
    });
});
```

The jQuery `data()` function is used to extract the thumbnail width from the HTML code that we created earlier. This value is then stored within the `imageWidth` variable for use later in the application. The `$('.gallery').find('img')` function is used to search for all the `img` elements within the `gallery` div element and store them as an array in the `images` variable. jQuery's `$.each()` function is used to iterate through each of the `img` elements in the images array. Inside the callback function of `$.each()`, we first use the `addClass()` function to add a class to the main image element based on the array index (that is, `img0`, `img1`, and so on). Then, an anchor element is created with an image inside and the width set using the `imageWidth` variable declared earlier. Using the `append()` function, the anchor element is then inserted into the DOM inside the `thumbs` div element. Additionally, the `data-index` property value of this anchor is set to match the class name of the larger image.

In the `$.each()` function, we call a custom function named `updateScrollButtons`, which is declared at the end of the JavaScript file. This function is used to determine whether the arrow buttons should be enabled based on the current position of the thumbnails. This prevents the user from scrolling the thumbnails out of the bottom section of the image gallery. Once the user has scrolled right to the last thumbnail, the right arrow button is disabled. Once the user has scrolled left to the first thumbnail, the left arrow button is disabled.

Next, using the following code we attach a click event handler to each of the arrow buttons so we can detect when the user wants to scroll through the thumbnail images.

```
$('.arrow').click(function(){
var element = $(this);
if (!element.hasClass('disabled')) {
  element.addClass('disabled');
  var scrollString = "-=";
  if ($(this).data("direction") == "left") {
    scrollString = "+=";
  }
  $('.thumbs').animate({
    marginLeft: scrollString + imageWidth + "px"
  }, "fast", function(){
    element.removeClass('disabled');
    updateScrollButtons();
  });
}
});
```

In the callback function of the click event handler, we first declare a variable and store the click element within it referring to $(this), meaning the clicked element. Using this variable, we can use the jQuery function hasClass to determine if the clicked element has the class disabled. We wrap all the code within this function inside an if statement so that none of this code will be executed if the clicked element has the disabled class. In the if statement, we use addClass to add the disabled class to the clicked element. This is to prevent the user from being able to spam-click on the scroll arrows and cause undesired animations.

We also have a variable declared named scrollString that has the default value of -=. This value will be used within the jQuery animate() function that will provide the scrolling animation to our thumbnails. Depending on the data-direction property value of the arrow that is clicked, this value will either stay as -=, meaning that the left margin of the thumbs div will be taken away from (that is, scrolled right), or the value will change to +=, meaning that the left margin will be added to (that is, scrolled left).

Finally, within this event handler callback function, the jQuery animate() function is used to modify the left margin of the thumbs div element, which provides the scrolling effect. The imageWidth variable is used once more to set the scroll position to match the width of the thumbnails as follows:

```
$('.gallery').on("click", ".thumb", function(){
var thumb = $(this);
var image = $('.' + thumb.attr('rel'));
$.each(images, function(index, value){
    if (!$(value).hasClass(thumb.attr('rel'))) {
        $(value).hide();
    }
});
if (image.css("display") != "block") {
    image.fadeIn();
}
});
```

The next section of code attaches a click event handler to the gallery div element. The click event handler listens for clicks on any element with the class thumb. This allows us to specify code to be executed once a thumbnail has been clicked. In the callback function, we select the clicked thumbnail and store the element reference in the thumb variable. We also use the clicked elements' data-index property value to select the larger image, storing its reference within image.

Once again, we use the $.each() function to iterate through all of the images. We hide each image that does not match the image in the clicked thumbnail. This is so that only the selected image appears in the main viewing panel. We also use the css() function to check the display property of the larger image to determine if the image is currently visible. If not, we use the jQuery fade in effect to show it, completing the image gallery functionality.

Creating a blinking button

Using jQuery's effect functions, we can create a blinking button that can be used in a web application or website to draw the user's attention.

Getting ready

Create a blank HTML document named `recipe-8.html` and ensure you have the latest version of jQuery downloaded and ready to be included in this HTML file.

How to do it...

Learn how jQuery can be used to create a simple blinking button effect by performing the following steps:

1. Add the following code to `recipe-8.html`, which you have just created, remembering to update the reference to the jQuery library.

```
<!DOCTYPE html>
<html>
<head>
  <script src="jquery.min.js"></script>
  <script src="recipe-8.js"></script>
  <title>Chapter 4 :: JQuery Effects :: Recipe 8 </title>
  <link type="text/css" media="screen" rel="stylesheet"
    href="recipe-8.css" />
</head>
<body>
<div class="frame">
  <h1>Newsletter!</h1>
  <p>Enter your email address below to sign-up for our
    monthly newsletter.</p>
  <form>
    <input type="text" class="email-input" name="email"
      placeholder="Your Email" />
    <button class="blinker">Sign-up Now!</button>
  </form>
</div>
</body>
</html>
```

2. Create a CSS file named `recipe-8.css` and add the following CSS code to add style to the newsletter form created in the HTML:

```
@import url(http://fonts.googleapis.com/css?family=Leckerli+One);
@import url(http://fonts.googleapis.com/css?family=Happy+Monkey);
```

```css
body {
  background-color: #333333;
  font-family: 'Happy Monkey', cursive;
}
h1 {
  font-family: 'Leckerli One', cursive;
  font-size: 60px;
  line-height: 80px;
  padding: 0;
  margin: 0;
  text-align: center;
  color: #333;
}
.frame {
  width: 500px;
  margin: 50px auto auto auto;
  height: 300px;
  background-color: #FFF;
  box-shadow: #000 3px 3px 2px;
  border-radius: 10px;
  padding: 20px;
  text-align: center;
}
.frame p {
  font-size: 18px;
  line-height: 25px;
}
.frame form .email-input {
  height: 40px;
  font-size: 30px;
  width: 400px;
  font-family: 'Happy Monkey', cursive;
}
.frame form .blinker {
  height: 40px;
  width: 150px;
  font-size: 20px;
  margin-top: 20px;
  font-family: 'Happy Monkey', cursive;
}
```

3. Create a JavaScript file in the same directory as the CSS and HTML files. Save this file as `recipe-8.js` and add the following jQuery code:

```javascript
$(function(){
  $('.email-input').on('focus', function(){
```

```
        $('.blinker').fadeTo(300, 0.1).fadeTo(300, 1);
    })
});
```

4. Open `recipe-8.html` in a web browser and you will be presented with a web page similar to the following screenshot:

5. Clicking inside the textbox will cause the **Sign-up Now!** button to blink to draw the user's attention.

How it works...

The HTML and CSS code used in this recipe creates a page that allows a user to sign up for a newsletter subscription. There are no complex elements in the HTML or CSS code, so no further explanation is necessary.

This recipe provides a simple example that demonstrates how we can use jQuery to give the appearance of a blinking button. The idea is that when the user clicks inside the textbox to input an e-mail address, the **Sign-up Now!** button will blink to draw their attention.

In our jQuery code, we first attach an event handler to the text input for focus. The `focus` event is triggered when an element on the page receives the attention of the user, either by tabbing to the form element or by clicking on it. In the callback function to this event handler, we use the `fadeTo()` jQuery effect function to sequentially fade out and fade in the button, creating the blinking effect. The `fadeTo()` function, in this example, takes two arguments, effect duration and element opacity. We specify the opacity of the element to be `0.1` within the first `fadeTo()` function to fade out the button. Then we specify `1.0` to fade the button back in. We can control the speed of the effect by altering the specified duration, which is set to `300` milliseconds.

There's more...

There are many ways to create the blinking effect with jQuery. In *Chapter 6, User Interface*, you will learn to alter the CSS attributes of elements, which will allow you to add drop-shadows and colored borders to greatly enhance the blinking effect. The `fadeTo()` function provides the easiest way to create this effect, but be aware that there are alternatives that can provide a greater impact that may be more suitable to your needs.

When forcing elements to blink, move, or flash to draw the user's attention, you must be very careful not to cause annoyance, as this may have the reverse effect of turning them away. Effects such as these should only be used as subtle hints to prompt the user's interaction with your user interface.

See also

► *Fading elements*

► *Creating a basic photo gallery*

Removing elements with effects

You will often create interfaces such as lists or tables that will be representing data from a database. If the interface is for management purposes, you will typically be able to add, edit, and remove these items. We can use jQuery effects to add to the user experience when these items are added, as described in the *Fading elements* recipe. We can also provide effects when removing an item from the DOM. Thanks to jQuery, it is very easy to do.

Getting ready

As with the other recipes in this chapter, you are going to need a blank HTML document. Save this document as `recipe-9.html` and ensure it is within the same directory as the latest version of jQuery.

How to do it...

Understand how you can remove DOM elements with effects by performing the following steps:

1. Add the following HTML code to the HTML document you have just created:

```
<!DOCTYPE html>
<html>
<head>
  <script src="jquery.min.js"></script>
  <script src="recipe-9.js"></script>
```

```
    <title>Chapter 4 :: JQuery Effects :: Recipe 9 </title>
    <link type="text/css" media="screen" rel="stylesheet"
      href="recipe-9.css" />
</head>
<body>
<div class="frame">
  <h1>User Management</h1>
  <table width="100%" id="user-table">
    <thead>
    <tr>
      <th>Username</th>
      <th>Email</th>
      <th>Full Name</th>
      <th>Date of Birth</th>
      <th></th>
    </tr>
    </thead>
    <tbody>
    <tr>
      <td>jd101</td>
      <td>j.doe@somewhere.com</td>
      <td>John Doe</td>
      <td>16-05-1987</td>
      <td><button class="delete">Delete</button></td>
    </tr>
    <tr>
      <td>msmith17</td>
      <td>smithy@nowhere.com</td>
      <td>Jane Smith</td>
      <td>18-08-1988</td>
      <td><button class="delete">Delete</button></td>
    </tr>
    <tr>
      <td>tommy22</td>
      <td>tom@idontknow.com</td>
      <td>Thomas Knowhow</td>
      <td>10-08-1980</td>
      <td><button class="delete">Delete</button></td>
    </tr>
    </tbody>
  </table>
</div>
</body>
</html>
```

2. You may have noticed the CSS file included in the header of the previous HTML code. Create `recipe-9.css` and add the following CSS code:

```css
@import url(http://fonts.googleapis.com/css?family=Lato:300,400);
body {
  background-color: #333333;
  font-family: 'Lato', sans-serif;
}
h1 {
  line-height: 60px;
  padding: 0;
  margin: 0 0 15px 0;
  text-align: center;
  color: #333;
  font-weight: 300;
}
.frame {
  width: 700px;
  margin: 50px auto auto auto;
  background-color: #FFF;
  box-shadow: #000 3px 3px 2px;
  border-radius: 10px;
  padding: 20px;
  text-align: center;
}
```

3. In addition to the CSS file, a JavaScript file is also included in the HTML page. Create a JavaScript file named `recipe-9.js` and save it in the same directory as the HTML and CSS files. Add the following jQuery code to this file:

```javascript
$(function(){
  $('#user-table').on("click", ".delete", function(){
    var response = confirm("Are you sure you want to delete
      this user?");
    if (response) {
      $(this).parent().parent().fadeOut().remove();
    }
  });
});
```

4. Open `recipe-9.html` in a web browser and you will be presented with a simple user management UI. Clicking on the **Delete** button next to any entry will prompt you to confirm that you would like to delete. When the user clicks on **OK**, the entry for that particular user will fade out and be removed from the DOM.

How it works...

This recipe too has basic HTML and CSS code that needs no explanation. Instead, let's concentrate on the jQuery code.

All of our jQuery code is wrapped in `$(function(){})`;, which is the jQuery on-load function, allowing us to execute on page load. We attach a click event handler to the user table and listen for clicks on any elements with the `delete` class as follows. From the HTML code, you will know these elements are the `delete` buttons.

```
$('#user-table').on("click", ".delete", function(){

});
```

Inside the callback function to this event handler, we use the native JavaScript function `confirm()` and assign its output to the `response` variable. This will display a pop-up window to the user that has the message **Are you sure you want to delete this user?**. If the user clicks on **OK**, the `response` variable will equal `true`. If they click on **Cancel**, it will be `false`. By using this `response` variable, we can determine whether they want to go ahead and delete the user. If they do, we can remove the table row from the DOM.

To remove the table row, we first need to select it. We can refer to `$(this)`, which is the clicked item (in this case, the button), then select its parents' parent, which is the `tr` table. This is done using the following code:

```
$(this).parent().parent().fadeOut().remove();
```

We then use the `fadeOut()` function to apply the effect and use the `remove()` function to remove the element from the DOM.

There's more...

This simple user interface would typically be coupled with server-side calls, which would also remove the user entry from the database. Take a look back at *Chapter 3, Loading and Manipulating Dynamic Content with AJAX and JSON*, to see how this can be done using jQuery and AJAX.

See also

- ▸ *Fading elements*

5
Form Handling

In this chapter, we will look at how to create robust and attractive web forms with animation, validation, and user feedback. We will cover:

- ▶ Implementing basic form validation
- ▶ Adding number validation
- ▶ Adding credit card number validation
- ▶ Adding date validation
- ▶ Adding e-mail address validation
- ▶ Implementing live form validation
- ▶ Adding a password strength indicator
- ▶ Adding anti-spam measures
- ▶ Implementing input character restrictions

Introduction

Collecting user data is a basic function of many websites and web applications, from simple data collection techniques such as registration or login information, to more complex scenarios such as payment or billing information. It is important that only relevant and complete information is collected from the user. To ensure this, the web developer must enforce validation on all data input. It is also important to provide a good user experience while enforcing this data integrity. This can be done by providing useful feedback to the user regarding any validation errors their data may have caused. This chapter will show you how to create an attractive web form that enforces data integrity while keeping a high-quality user experience.

A very important point to note is that any JavaScript or jQuery validation is open to manipulation by the user. JavaScript and jQuery resides within the web browser, so a user with little knowledge can easily modify the code to bypass any client-side validation techniques. This means that client-side validation cannot be totally relied on to prevent the user from submitting invalid data. Any validation done within the client side must be replicated on the server, which is not open for manipulation by the user.

We use client-side validation to improve the user experience. Because of this, the user does not need to wait for a server response.

Implementing basic form validation

At the most basic level of form validation, you will need to be able to prevent the user from submitting empty values. This recipe will provide the HTML and CSS code for a web form that will be used for recipes 1 through 8 of this chapter.

Getting ready

Using your favorite text editor or IDE, create a blank HTML page in an easily accessible location and save this file as `recipe-1.html`. Ensure that you have the latest version of jQuery downloaded to the same location as this HTML file.

This HTML page will form the basis of most of this chapter, so remember to keep it after you have completed this recipe.

How to do it...

Learn how to implement basic form validation with jQuery by performing the following steps:

1. Add the following HTML code to `index.html`. Be sure to change the source location of the JavaScript included for the jQuery library, pointing it to where the latest version of jQuery is downloaded on your computer.

```
<!DOCTYPE html>
<html xmlns="http://www.w3.org/1999/html">
<head>
    <title>Chapter 5 :: Recipe 1</title>
    <link type="text/css" media="screen" rel="stylesheet"
href="styles.css" />
    <script src="jquery.min.js"></script>
    <script src="validation.js"></script>
</head>
<body>
    <form id="webForm" method="POST">
        <div class="header">
```

```
      <h1>Register</h1>
    </div>
    <div class="input-frame">
       <label for="firstName">First Name:</label>
       <input name="firstName" id="firstName" type="text"
          class="required" />
    </div>
    <div class="input-frame">
       <label for="lastName">Last Name:</label>
       <input name="lastName" id="lastName" type="text"
          class="required" />
    </div>
    <div class="input-frame">
       <label for="email">Email:</label>
       <input name="email" id="email" type="text"
          class="required email" />
    </div>
    <div class="input-frame">
       <label for="number">Telephone:</label>
       <input name="number" id="number" type="text"
          class="number" />
    </div>
    <div class="input-frame">
       <label for="dob">Date of Birth:</label>
       <input name="dob" id="dob" type="text"
          class="required date"
          placeholder="DD/MM/YYYY"/>
    </div>
    <div class="input-frame">
       <label for="creditCard">Credit Card #:</label>
       <input name="creditCard" id="creditCard"
          type="text" class="required credit-card" />
    </div>
    <div class="input-frame">
       <label for="password">Password:</label>
       <input name="password" id="password"
          type="password" class="required" />
    </div>
    <div class="input-frame">
       <label for="confirmPassword">Confirm
          Password:</label>
          <input name="confirmPassword"
             id="confirmPassword" type="password"
             class="required" />
    </div>
```

```
        <div class="actions">
            <button class="submit-btn">Submit</button>
        </div>
    </form>
</body>
</html>
```

2. Create a CSS file named `styles.css` in the same directory and add the following CSS code to add style to our HTML page and form:

```css
@import url(http://fonts.googleapis.com/css?family=Ubuntu);
body {
    background-color: #FFF;
    font-family: 'Ubuntu', sans-serif;
}
form {
    width: 500px;
    padding: 20px;
    background-color: #333;
    border-radius: 5px;
    margin: 10px auto auto auto;
    color: #747474;
    border: solid 2px #000;
}
form label {
    font-size: 14px;
    line-height: 30px;
    width: 27%;
    display: inline-block;
    text-align: right;
}
.input-frame {
    clear: both;
    margin-bottom: 25px;
    position: relative;
}
form input {
    height: 30px;
    width: 330px;
    margin-left: 10px;
    background-color: #191919;
    border: solid 1px #404040;
    padding-left: 10px;
    color: #DB7400;
}
```

```css
form input:hover {
   background-color: #262626;
}
form input:focus {
   border-color: #DB7400;
}
form .header {
   margin: -20px -20px 25px -20px;
   padding: 10px 10px 10px 20px;
   position: relative;
   background-color: #DB7400;
   border-top-left-radius: 4px;
   border-top-right-radius: 4px;
}
form .header h1 {
   line-height: 50px;
   margin: 0px;
   padding: 0px;
   color: #FFF;
   font-weight: normal;
}
.actions {
   text-align: right;
}
.submit-btn {
   background-color: #DB7400;
   border: solid 1px #000;
   border-radius: 5px;
   color: #FFF;
   padding: 10px 20px 10px 20px;
   text-decoration: none;
   cursor: pointer;
}
.error input {
   border-color: red;
}
.error-data {
   color: red;
   font-size: 11px;
   position: absolute;
   bottom: -15px;
   left: 30%;
}
```

3. In addition to the jQuery library, the previous HTML page also uses another JavaScript file. Create a blank JavaScript file in the directory where the `index.html` file is saved. Save this file as `validation.js` and add the following JavaScript code:

```
$(function(){
    $('.submit-btn').click(function(event){
        //Prevent form submission
        event.preventDefault();
        var inputs = $('input');
        var isError = false;
        //Remove old errors
        $('.input-frame').removeClass('error');
        $('.error-data').remove();
        for (var i = 0; i < inputs.length; i++) {
            var input = inputs[i];
            if ($(input).hasClass('required') &&
                !validateRequired($(input).val())) {
                addErrorData($(input), "This is a required
                field");
                isError = true;
            }

        }
        if (isError === false) {
            //No errors, submit the form
            $('#webForm').submit();
        }
    });
});

function validateRequired(value) {
    if (value == "") return false;
    return true;
}

function addErrorData(element, error) {
    element.parent().addClass("error");
    element.after("<div class='error-data'>" + error + "</div>");
}
```

4. Open `index.html` in a web browser and you should see a form similar to the following screenshot:

5. If you click on the **Submit** button to submit an empty form, you will be presented with error messages under the required fields.

How it works...

Now, let us understand the steps performed previously in detail.

HTML

The HTML creates a web form with various fields that will take a range of data inputs, including text, date of birth, and credit card number. This page forms the basis for most of this chapter. Each of the input elements has been given different classes depending on what type of validation they require. For this recipe, our JavaScript will only look at the `required` class, which indicates a required field and therefore cannot be blank. Other classes have been added to the input fields, such as `date` and `number`, which will be used in the later recipes in this chapter.

CSS

Basic CSS has been added to create an attractive web form. The CSS code styles the input fields so they blend in with the form itself and adds a hover effect. The Google Web Font Ubuntu has also been used to improve the look of the form.

jQuery

The first part of the jQuery code is wrapped within `$(function(){});`, which will ensure the code is executed on page load. Inside this wrapper, we attach a click event handler to the form submit button, shown as follows:

```
$(function(){
    $('.submit-btn').click(function(event){
        //Prevent form submission
        event.preventDefault();

    });
});
```

As we want to handle the form submission based on whether valid data has been provided, we use `event.preventDefault();` to initially stop the form from submitting, allowing us to perform the validation first, shown as follows:

```
var inputs = $('input');
var isError = false;
```

After the `preventDefault` code, an `inputs` variable is declared to hold all the input elements within the page, using `$('input')` to select them. Additionally, we create an `isError` variable, setting it to `false`. This will be a flag to determine if our validation code has discovered an error within the form. These variable declarations are shown previously. Using the length of the `inputs` variable, we are able to loop through all of the inputs on the page. We create an input variable for each input that is iterated over, which can be used to perform actions on the current input element using jQuery. This is done with the following code:

```
for (var i = 0; i < inputs.length; i++) {
var input = inputs[i];
}
```

After the input variable has been declared and assigned the current input, any previous error classes or data is removed from the element using the following code:

```
$(input).parent().removeClass('error');
$(input).next('.error-data').remove();
```

The first line removes the `error` class from the input's parent (`.input-frame`), which adds the red border to the input element. The second line removes the error information that is displayed under the input if the validation check has determined that this input has invalid data.

Next, jQuery's `hasClass()` function is used to determine if the current input element has the `required` class. If the current element does have this class, we need to perform the required validation to make sure this field contains data. We call the `validateRequired()` function within the `if` statement and pass through the value of the current input, shown as follows:

```
if ($(input).hasClass('required') && !validateRequired($(input).
val())) {
addErrorData($(input), "This is a required field");
    isError = true;
}
```

We call the `validateRequired()` function prepended with an exclamation mark to check to determine if this function's results are equal to `false`; therefore, if the current input has the `required` class and `validateRequired()` returns `false`, the value of the current input is invalid. If this is the case, we call the `addErrorData()` function inside the `if` statement with the current input and the error message, which will be displayed under the input. We also set the `isError` variable to `true`, so that later on in the code, we will know a validation error occurred.

The JavaScript's `for` loop will repeat these steps for each of the selected input elements on the page. After the `for` loop has completed, we check if the `isError` flag is still set to `false`. If so, we use jQuery to manually submit the form, shown as follows:

```
if (isError === false) {
    //No errors, submit the form
    $('#webForm').submit();
}
```

Note that the operator `===` is used to compare the variable type of `isError` (that is, `Boolean`) as well as its value. At the bottom of the JavaScript file, we declare our two functions that have been called earlier in the script. The first function, `validateRequired()`, simply takes the input value and checks to see if it is blank or not. If the value is blank, the function returns `false`, meaning validation failed; otherwise, the function returns `true`. This can be coded as follows:

```
function validateRequired(value) {
    if (value == "") return false;
    return true;
}
```

The second function used is the `addErrorData()` function, which takes the current input and an error message. It uses jQuery's `addClass()` function to add the error class to the input's parent, which will display the red border on the input element using CSS. It then uses jQuery's `after()` function to insert a division element into the DOM, which will display the specified error message under the current input field, shown as follows:

```
function validateRequired(value) {
    if (value == "") return false;
    return true;
}
function addErrorData(element, error) {
    element.parent().addClass("error");
    element.after("<div class='error-data'>" + error + "</div>");
}
```

There's more...

This structure allows us to easily add additional validation to our web form. Because the JavaScript is iterating over all of the input fields in the form, we can easily check for additional classes, such as `date`, `number`, and `credit-card`, and call extra functions to provide the alternative validation. The other recipes in this chapter will look in detail at the additional validation types and add these functions to the current `validation.js` file.

See also

▶ *Implementing input character restrictions*

Adding number validation

When collecting data from a user, there are many situations when you will want to only allow numbers in a form field. Examples of this could be telephone numbers, PIN codes, or ZIP codes, to name a few. This recipe will show you how to validate the telephone number field within the form we created in the previous recipe.

Getting ready

Ensure that you have completed the previous recipe and have the same files available. Open `validation.js` in your text editor or IDE of choice.

How to do it...

Add number validation to the form you created in the previous recipe by performing the following steps:

1. Update `validation.js` to be as follows, adding the `valdiateNumber()` function with an additional `hasClass('number')` check inside the `for` loop:

```
$(function(){
    $('.submit-btn').click(function(event){
        //Prevent form submission
        event.preventDefault();
        var inputs = $('input');
        var isError = false;
        //Remove old errors
        $('.input-frame').removeClass('error');
        $('.error-data').remove();
        for (var i = 0; i < inputs.length; i++) {
            var input = inputs[i];

            if ($(input).hasClass('required') &&
                !validateRequired($(input).val())) {
                addErrorData($(input), "This is a required
                    field");
                isError = true;
            }
/* Code for this recipe */
            if ($(input).hasClass('number') &&
                !validateNumber($(input).val())) {
                addErrorData($(input), "This field can only
                    contain numbers");
                isError = true;
            }
/* --- */

        }
        if (isError === false) {
            //No errors, submit the form
            $('#webForm').submit();
        }
    });
});

function validateRequired(value) {
    if (value == "") return false;
```

```
        return true;
    }

    /* Code for this recipe */
    function validateNumber(value) {
        if (value != "") {
            return !isNaN(parseInt(value, 10)) && isFinite(value);
            //isFinite, in case letter is on the end
        }
        return true;
    }
    /* --- */
    function addErrorData(element, error) {
        element.parent().addClass("error");
        element.after("<div class='error-data'>" + error + "</div>");
    }
```

2. Open `index.html` in a web browser, input something other than a valid integer into the telephone number field, and click on the **Submit** button. You will be presented with a form similar to the following screenshot:

How it works...

First, we add an additional `if` statement to the main `for` loop of `validation.js` to check to see if the current input field has the class `number`, as follows:

```
if ($(input).hasClass('number') &&
    !validateNumber($(input).val())) {
    addErrorData($(input), "This field can only contain numbers");
    isError = true;
}
```

If it does, this input value needs to be validated for a number. To do this, we call the `validateNumber` function inline within the `if` statement:

```
function validateNumber(value) {
    if (value != "") {
        return !isNaN(parseInt(value, 10)) && isFinite(value);
        //isFinite, in case letter is on the end
    }
    return true;
}
```

This function takes the value of the current input field as an argument. It first checks to see if the value is blank. If it is, we do not need to perform any validation here because this is handled by the `validateRequired()` function from the first recipe of this chapter.

If there is a value to validate, a range of actions are performed on the `return` statement. First, the value is parsed as an integer and passed to the `isNaN()` function. The JavaScript `isNaN()` function simply checks to see if the provided value is **NaN (Not a Number)**. In JavaScript, if you try to parse a value as an integer and that value is not actually an integer, you will get the `NaN` value. The first part of the `return` statement is to ensure that the provided value is a valid integer. However, this does not prevent the user from inputting invalid characters. If the user was to input `12345ABCD`, the `parseInt` function would ignore `ABCD` and just parse `12345`, and therefore the validation would pass. To prevent this situation, we also use the `isFinite` function, which returns `false` if provided with `12345ABCD`.

See also

▶ *Adding credit card number validation*

Adding credit card number validation

Number validation could be enough validation for a credit card number; however, using regular expressions, it is possible to check for number combinations to match credit card numbers from Visa, MasterCard, American Express, and more.

Getting ready

Make sure that you have `validation.js` from the previous two recipes in this chapter open and ready for modification.

How to do it...

Use jQuery to provide form input validation for credit card numbers by performing the following step-by-step instructions:

1. Update `validation.js` to add the credit card validation function and the additional class check on the input fields:

```
$(function(){
    $('.submit-btn').click(function(event){
        //Prevent form submission
        event.preventDefault();
        var inputs = $('input');
        var isError = false;
        for (var i = 0; i < inputs.length; i++) {

// -- JavaScript from previous two recipes hidden

            if ($(input).hasClass('credit-card') &&
                !validateCreditCard($(input).val())) {
                addErrorData($(input), "Invalid credit card
                    number");
                isError = true;
            }

        }
// -- JavaScript from previous two recipes hidden
    });
});

// -- JavaScript from previous two recipes hidden

function validateCreditCard(value) {
```

```
    if (value != "") {
        return /^(?:4[0-9]{12}(?:[0-9]{3})?|5[1-5][0-9]
{14}|6(?:011|5[0-9][0-9])[0-9]{12}|3[47][0-9]{13}|3(?:0[0-5]|[68]
[0-9])[0-9]{11}|(?:2131|1800|35\d{3})\d{11})$/.test(value);
    }
    return true;
}
// -- JavaScript from previous two recipes hidden
}
```

2. Open `index.html` and input an invalid credit card number. You will be presented with the following error information in the form:

How it works...

To add credit card validation, as with the previous two recipes, we added an additional check in the main `for` loop to look for the `credit-card` class on the input elements, as follows:

```
if ($(input).hasClass('credit-card') &&
    !validateCreditCard($(input).val())) {
    addErrorData($(input), "Invalid credit card number");
    isError = true;
}
```

The `validateCreditCard` function is also added, which uses a regular expression to validate the input value, as follows:

```
function validateCreditCard(value) {
    if (value != "") {
        return /^(?:4[0-9]{12}(?:[0-9]{3})?|5[1-5][0-
            9]{14}|6(?:011|5[0-9][0-9])[0-9]{12}|3[47][0-
            9]{13}|3(?:0[0-5]|[68][0-9])[0-
            9]{11}|(?:2131|1800|35\d{3})\d{11})$/.test(value);
    }
    return true;
}
```

The first part of this function determines if the provided value is blank. If it isn't, the function will perform further validation; otherwise, it will return `true`. Most credit card numbers start with a prefix, which allows us to add additional validation to the inputted value on top of numeric validation. The regular expression used in this function will allow for Visa, MasterCard, American Express, Diners Club, Discover, and JCB cards.

See also

▸   *Adding number validation*

Adding date validation

Dates are common items of data, and it is important that the user be able to easily input a date into your web form. Typically, you would use a date picker that has date validation included to provide an easy input method. This recipe shows you how to manually validate a date in the UK format (that is, DD/MM/YYYY). Date pickers are covered in *Chapter 9, jQuery UI,* using the popular jQuery UI framework. Refer to the *See also* section of this recipe for more information.

Getting ready

Continuing the trend of the previous recipes of this chapter, ensure that you have `validation.js` open and ready for modification and that you have completed the previous three recipes.

How to do it...

Add date validation to your web form by performing the following simple steps:

1.   Update `validation.js` to add the additional date validation function and class check within the main `for` loop, shown as follows:

```
$(function(){
   $('.submit-btn').click(function(event){

// -- JavaScript from previous three recipes hidden

      for (var i = 0; i < inputs.length; i++) {

// -- JavaScript from previous three recipes hidden

          if ($(input).hasClass('date') &&
              !validateDate($(input).val())) {
              addErrorData($(input), "Invalid date
              provided");
              isError = true;
          }

          // -- JavaScript from previous three recipes hidden

      }
      // -- JavaScript from previous three recipes hidden    });
});

// -- JavaScript from previous three recipes hidden

function validateDate(value) {
    if (value != "") {
       if (/^\d{2}([.\/-])\d{2}\1\d{4}$/.test(value)) {
           // Remove leading zeros
           value = value.replace(/0*(\d*)/gi,"$1");
           var dateValues = value.split(/[\.|\/|-]/);
           // Correct the month value as month index starts
              at 0 now 1 (e.g. 0 = Jan, 1 = Feb)
           dateValues[1]--;
           var date = new Date(dateValues[2], dateValues[1],
              dateValues[0]);
           if (
              date.getDate() == dateValues[0] &&
                 date.getMonth() == dateValues[1] &&
              date.getFullYear() == dateValues[2]
              ) {
              return true;
           }
       }
       return false;
    } else {
```

```
            return true;
        }
    }

    // -- JavaScript from previous three recipes hidden
```

2. Open `index.html` in a web browser, input an invalid date, and click on **Submit** to generate the invalid date error, shown in the following screenshot:

How it works...

Once again, we add an additional class check to the main `for` loop to see if the current input needs to have date validation applied. If it does, the `validateDate()` function is called.

Just like the other validation functions, we first check to see if the value is blank. If it is not blank, the value can be validated. A regular expression is used to determine if the string value provided is of a valid date format, as follows:

```
    if (/^\d{2}([.\/-])\d{2}\1\d{4}$/.test(value)) {
```

This test will pass if the provided value is separated with a slash, a hyphen, or a full stop and where the first two parts consist of two numbers and the last part consists of four numbers. This will ensure the provided value is DD/MM/YYYY, as required.

If this test passes, the next step is to remove all of the leading zeros so that the provided date string can be converted into a date object with JavaScript (for example, `08-08-1989` will become `8-8-1989`). The code for the same is as follows:

```
value = value.replace(/0*(\d*)/gi,"$1");
```

After this, an array is created as follows, splitting the date string on either -, /, or:

```
var dateValues = value.split(/[\.|\/|-]/);
```

Now, it is possible to use these date values to create a JavaScript date object and test its validity. Before this can happen, we must convert the month value. JavaScript months start from `0`, whereas our user will have started from `1`. For example, the user will use `1` for January, `2` for February, and so on, whereas JavaScript uses `0` for January, `1` for February, and so on. To account for this, we simply subtract `1` from the provided date value, shown as follows:

```
dateValues[1]--;
```

With this done, it is possible to create the JavaScript date object and check that the outcome matches the input date, proving its validity:

```
var date = new Date(dateValues[2], dateValues[1], dateValues[0]);
if (
    date.getDate() == dateValues[0] &&
    date.getMonth() == dateValues[1] &&
    date.getFullYear() == dateValues[2]
) {
    return true;
}
```

See also

▶ The *Adding date picker interfaces to input boxes quickly* recipe in Chapter 9, jQuery UI

Adding e-mail address validation

E-mail address validation is one of the most common types of validation on the Web. Most people would believe that a valid e-mail address only contains alphanumeric characters with the exception of the @ symbol and a full stop. While most e-mail addresses are typically of this format, a valid e-mail address can actually contain a variety of other characters. This recipe will show you how to add e-mail validation to the web form we have been using in the last four recipes.

How to do it...

Create e-mail validation that can be reused again and again by performing the following instructions:

1. Add the additional `hasClass` check and `if` statement to the main `for` loop in `validation.js` as follows:

```
if ($(input).hasClass('email') &&
    !validateEmail($($(input)).val())) {
    addErrorData($(input), "Invalid email address
    provided");
    isError = true;
}
```

2. Add the following `validateEmail()` function to the end of `validation.js`:

```
function validateEmail(value) {
    if (value != "") {
        return /[a-z0-9!#$%&'*+/=?^_`{|}~-]+(?:\.[a-z0-
9!#$%&'*+/=?^_`{|}~-]+)*@(?:[a-z0-9](?:[a-z0-9-]*[a-z0-
9])?\.)+[a-z0-9](?:[a-z0-9-]*[a-z0-9])?/i.test(value);
    }
    return true;
}
```

3. Open `index.html` in a web browser, input an invalid e-mail address, and submit the form. You will be presented with an appropriate error in the same fashion as the other types of validation errors.

How it works...

The e-mail validation function, however simple, contains a complex regular expression to validate an e-mail address to a practical version of RFC 5322 standards, which was provided by `http://www.regular-expressions.info/email.html`.

The first part of the `validateEmail()` function checks to see if there is a value to validate. If so, it uses the complex regular expression to test the string values' validity, returning `true` or `false` accordingly.

Finally, as with the other validation functions, there is the class check inside the main `for` loop, which determines which inputs need to be validated for e-mail addresses. If these input fields fail validation, it will provide the appropriate error output on screen.

There's more...

It is important to understand that this method of e-mail validation only validates the syntax to cut down on the amount of rubbish data provided by users. To truly validate an e-mail address, you would have to actually send an e-mail to verify that it exists and is ready to receive e-mail.

Implementing live form validation

It can be very useful for the user to get real-time feedback regarding validation errors as they type in your web form. If you are performing client-side validation with JavaScript as well as server-side validation, this can be achieved easily as you do not need to send a request to the server every time the user types in an input—you can do it all within the client. Once again, it is very important that the same data undergoes additional validation on the server side. The server-side validation can then be fed back to the web form after the user has submitted the form.

Getting ready

This recipe will adapt the client-side validation that has been created as part of the last five recipes. Ensure that you have completed these recipes beforehand.

How to do it...

Provide real-time validation to users by performing the following steps:

1. First, we need to move all of the class checks from the `for` loop into their own function so that they can be reused. Move all of the `if` statements, which perform the `hasClass` checks for `required`, `email`, `number`, `date`, and `credit-card`, into a function called `doValidation()`, shown as follows:

```
// --- Hidden JavaScript from previous recipes

function doValidation(input) {
    //Remove old errors
    $(input).parent().removeClass('error');
    $(input).next('.error-data').remove();
    if ($(input).hasClass('required') &&
        !validateRequired($(input).val())) {
        addErrorData($(input), "This is a required field");
    }
    if ($(input).hasClass('email') &&
        !validateEmail($($(input)).val())) {
        addErrorData($(input), "Invalid email address
            provided");
```

```
    }
    if ($(input).hasClass('number') &&
        !validateNumber($(input).val())) {
        addErrorData($(input), "This field can only contain
            numbers");
    }
    if ($(input).hasClass('date') &&
        !validateDate($(input).val())) {
        addErrorData($(input), "Invalid date provided");
    }
    if ($(input).hasClass('credit-card') &&
        !validateCreditCard($(input).val())) {
        addErrorData($(input), "Invalid credit card number");
    }
}

// --- Hidden JavaScript
```

2. Now, we need to update the main `for` loop to use this function so that the form validation is still performed when the user clicks on the submit button, as follows:

```
for (var i = 0; i < inputs.length; i++) {
    var input = inputs[i];
    doValidation(input);
}
```

3. Update the `isError` check after the `for` loop to use an alternative method to determine if there were errors so that the form can still be submitted, as follows:

```
if ($('.error-data').length == 0) {
    //No errors, submit the form
    $('#webForm').submit();
}
```

4. To perform validation on the field that the user is typing into, we need to call the `doValidation()` function on the `keyup` event. Add the following code inside the `$(function(){});` block to attach a `keyup` event handler to each of the form inputs:

```
$('input').on("keyup", function(){
    doValidation($(this));
});
```

5. Open `index.html` in a web browser, start typing inside the e-mail field, and you will be provided with the appropriate error message as you type until you have entered a valid e-mail address.

How it works...

It is easy to adapt the previous validation code to provide real-time validation for the user. Moving the main validation triggers to another function means that the code can be reused without the need for duplication. The function that holds these triggers takes one argument, which is the input it needs to perform the validation checks on. The `for` loop is still used to provide this input, shown as follows:

```
for (var i = 0; i < inputs.length; i++) {
    var input = inputs[i];
    doValidation(input);
}
```

Instead of relying on the `doValidation` function to return an `isError` value, we look to the DOM directly to see if there are any errors being displayed on screen by looking for any elements with the `error-data` class, as follows:

```
if ($('.error-data').length == 0) {
    //No errors, submit the form
    $('#webForm').submit();
}
```

If there are no errors, the form is submitted manually as before.

To provide real-time validation, a `keyup` event handler is attached to each of the form inputs using the following jQuery code:

```
$('input').on("keyup", function(){
    doValidation($(this));
});
```

The callback function for the `on()` method will be executed every time the user presses and releases a key inside one of the input fields. It is then possible to use `$(this)`, which refers to the input that triggered the event, thereby providing the `doValidation()` function with the input object it requires to perform the validation checks.

Adding a password strength indicator

Users like to create a really simple password that is easy to remember, such as cat, john, or even password. However, most people, especially web developers, know that these types of passwords are too insecure and are incredibly easy to decrypt from an encrypted database using techniques such as a dictionary attack, for example. Password strength indicators are useful to nudge the user in the right direction of using more complex passwords.

Getting ready

To be able to validate password strength, we need to create some rules that our code will use. There are no hard-and-fast rules regarding this, but plenty of information can be found online about what types of passwords are best. We will give the password a score out of five, one point for each of the following rules:

- ▸ It is greater than six characters in length
- ▸ It is greater than eight characters
- ▸ It has both upper and lowercase characters
- ▸ It has at least one number
- ▸ It has one of the following symbols: @, $, !, &, and ^

This recipe will add password strength indicator to the web form that we have been creating over the last six recipes. Ensure that you have the code from these recipes available before you begin this recipe.

How to do it...

Create an effective password strength indicator for web forms by performing each of the following steps:

1. Update `index.html`, adding some additional classes to the password form elements and also some additional HTML, which will create the password strength indicator, as follows:

```
// --- ADDITIONAL HTML HIDDEN
<div class="input-frame">
<label for="password">Password:</label>
<input name="password" id="password" type="password"
class="required password" />
<div class="password-strength">
    <div class="inner"></div>
    <div class="text"></div>
</div>
</div>
<div class="input-frame">
<label for="confirmPassword">Confirm Password:</label>
<input name="confirmPassword" id="confirmPassword" type="password"
class="confirm-password" />
</div>
// --- ADDITIONAL HTML HIDDEN
```

2. Add the following styles to the end of `styles.css` to position the strength indicator under the password field. These styles will also allow the strength indicator to act as a load bar showing the percentage of password strength.

```css
.password-strength {
    position: absolute;
    width: 150px;
    height: 20px;
    left: 69%;
    top: 35px;
    line-height: 20px;
    border: solid 1px #191919;
}
.password-strength .inner {
    position: absolute;
    left: 0;
    top: 0;
}
.password-strength .text {
    font-size: 11px;
    color: #FFF;
    text-align: center;
    position: relative;
    z-index: 10;
}
```

3. Add the `validatePasswords()` function to the end of `validation.js`, which will be used to ensure both passwords are entered and that they match, as follows:

```javascript
// --- HIDDEN JAVASCRIPT
function validatePasswords(value) {
    var password = $('.password').val();
    if (value == "") {
        return "Both passwords are required";
    } else if (value != password) {
        return "Passwords do not match";
    }
    return true;
}
```

4. Add the following code to the end of the `doValidation()` function to run the `validatePasswords()` function on the `confirm-password` input:

```javascript
function doValidation(input) {
// --- HIDDEN JAVASCRIPT
if ($(input).hasClass('confirm-password')) {
    var result = validatePasswords($(input).val());
```

```
        if (result != true) {
            addErrorData($(input), result);
        }
    }
}
```

5. Add the following `keyup` event handler inside the `$(function(){});` block in `validation.js` to score the password strength when the user types in the first password field:

```
$('.password').on("keyup", function(){
    var score = 0;
    var password = $('.password');
    var passwordAgain = $('.confirm-password');
    //Remove any old errors for the password fields
    password.parent().removeClass('error');
    password.next('.error-data').remove();
    passwordAgain.parent().removeClass('error');
    passwordAgain.next('.error-data').remove();
    //Password is greater than 6 characters
    if (password.val().length > 6) {
        score++;
    }
    //Password is greater than 8 characters
    if (password.val().length > 8) {
        score++;
    }
    //Password has both uppercase and lowercase characters
    if (/(?=.*[A-Z])(?=.*[a-z])/.test(password.val())) {
        score++;
    }
    //Password has at least one number
    if (/(?=.*[0-9])/.test(password.val())) {
        score++;
    }
    //Password has at least one symbol (@$!&^) character
    if (/@|\$|\!|&|\^/.test(password.val())) {
        score++;
    }
    var fill = (100 - ((score * 2) * 10));
    var percent = (100 - fill);
    var level,
    colour;
    switch (score) {
    case 0:
```

```
case 1:
level = "Weak";
colour = "green";
break;
case 2:
case 3:
level = "Medium";
colour = "orange";
break;
case 4:
level = "Strong";
colour = "red";
break;
case 5:
level = "Excellent";
colour = "purple";
break;
}
$('.password-strength .inner').css('right', fill +
    "%").css('background-color', colour);
$('.password-strength .text').html(level + " (" + percent +
    "%)");
});
```

6. Open index.html in a web browser and you will see an additional black box
    under the first password field. Start typing in a password and this field will provide
    information on the password strength as you type. This is illustrated in the
    following screenshot:

How it works...

The HTML for the indicator itself has an inner element and a text element. The text
element is used by jQuery to display the password strength and percentage based on the
calculated score of the inputted password. The inner element is used to form the colored
bar. Based on the calculated score, jQuery is used to change the inner element's color and
positioning, creating the load bar impression, which can be seen in the previous screenshot.

The CSS used needs little explanation since it provides basic styles and positioning. The `inner` element has an absolute position so that it can fill the `password-strength` element at different percentages. The `text` division has its `z-index` parameter set to ensure that the text will always display above the `inner` element.

The `validatePasswords` function, which was created as part of this recipe, simply adds basic password validation to our application. It checks to ensure that the `confirm-password` field has been filled and that the value matches the first `password` field. An additional check is added to the `doValdiation` function to ensure this validation gets applied along with the other validation methods created in earlier recipes.

To update the password strength indicator as the user types within the password field, the same method is used as that used in the *Implementing live form validation* recipe, which is to use the `keyup` event. An event handler is attached to the `password` field using the jQuery `on()` function, shown as follows:

```
$('.password').on("keyup", function(){
});
```

The code to calculate the score and update the `password-strength` HTML element is then placed within the callback function to this event handler. The first part of this code is to remove any current errors displayed for the password fields.

After this, there are a series of `if` statements which validate the password against the rules that were defined at the beginning of this recipe. The first basic validation is the password length, shown as follows:

```
//Password is greater than 6 characters
if (password.val().length > 6) {
    score++;
}
//Password is greater than 8 characters
if (password.val().length > 8) {
    score++;
}
```

The score variable is incremented by 1 using `score++` every time a validation condition is met.

The more complex rules use regular expressions to determine whether the password value meets the requirements for the additional score points, shown as follows:

```
//Password has both uppercase and lowercase characters
if (/(?=.*[A-Z])(?=.*[a-z])/.test(password.val())) {
    score++;
}
//Password has at least one number
```

```
if (/(?=.*[0-9])/.test(password.val())) {
    score++;
}
//Password has at least one symbol (@$!&^) character
if (/@|\$|\!|&|\^/.test(password.val())) {
    score++;
}
```

After all five rules have been considered, the final score is used to calculate the fill value. The fill value is the percentage of the `inner` element that needs to be filled from the right-hand side of the strength indicator. This allows us to create the load bar effect. In addition to the fill value, a normal percentage is calculated to be displayed along with the strength level text as follows:

```
var fill = (100 - ((score * 2) * 10));
var percent = (100 - fill);
```

After this, the score value is used once more to determine the background color of the `inner` element and the strength level text as follows:

```
var level,
colour;
switch (score) {
case 0:
case 1:
    level = "Weak";
    colour = "green";
break;
case 2:
case 3:
    level = "Medium";
    colour = "orange";
    break;
case 4:
    level = "Strong";
    colour = "red";
break;
case 5:
    level = "Excellent";
    colour = "purple";
break;
}
```

Finally, using the jQuery `password-strength`, the HTML code is updated with the acquired information to display the results to the user, as follows:

```
$('.password-strength .inner').css('right', fill +
    "%").css('background-color', colour);
$('.password-strength .text').html(level + " (" + percent + "%)");
```

There's more...

This code should be easily adaptable so that you can add your own rules regarding password strength. There are many discussions and resources online to point you to what a strong password should look like.

See also

> ▸ *Implementing live form validation*

Adding anti-spam measures

Most web developers will know that if you have a contact form or any kind of web form publically available on your website, there will be web bot submissions and a lot of spam. Most web bots will be thwarted by the JavaScript-only web form we have been creating over the last seven recipes, but with browser automation and web bots becoming ever cleverer, it is still important to add anti-spam measures to your web forms.

Getting ready

Ensure that you have completed the last seven recipes and have the code readily available. Remember that if you would just like to use the code without fully understanding how it works, skip to the end of this chapter, to the *How it works...* section, to grab it all.

How to do it...

Add simple anti-spam measures to your web form by performing each of the following steps:

1. Update `index.html` to have an additional form input under the input labeled `Confirm Password` as follows:

```
<!-- HIDDEN HTML CODE -->
<div class="input-frame">
    <label>Confirm Password:</label>
    <input type="password" class="confirm-password" />
</div>
<div class="input-frame">
```

```
<label>Enter the number <span class="anti-spam-
    number"></span>:</label>
<input type="text" class="required anti-spam-input" />
</div>
<!-- HIDDEN HTML CODE -->
```

2. Using JavaScript, generate a random number between `1` and `100` at the top of `validation.js` using the following code:

```
var spamNumber = Math.floor(Math.random() * (100 - 1 + 1))
    + 1;
$(function(){
// --- HIDDEN JAVASCRIPT CODE
```

3. At the very end of the `$(function(){});` jQuery block, add the following code to update the HTML `anti-spam-number` span element with the random number:

```
// --- HIDDEN JAVASCRIPT CODE
$('.anti-spam-number').html(spamNumber);
});
```

4. Add the following additional validation check to the end of the `doValidation()` function:

```
if ($(input).hasClass('anti-spam-input') &&
    !validateAntiSpam($(input).val())) {
    addErrorData($(input), "Incorrect Anti-Spam answer");
}
```

5. Finally, at the end of `validation.js`, add the `validateAntiSpam()` function, which is called by the previous code:

```
// --- HIDDEN JAVASCRIPT CODE
function validateAntiSpam(value) {
    if (value != "") {
        if (parseInt(value) != spamNumber) return false;
    }
    return true;
}
```

6. Open `index.html` in a web browser and you will see the additional anti-spam form input field. Every time you refresh the page, it will ask you to input a different number.

How it works...

By declaring the `spamNumber` global variable outside any function, it is available for use by the whole JavaScript file. A new number between `1` and `100` is generated on every page load so that a web bot cannot store the answer and submit the form. Within the HTML code, there is a span element with the class `anti-spam-number`, which is updated with a random number on page load using the following code:

```
$('.anti-spam-number').html(spamNumber);
```

This will ensure the user is being told to input the correct number. We created an additional validation function named `validateAntiSpam` and called it from the `doValidation()` function for all inputs that have the `anti-spam-input` class. This will then validate the user-entered number with the globally available `spamNumber` variable, shown as follows:

```
function validateAntiSpam(value) {
    if (value != "") {
        if (parseInt(value) != spamNumber) return false;
    }
    return true;
}
```

Note that the input is parsed as an integer to ensure a number-on-number comparison. If the values do not match, this function will return `false` so that the `doValidation()` function can create the appropriate error message on-screen for the user.

There's more...

This type of client-side spam validation cannot be completely relied upon. It is effective towards general web bots that are not directly targeting your website. If someone wants to write a bot script specific to your site, bypassing this JavaScript would not be a difficult process. If you think this is possible, more extreme server-side spam prevention must be used.

There are many effective spam-prevention methods available for free on the Internet. The most popular are CAPTCHAs. One of the most popular CAPTCHAs is available for free by Google at `http://www.google.com/recaptcha`.

See also

▸ *Adding a password strength indicator*

Implementing input character restrictions

Until now, all of the recipes in this chapter have concentrated on input validation and providing appropriate feedback to the user. There are situations where it is better to simply prevent the user from inputting invalid characters in the first place. This method would not typically be used, because it can be confusing for some users; for example, if they are not being told why they cannot input %. A situation where this would work is a login form. If you know your registration system does not allow % in the username, you know that the user would be inputting % by mistake, and therefore preventing the input is acceptable. This recipe provides a method to prevent users from inputting non-alphanumeric characters into an input field.

Getting ready

This recipe does not use any code from the last eight recipes; however, there are similarities in the CSS code. To complete this recipe, you are going to need three files. Create `recipe-9.html`, `recipe-9.js`, and `recipe-9.css` in the same directory as you have stored the latest version of jQuery.

How to do it...

Use jQuery to prevent users from inputting invalid chapters into text inputs by performing the following steps:

1. Add the following HTML code to `recipe-9.html`. This creates a basic login form and includes the two other files along with the jQuery library:

```
<!DOCTYPE html>
<html xmlns="http://www.w3.org/1999/html">
<head>
    <title>Chapter 5 :: Recipe 7</title>
    <link type="text/css" media="screen" rel="stylesheet"
href="recipe-9.css" />
    <script src="jquery.min.js"></script>
    <script src="recipe-9.js"></script>
</head>
<body>
<form id="webForm" method="POST">
    <div class="header">
        <h1>Register</h1>
    </div>
    <div class="input-frame">
        <label for="username">Username:</label>
```

```
        <input name="username" id="username" type="text"
class="username" />
    </div>
    <div class="input-frame">
        <label for="password">Password:</label>
        <input name="password" id="password" type="text"
class="required" />
    </div>
    <div class="actions">
        <button class="submit-btn">Submit</button>
    </div>
</form>
</body>
</html>
```

2. Add the following CSS code to `recipe-9.css`, which adds style to the login form:

```
@import url(http://fonts.googleapis.com/css?family=Ubuntu);
body {
    background-color: #FFF;
    font-family: 'Ubuntu', sans-serif;
}
form {
    width: 500px;
    margin: 10px auto auto auto;
    padding: 20px;
    background-color: #333;
    border-radius: 5px;
    color: #747474;
    border: solid 2px #000;
}
form label {
    font-size: 14px;
    line-height: 30px;
    padding-bottom: 8px;
    width: 140px;
    display: inline-block;
    text-align: right;
}
.input-frame {
    clear: both;
    margin-bottom: 25px;
    position: relative;
}
form input {
```

```css
    height: 30px;
    width: 330px;
    margin-left: 10px;
    background-color: #191919;
    border: solid 1px #404040;
    padding-left: 10px;
    color: #DB7400;
}
form input:hover {
    background-color: #262626;
}
form input:focus {
    border-color: #DB7400;
}
form .header {
    margin: -20px -20px 25px -20px;
    padding: 10px 10px 10px 20px;
    position: relative;
    background-color: #DB7400;
    border-top-left-radius: 4px;
    border-top-right-radius: 4px;
}
form .header h1 {
    line-height: 50px;
    margin: 0;
    padding: 0;
    color: #FFF;
    font-weight: normal;
}
.actions {
    text-align: right;
}
.submit-btn {
    background-color: #DB7400;
    border: solid 1px #000;
    border-radius: 5px;
    color: #FFF;
    padding: 10px 20px 10px 20px;
    text-decoration: none;
    cursor: pointer;
}
```

3. Add the following JavaScript code to `recipe-9.js` in order to watch for user input on the `username` field and ensure non-alphanumeric characters are not inputted:

```
$(function(){
    $('.username').on("keypress", function(event){
        //Get key press character code
        var key = String.fromCharCode(event.which);
        if (/[^a-zA-Z\d\s:]/.test(key)) {
            event.preventDefault();
            return false;
        }
    });
});
```

4. Open `recipe-9.html` in a web browser and attempt to input a non-alphanumeric character (for example, $) inside the `username` field. You will see it will not be placed inside the field.

How it works...

A key press event handler is attached to the `username` field on page load. The callback function for this event handler has a single argument, which is the `event` object. This `event` object provides access to the key code of the key that the user is pressing. When the `username` field has focus and the user presses a key, the callback function is executed.

First, `String.fromCharCode(event.which);` is used to get the string value of the pressed key; for example, D, H, and 4. A regular expression is then used to determine whether or not this character is alphanumeric. If not, the character is prevented from being inputted into the form field using the following code:

```
if (/[^a-zA-Z\d\s:]/.test(key)) {
    event.preventDefault();
    return false;
}
```

There's more...

Ensure that the event used in this recipe is the `keypress` event. If an alternative event is used, such as `keydown`, you may not achieve the desired result. If the `keydown` event is used, when the user presses *Shift + 4* to input a $ symbol, the `keydown` event will provide its event handler as just 4, and not $, therefore passing validation.

6
User Interface

In this chapter, we will cover the following topics:

- ▸ Manipulating element CSS
- ▸ Creating a news ticker
- ▸ Creating sticky elements
- ▸ Implementing smooth scrolling
- ▸ Creating a dynamic table of contents
- ▸ Creating a basic drag-and-drop functionality
- ▸ Creating a dynamic animated tree menu
- ▸ Creating an accordion content slider
- ▸ Creating tabbed content
- ▸ Creating a modal pop up
- ▸ Creating a draggable content pop up

Introduction

jQuery empowers developers with the ability to easily create complex user interface elements. Because of this, there are a vast amount of jQuery plugins that allow developers to quickly add such interfaces to their site. Additionally, jQuery's own UI framework houses many popular interface elements, such as accordions, tabular content, modals, and more. If you would like to know how to use jQuery UI for your own site, skip directly to *Chapter 9, jQuery UI*. This chapter will focus on developing some of these popular UI elements from scratch, providing for unlimited customizability and allowing you to gain an understanding of how these other plugins work.

Manipulating element CSS

jQuery allows developers to access the CSS properties of DOM elements directly. This provides an easy way to alter the look and feel of your application based on data within your JavaScript. This recipe will show you how to manipulate DOM CSS in various elements.

Getting ready

You are going to need three files for this recipe. Using your editor of choice, create `recipe-1.html`, `recipe-1.js`, and `recipe-1.css` in the same directory as the latest version of the jQuery library.

How to do it...

Of the three files you have just created, open each one for editing and perform the following steps:

1. Add the following HTML code to `recipe-1.html`; be sure to change the source location of the JavaScript included for the jQuery library, pointing it to where the latest version of jQuery is downloaded on your computer:

```
<!DOCTYPE html>
<html>
<head>
    <title>Chapter 6 :: Recipe 1</title>
    <link href="recipe-1.css" rel="stylesheet"
        type="text/css" />
    <script src="jquery.min.js"></script>
    <script src="recipe-1.js"></script>
</head>
<body>
    <div class="header">
        <h1>ALTER ELEMENT CSS WITH JQUERY</h1>
    </div>
    <div class="content-frame">
        <div class="left">
            <h1>SOME TITLE HERE</h1>
            <p>Lorem ipsum dolor sit amet, consectetur adipisicing
elit, sed do eiusmod tempor incididunt ut labore et dolore magna
aliqua. Ut enim ad minim veniam, quis nostrud exercitation ullamco
laboris nisi ut aliquip ex ea commodo consequat. Duis aute irure
dolor in reprehenderit in voluptate velit esse cillum dolore
eu fugiat nulla pariatur. Excepteur sint occaecat cupidatat non
proident, sunt in culpa qui officia deserunt mollit anim id est
laborum.</p>
```

```
        <h2>SOME KIND OF SUBTITLE HERE</h2>
            <p>Lorem ipsum dolor sit amet, consectetur adipisicing
elit, sed do eiusmod tempor incididunt ut labore et dolore magna
aliqua. Ut enim ad minim veniam, quis nostrud exercitation ullamco
laboris nisi ut aliquip ex ea commodo consequat. Duis aute irure
dolor in reprehenderit in voluptate velit esse cillum dolore
eu fugiat nulla pariatur. Excepteur sint occaecat cupidatat non
proident, sunt in culpa qui officia deserunt mollit anim id est
laborum.</p>
            <p>Lorem ipsum dolor sit amet, consectetur adipisicing
elit, sed do eiusmod tempor incididunt ut labore et dolore magna
aliqua. Ut enim ad minim veniam, quis nostrud exercitation ullamco
laboris nisi ut aliquip ex ea commodo consequat. Duis aute irure
dolor in reprehenderit in voluptate velit esse cillum dolore
eu fugiat nulla pariatur. Excepteur sint occaecat cupidatat non
proident, sunt in culpa qui officia deserunt mollit anim id est
laborum.</p>
        </div>
        <div class="right">
            <h3>TITLE COLOUR</h3>
            <select class="title-colour">
                <option value="#">Default</option>
                <option value="red">Red</option>
                <option value="green">Green</option>
                <option value="orange">Orange</option>
                <option value="blue">Blue</option>
            </select>
            <h3>PARAGRAPH SIZE</h3>
            <select class="p-size">
                <option value="#">Default</option>
                <option value="10px">10px</option>
                <option value="15px">15px</option>
                <option value="20px">20px</option>
                <option value="25px">25px</option>
            </select>
        </div>
    </div>
</body>
</html>
```

2. Add the following CSS code to `recipe-1.css`:

```
body {
    margin: 0;
    background-color: #5dace7;
}
.header {
```

```
        height: 150px;
        background-color: #0174cd;
}
.header h1 {
        margin: 0 50px 0 50px;
        padding: 0;
        line-height: 100px;
        font-size: 40px;
        color: #FFFFFF;
}
.content-frame {
        margin: -50px 50px 0 50px;
        background-color: #FFFFFF;
        border-radius: 10px;
        min-height: 500px;
        position: relative;
}
.content-frame .left {
        margin-right: 20%;
        padding: 20px;
}
.content-frame .left h1 {
        margin: 0;
}
.content-frame .right {
        width: 16%;
        padding: 2%;
        position: absolute;
        top: 0;
        right: 0;
        background-color: #F1F1F1;
        border-top-right-radius: 10px;
        border-bottom-right-radius: 10px;
}
.content-frame .right h3 {
        margin: 0;
        line-height: 30px;
        color: #333333;
}
.content-frame .right select {
        width: 100%;
}
```

3. Add the following jQuery code to `recipe-1.js` to add functionality to the select dropdowns within the HTML code:

```
$(function(){
    $('.title-colour').on("change", function(){
        var colour = $(this).val();
        if (colour == "#") {
            colour = "";
        }
        $('h1, h2').css("color", colour);
    });
    $('.p-size').on("change", function(){
        var size = $(this).val();
        if (size == "#") {
            size = "";
        }
        $('p').css("font-size", size);
    });
});
```

4. Open `recipe-1.html` in a web browser and you should see the following simple web page:

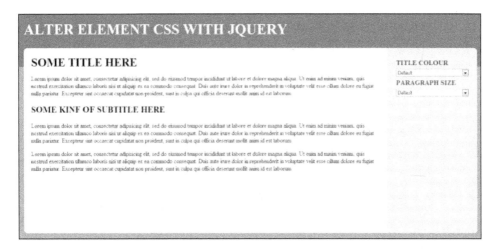

5. Use the drop-down menus on the right-hand side to alter the CSS for the header and paragraph elements.

How it works...

The HTML creates a basic web page to provide elements such that their CSS can be manipulated by jQuery and a simple interface to initiate these changes. The CSS code in `recipe-1.css` adds basic styling to create our web page layout.

To change an element's CSS, a `change` event handler is attached to both select dropdowns using their respective class names:

```
$(function(){
    $('.title-colour').on("change", function(){

});
$('.p-size').on("change", function(){

});
});
```

This will allow us to execute some code when the user changes the values of either the title color (`title-colour`) or paragraph size (`p-size`) dropdowns. Using `$(this).val()`, it is possible to get the value of the selected option, as shown in the following code snippet:

```
$(function(){
    $('.title-colour').on("change", function(){
        var colour = $(this).val();
        if (colour == "#") {
            colour = "";
        }
        $('h1, h2').css("color", colour);
    });
    $('.p-size').on("change", function(){
        var size = $(this).val();
        if (size == "#") {
            size = "";
        }
        $('p').css("font-size", size);
    });
});
```

Using either the `colour` or `size` variable, which hold the selected values of their respective dropdowns, we determine whether or not the default option has been selected using its value #. If it has been selected, we set the `colour` or `size` value to blank, allowing the user to reset the manipulated CSS to the default values.

If an option other than the default has been chosen, the value will be used in conjunction with the appropriate CSS option in the jQuery `css()` function as highlighted in the following code snippet:

```
$(function(){
    $('.title-colour').on("change", function(){
        var colour = $(this).val();
        if (colour == "#") colour = "";
        $('h1, h2').css("color", colour);
    });
    $('.p-size').on("change", function(){
        var size = $(this).val();
        if (size == "#") size = "";
        $('p').css("font-size", size);
    });
});
```

Creating a news ticker

This recipe will show you how to create a simple news ticker with a stop/pause functionality. A news ticker is a great way to display a lot of information such as tweets, quotes, or general news items in a small space.

Getting ready

Once again, you are going to need to create three files. Create `recipe-2.html`, `recipe-2.css`, and `recipe-2.js` in the same directory as the latest version of jQuery.

How to do it...

Carry out the following step-by-step instructions to create an animated news ticker:

1. Add the following HTML code to `recipe-2.html` to create a simple web page and content for our ticker:

```
<!DOCTYPE html>
<html>
<head>
    <title>Chapter 6 :: Recipe 2</title>
    <link href="recipe-2.css" rel="stylesheet" type="text/css" />
    <script src="jquery.min.js"></script>
    <script src="recipe-2.js"></script>
</head>
<body>
```

```
<div class="header">
    <h1>CONTENT TICKER</h1>
</div>
<div class="content-frame">
    <ul id="ticker">
        <li>Learn from yesterday, live for today, hope for
tomorrow. The important thing is not to stop questioning</li>
        <li>Try not to become a man of success, but rather try to
become a man of value</li>
        <li>Logic will get you from A to B. Imagination will take
you everywhere</li>
        <li>Reality is merely an illusion, albeit a very
persistent one</li>
    </ul>
</div>
</body>
</html>
```

2. Add the following simple CSS to `recipe-2.css` to add styles to our web page:

```
body {
    margin: 0;
    background-color: #5dace7;
}
.header {
    height: 130px;
    background-color: #0174cd;
}
.header h1 {
    margin: 0 50px 0 50px;
    padding: 0;
    line-height: 100px;
    font-size: 40px;
    color: #FFFFFF;
}
.content-frame {
    margin: -30px 50px 0 50px;
    background-color: #FFFFFF;
    border-radius: 10px;
    height: 50px;
    position: relative;
    padding: 0 20px 0 20px;
    overflow: hidden;
}
.content-frame ul {
    list-style: none;
```

```
        margin: 0;
        padding: 0;
    }
    .content-frame ul li {
        line-height: 50px;
    }
```

3. Add the following jQuery code to `recipe-2.js` to make our ticker active:

```
var tick = null;
var interval = 2000;
$(function(){
    tick = setInterval(function(){
        ticker()
    }, interval);
    $('.content-frame').on("mouseover", function(){
        clearInterval(tick);
    });
    $('.content-frame').on("mouseout", function(){
        tick = setInterval(function(){
            ticker()
        }, interval);
    });
});
function ticker() {
    $('#ticker li:first-child').slideUp(function(){
        $(this).appendTo($('#ticker')).slideDown();
    });
}
```

4. Opening `recipe-2.html` in a web browser will present you with a simple web page and an animated ticker that shows a different quote by Einstein every two seconds.

How it works...

Because the HTML and CSS code are very simple, the only explanation needed is for the jQuery code. Note that the HTML web page holds an unordered list element with four Einstein quotes inside a division element called `content-frame`. The `content-frame` element has its `overflow` attribute set to `hidden` so that only one quote is visible at a time.

At the top of the `recipe-2.js` file, two variables are declared: `tick` and `interval`. The `tick` variable is where the JavaScript `setInterval()` function will be declared. The JavaScript `setInterval()` function allows us to specify a function and an interval. The specified function will then be called again over the specified interval. This allows us to loop through the news ticker content.

By declaring the `tick` variable at the top of the JavaScript file, we can stop the interval at a later point to add the pause functionality. The `interval` variable simply holds the number of milliseconds we want the `setInterval()` function to wait before it calls the specified function again:

```
var tick = null;
var interval = 2000;
$(function(){

});
```

Inside the jQuery on-load function, we assign the `tick` variable to the `setInterval()` function, specify that the function be called again, and then use the `interval` variable to set the interval duration, as shown in the following code snippet:

```
$(function(){
    tick = setInterval(function(){
        ticker();
    }, interval);
});
```

To add the stop/start functionality, according to which the ticker will stop when the user hovers over it and start up again when they move their mouse away, we need to attach two event handlers to the `content-frame` division element as follows:

```
$(function(){
    tick = setInterval(function(){
        ticker()
    }, interval);
    $('.content-frame').on("mouseover", function(){
        clearInterval(tick);
    });
    $('.content-frame').on("mouseout", function(){
        tick = setInterval(function(){
            ticker()
        }, interval);
    });
});
```

The `mouseover` event handler uses the JavaScript `clearInterval()` function and is passed the `tick` variable as an argument. This will stop the `setInterval()` function from calling the `ticker()` function again when the user hovers over the `content-frame` element. Within the callback function to the `mouseout` event, the `tick` variable is declared again with the same `setInterval()` function as before, reinitializing the news ticker and starting it again.

Finally, there is the `ticker()` function itself. This function takes the first list element and slides it upwards using the jQuery `slideUp()` function. This provides the effect of the next element moving into view. It then takes the element that has been hidden using the `slideUp()` function and moves it to the end of the ticker list using `appendTo()`. Finally, it slides this element back down using `slideDown()`, so it is ready for display when it eventually moves to the top of the list again. This is shown in the following code snippet:

```
function ticker() {
    $('#ticker li:first-child').slideUp(function(){
        $(this).appendTo($('#ticker')).slideDown();
    });
}
```

There's more...

It is possible to adopt the start and stop functionality any way you like, for example, using start and stop buttons or even a single pause button to make it more obvious that it is possible to pause the ticker. The benefit of the method used in this recipe is that links will often be displayed within the ticker content. When the user goes to click on a link within the ticker, the ticker will stop, allowing them to click on the link instead of the link moving away before they can initiate the click.

See also

▶ *Creating a dynamic table of contents*

Creating sticky elements

Sticky elements are page elements that stick to a position within the user's browser, even as they scroll. Sticky elements are used to always keep content within the user's line of sight. This content could be navigation, important information, or even advertising. This recipe will show you how to create sticky elements and also use jQuery to activate them when the user scrolls to a certain point on the page.

Getting ready

Using your favorite editor, create three files named `recipe-3.html`, `recipe-3.css`, and `recipe-3.js`, ensuring that they are in the same directory as your jQuery library.

How to do it...

For each of the newly created files, perform the following steps:

1. Add the following HTML code to `recipe-3.html`; it creates a long web page that is scrollable and a `div` element with some important content that needs to stay within the user's view at all times:

```
<!DOCTYPE html>
<html>
<head>
    <title>Chapter 6 :: Recipe 3</title>
    <link href="recipe-3.css" rel="stylesheet" type="text/css" />
    <script src="jquery.min.js"></script>
    <script src="recipe-3.js"></script>
</head>
<body>
<div class="header">
    <h1>STICKY ELEMENTS RECIPE</h1>
</div>
<div class="content-frame">
    <div class="left">
        <h1>STICKY ELEMENTS</h1>
        <p>Sticky elements are great to keep important content
within the users view, such as share buttons, navigation and also
table of contents.</p>
        <p>Scroll down this page and when you are about to go past
the important content on the right hand side, it will start to
follow you down the screen.</p>
    </div>
    <div class="right">
        <ul>
            <li><a href="#">Navigation Item 1</a></li>
            <li><a href="#">Navigation Item 2</a></li>
            <li><a href="#">Navigation Item 3</a></li>
            <li><a href="#">Navigation Item 4</a></li>
            <li><a href="#">Navigation Item 5</a></li>
            <li><a href="#">Navigation Item 6</a></li>
        </ul>
        <div class="important">
            <p>Here is some important content.</p>
        </div>
    </div>
</div>
</body>
</html>
```

2. To style this page, add the following CSS code to `recipe-3.css`; there is also a `sticky` class within this code, which will be applied to the important elements by jQuery when users scroll down the page:

```css
@import url(http://fonts.googleapis.com/css?family=Ubuntu);
body {
    margin: 0;
    background-color: #5dace7;
    font-family: 'Ubuntu', sans-serif;
}
.header {
    height: 150px;
    background-color: #0174cd;
}
.header h1 {
    width: 1000px;
    margin: auto;
    padding: 0;
    line-height: 100px;
    font-size: 40px;
    color: #FFFFFF;
}
.content-frame {
    margin: -50px auto auto auto;
    width: 1000px;
    background-color: #FFFFFF;
    border-radius: 10px;
    min-height: 1300px;
    position: relative;
}
.content-frame .left {
    margin-right: 240px;
    padding: 20px;
}
.content-frame .left h1 {
    margin: 0;
}
.content-frame .right {
    width: 200px;
    padding: 10px;
    position: absolute;
    top: 0;
    right: 0;
    background-color: #F1F1F1;
    border-top-right-radius: 10px;
```

```
        border-bottom-right-radius: 10px;
    }
    .content-frame .right .important {
        border: solid 1px #CCCCCC;
        text-align: center;
        width: 200px;
    }
    .sticky {
        position: fixed;
        top: 10px;
    }
}
```

3. Finally, add the following jQuery code to `recipe-3.js`, which will activate the sticky element when the user tries to scroll past it:

```
var importantOrigin = {};
$(function(){
    importantOrigin = $('.important').offset();
    $(window).scroll(function(){
        sticky();
    });
});
function sticky() {
    var _important = $('.important');
    var scrollPosition = $('body, html').scrollTop();
    if (importantOrigin.top < scrollPosition) {
        _important.addClass("sticky");
    } else {
        _important.removeClass("sticky");
    }
}
```

How it works...

At the top of `recipe-3.js`, there is a variable called `importantOrigin`, which will be used to store the original position of the important division element. Within the jQuery on-load block, `$('.important').offset()` is used to get the top and left positions of the important element and stores these values in the previously created `importantOrigin` variable. This is shown in the following code snippet:

```
var importantOrigin = {};
$(function(){
    importantOrigin = $('.important').offset();
    $(window).scroll(function(){
```

```
        sticky();
    });
});
```

The jQuery `scroll()` function is used to execute the `sticky()` method every time the user scrolls on the page:

```
function sticky() {
    var _important = $('.important');
    var scrollPosition = $('body, html').scrollTop();
    if (importantOrigin.top < scrollPosition) {
        _important.addClass("sticky");
    } else {
        _important.removeClass("sticky");
    }
}
```

The `sticky()` method gets the current vertical position of the page using `$('body, html').scrollTop()` and then uses this to compare against the important element's top position. If the user has scrolled past the important element, the `sticky` CSS class is applied to the important element using the `addClass()` method:

```
.sticky {
    position: fixed;
    top: 10px;
}
```

If the page's current vertical position is lower than the top of the `sticky` element, the `sticky` class is removed with `removeClass()`, setting the important element back into its original state. Using `position: fixed;` in the CSS, it is possible to make an element stick to a certain point on the page. Using jQuery to conditionally apply this CSS, we can control when the element sticks, because it is typically not desired until the user scrolls past the element so that it is no longer visible on the screen.

There's more...

There is a popular jQuery plugin called `sticky.js`, which can be found at `http://stickyjs.com/`. This plugin uses the same principles that you have learned as part of this recipe and bundles all of the functionality into a plugin so that it is easy to reuse.

See also

 ► *Creating a dynamic table of contents*

Implementing smooth scrolling

Anchor links to navigate to different sections of the page are useful to allow users to easily bypass the information in which they are not interested and go directly to that in which they are. However, when there is a lot of textual data on the screen, jumping between these different sections can often be confusing for the user. Using smooth scrolling and animating the screen to slowly move up or down to the selected section, it is easier for a user to visualize where they have navigated to without getting disorientated.

Getting ready

Simply create the three standard recipe files, `recipe-4.html`, `recipe-4.css`, and `recipe-4.js`, and save them to the same directory as the latest version of the jQuery library.

How to do it...

Perform the following simple steps to add smooth scrolling to a website or web page:

1. Create a long web page by adding the following HTML code to `recipe-4.html`:

```
<!DOCTYPE html>
<html>
<head>
    <title>Chapter 6 :: Recipe 4</title>
    <link href="recipe-4.css" rel="stylesheet" type="text/css" />
    <script src="jquery.min.js"></script>
    <script src="recipe-4.js"></script>
</head>
<body>
<div class="header">
    <h1 id="top">SMOOTH SCROLLING RECIPE</h1>
</div>
<div class="content-frame">
    <div class="left">
        <h2 id="one">SECTION 1 <a href="#top" class="top-
link">[TOP]</a></h2>
        <div class="section"></div>
        <h2 id="two">SECTION 2 <a href="#top" class="top-
link">[TOP]</a></h2>
        <div class="section"></div>
        <h2 id="three">SECTION 3 <a href="#top" class="top-
link">[TOP]</a></h2>
        <div class="section"></div>
```

```
        <h2 id="four">SECTION 4 <a href="#top" class="top-
link">[TOP]</a></h2>
            <div class="section"></div>
    </div>
    <div class="right">
        <h2>NAVIGATION</h2>
        <ul>
            <li><a href="#one">SECTION ONE</a></li>
            <li><a href="#two">SECTION TWO</a></li>
            <li><a href="#three">SECTION THREE</a></li>
            <li><a href="#four">SECTION FOUR</a></li>
            <li><a href="http://www.google.com" target="_
blank">EXTERNAL LINK</a></li>
            <li><a href="#">EMPTY LINK</a></li>
        </ul>
    </div>
</div>
</body>
</html>
```

2. Style this page by adding the following CSS code to `recipe-4.css`, which is included in the preceding HTML page:

```css
@import url(http://fonts.googleapis.com/css?family=Ubuntu);
body {
    margin: 0;
    background-color: #5dace7;
    font-family: 'Ubuntu', sans-serif;
}
.header {
    height: 150px;
    background-color: #0174cd;
}
.header h1 {
    width: 1000px;
    margin: auto;
    padding: 0;
    line-height: 100px;
    font-size: 40px;
    color: #FFFFFF;
}
.content-frame {
    margin: -50px auto auto auto;
    width: 1000px;
    background-color: #FFFFFF;
```

```css
        border-radius: 10px;
        min-height: 1300px;
        position: relative;
    }
    .content-frame .left {
        margin-right: 240px;
        padding: 20px;
    }
    .content-frame .left h1 {
        margin: 0;
    }
    .content-frame .right {
        width: 200px;
        padding: 10px;
        position: absolute;
        top: 0;
        right: 0;
        background-color: #F1F1F1;
        border-top-right-radius: 10px;
        border-bottom-right-radius: 10px;
    }
    .content-frame .right h2 {
        margin: 0;
        padding: 0;
    }
    .section {
        height: 400px;
        background-color: #CCCCCC;
        margin-bottom: 20px;
    }
    .top-link {
        width: 50px;
        text-align: right;
        float: right;
        font-size: 12px;
    }
```

3. Add the following jQuery code to `recipe-4.js` to catch anchor element clicks and provide the smooth-scrolling effect:

```javascript
$(function(){
    $('a[href*=#]:not([href=#])').click(function(){
        if (this.hash.length > 0) {
            $('body, html').animate({
                scrollTop: $(this.hash).offset().top
```

```
            }, 1000);
        }
        return false;
    });
});
```

How it works...

The jQuery code first attaches a `click` event handler to certain anchor elements:

```
$(function(){
    $('a[href*=#]:not([href=#])').click(function(){

    });
});
```

The preceding code will only attach a `click` event handler to anchors with a hash (#) in their `href` attribute. The `:not([href=#])` is also used so that event handlers will not be attached to anchors that have only a hash as their `href` attribute. Now we can specify code to be executed for the links on the page that navigate to other sections on the same page. Blank and external links will be ignored and operate as usual.

Within the `click` event handler `callback()` function, we can use `this.hash` to retrieve the hash value in the `href` attribute of the clicked anchor element. If the anchor links to `#two`, we would receive the string value `"#two"`. Using `this.hash.length`, we can ensure that the value is valid and that we can continue to provide the smooth scroll animation:

```
$(function(){
    $('a[href*=#]:not([href=#])').click(function(){
        if (this.hash.length > 0) {

        }
        return false;
    });
});
```

Inside the `if` statement of `this.hash.length`, we use the jQuery `animate()` function as follows to animate and scroll the user to the location of the anchor target:

```
$('body, html').animate({
    scrollTop: $(this.hash).offset().top
}, 1000);
```

The `scrollTop` parameter is the location to which the animation should scroll. We get this location by selecting the target element using `$(this.hash)` and then using the jQuery `offset()` function to get its top position.

Finally, we return `false` after the `if` statement of `this.hash.length` to prevent the default action of the click event. If you remove `return false`, you will get a flicker on the screen because the default action of the click event (which would send the user to the linked section) occurs just before the animation kicks in.

See also

▸   *Creating a dynamic table of contents*

Creating a dynamic table of contents

A table of contents is a common way to allow users to quickly get to the section of content they are looking for. With jQuery, it is possible to create a table of contents dynamically, based on the HTML header elements on the page. This is very useful for blog posts or other sites that have lots of different content pages.

Getting ready

Create `recipe-5.html`, `recipe-5.css`, and `recipe-5.js` as before and have all three open and ready for editing.

How to do it...

With the required files created, perform the following steps to create a dynamic table of contents:

1. Create a basic web page using the following HTML code, adding it to `recipe-5.html`:

```
<!DOCTYPE html>
<html>
<head>
    <title>Chapter 6 :: Recipe 5</title>
    <link href="recipe-5.css" rel="stylesheet" type="text/css" />
    <script src="jquery.min.js"></script>
    <script src="recipe-5.js"></script>
</head>
<body>
</body>
</html>
```

2. Add the following HTML code to `recipe-5.html` within the `body` tags you have just added; this will create a page with sectioned content and an ordered list element that can be populated with content:

```html
<div class="header">
    <h1>DYNAMIC TABLE OF CONTENTS</h1>
</div>
<div class="content-frame">
    <div class="left">
        <h1 id="one">MAIN HEADING</h1>
        <p>Lorem ipsum dolor sit amet, consectetur adipisicing
elit, sed do eiusmod tempor incididunt ut labore et dolore magna
aliqua. Ut enim ad minim veniam, quis nostrud exercitation ullamco
laboris nisi ut aliquip ex ea commodo consequat.</p>
        <h2 id="two">SUBTITLE</h2>
        <p>Lorem ipsum dolor sit amet, consectetur adipisicing
elit, sed do eiusmod tempor incididunt ut labore et dolore magna
aliqua.</p>
        <h3 id="three">SUB-SUBTITLE</h3>
        <p>Lorem ipsum dolor sit amet, consectetur adipisicing
elit, sed do eiusmod tempor incididunt ut labore et dolore magna
aliqua. Ut enim ad minim veniam, quis nostrud exercitation ullamco
laboris nisi ut aliquip ex ea commodo consequat.</p>
        <h2 id="four">SUBTITLE</h2>
        <p>Ut enim ad minim veniam, quis nostrud exercitation
ullamco laboris nisi ut aliquip ex ea commodo consequat.</p>
        <h3 id="five">SUB-SUBTITLE</h3>
        <p>Ut enim ad minim veniam, quis nostrud exercitation
ullamco laboris nisi ut aliquip ex ea commodo consequat.</p>
        <p>Ut enim ad minim veniam, quis nostrud exercitation
ullamco laboris nisi ut aliquip ex ea commodo consequat.</p>
        <h4 id="six">SUB-SUB-SUBTITLE</h4>
        <p>Ut enim ad minim veniam, quis nostrud exercitation
ullamco laboris nisi ut aliquip ex ea commodo consequat.</p>
    </div>
    <div class="right">
        <h2>CONTENTS</h2>
        <ol class="contents"></ol>
    </div>
</div>
```

3. Add the following CSS to `recipe-5.css` to add basic styles to this page. This CSS code is once again very similar to that in the last two recipes of this chapter:

```css
@import url(http://fonts.googleapis.com/css?family=Ubuntu);
body {
    margin: 0;
    background-color: #5dace7;
```

```
        font-family: 'Ubuntu', sans-serif;
    }
    .header {
        height: 150px;
        background-color: #0174cd;
    }
    .header h1 {
        width: 1000px;
        margin: auto;
        padding: 0;
        line-height: 100px;
        font-size: 40px;
        color: #FFFFFF;
    }
    .content-frame {
        margin: -50px auto auto auto;
        width: 1000px;
        background-color: #FFFFFF;
        border-radius: 10px;
        min-height: 1300px;
        position: relative;
    }
    .content-frame .left {
        margin-right: 240px;
        padding: 20px;
    }
    .content-frame .left h1 {
        margin: 0;
    }
    .content-frame .right {
        width: 200px;
        padding: 10px;
        position: absolute;
        top: 0;
        bottom: 0;
        right: 0;
        background-color: #F1F1F1;
        border-top-right-radius: 10px;
        border-bottom-right-radius: 10px;
    }
    .content-frame .right h2 {
        margin: 0;
        padding: 0;
    }
```

4. Add the following jQuery code to `recipe-5.js`, which will populate the ordered list based on the headed sections in the HTML page we have just created:

```
$(function(){
    var _contents = $('.content-frame .left');
    var _headers = _contents.find("h1, h2, h3, h4");
    _headers.each(function(index, value){
        var _header = $(value);
        var level = parseInt(_header.context.localName.
replace("h", ""));
        if (typeof _header.attr("id") != "undefined") {
            var listItem = $("<li><a href='#" + _header.attr("id")
+ "'>" + _header.html() + "</a></li>");
        } else {
            var listItem = $("<li>" + _header.html() + "</li>");
        }
        listItem.css("padding-left", (level * 5));
        $('.contents').append($(listItem));
    });
});
```

5. Opening `recipe-5.html` in a web page will present you with the content to the left-hand side of the screen and the dynamically-generated contents list to the right-hand side as shown in the following screenshot:

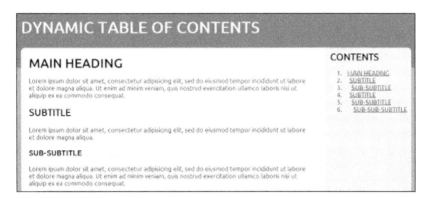

How it works...

The HTML code provides a content pane with various sections headed by h1, h2, h3, and h4 tags and an empty ordered list element.

Our jQuery code first selects the content section and then finds all of the header elements inside it using the jQuery `find()` function and specifying `h1, h2, h3, h4` as the only argument. This will create an array of the found elements and store them in the `_headers` array as shown in the following code snippet:

```
$(function(){
    var _contents = $('.content-frame .left');
    var _headers = _contents.find("h1, h2, h3, h4");
// --- HIDDEN CODE
});
```

Using the jQuery `each()` function, it is then possible to iterate through all of the found header elements and construct the table of contents. The local variable `_header` is first declared and the current header element is stored in this variable.

To be able to indent subsections in the table of contents, making it easier for the user to see the content structure, the code needs to determine what level the current header is at: `h1` being the top level and `h5` being the bottom. Using `_header.context.localName`, we can get the tag of the header element (for example, `h1`) and remove the "h" with the JavaScript `replace()`. Then, we can convert the remaining value to an integer using `parseInt()`. We are left with a value we can use to determine the level of the header element. This process is shown in the following code snippet:

```
$(function(){
    var _contents = $('.content-frame .left');
    var _headers = _contents.find("h1, h2, h3, h4");
    _headers.each(function(index, value){
        var _header = $(value);
        var level = parseInt(_header.context.localName.replace("h",
""));
        // --- HIDDEN CODE
    });
});
```

Now we can create the list element, which we will insert into the ordered list. In order to link the items in the table of contents to the appropriate section of content, we need to check to see whether or not the header element has an ID that we can link to. If it does, we create a list element with a link; otherwise, we create a basic list element by executing the following code:

```
$(function(){
    var _contents = $('.content-frame .left');
    var _headers = _contents.find("h1, h2, h3, h4");
    _headers.each(function(index, value){
        var _header = $(value);
        var level = parseInt(_header.context.localName.replace("h",
""));
```

```
        if (typeof _header.attr("id") != "undefined") {
            var listItem = $("<li><a href='#" + _header.attr("id") +
    "'>" + _header.html() + "</a></li>");
        } else {
            var listItem = $("<li>" + _header.html() + "</li>");
        }
        listItem.css("padding-left", (level * 5));
        $('.contents').append($(listItem));
    });
});
```

Finally, once the list item has been created, the `css()` function and the `level` variable are used to add the required padding for indentation and the created list item is appended to the content's ordered list.

There's more...

You could combine this recipe with both the *Implementing smooth scrolling* and *Creating sticky elements* recipes to force the table of contents to follow the user down the page and also provide scrolling animation for a better user experience.

See also

▶ *Creating sticky elements*

▶ *Implementing smooth scrolling*

Creating a basic drag-and-drop functionality

It is possible to create interesting and intuitive interfaces by adding drag-and-drop elements to your site. jQuery UI comes with a built-in plugin for drag-and-drop interfaces. This recipe will show you how to create a basic drag-and-drop functionality without the use of any plugins, giving you the freedom and understanding to expand the code.

Getting ready

Create a blank HTML page called `recipe-6.html` with the `recipe-6.css` and `recipe-6.js` files in the same directory as the latest version of the jQuery library.

How to do it...

Carry out the following step-by-step instructions to complete this recipe:

1. Add the following HTML code to `recipe-6.html`, creating a basic HTML page with three `draggable` elements in a container `div`:

```html
<!DOCTYPE html>
<html>
<head>
    <title>Chapter 6 :: Recipe 6</title>
    <link href="recipe-6.css" rel="stylesheet" type="text/css" />
    <script src="jquery.min.js"></script>
    <script src="recipe-6.js"></script>
</head>
<body>
    <div class="container">
        <div class="draggable"></div>
        <div class="draggable"></div>
        <div class="draggable"></div>
    </div>
</body>
</html>
```

2. Add the following CSS code to `recipe-6.css` to style the HTML page and `draggable` elements:

```css
.container {
    width: 800px;
    height: 500px;
    border: solid 2px #333333;
    margin: 20px auto auto auto;
}
.draggable {
    width: 120px;
    height: 120px;
    margin: 10px;
    background-color: darkred;
        cursor: pointer;
}
.draggable.dragging {
    box-shadow: 5px 5px 5px #CCC;
}
```

3. Insert the following jQuery code in `recipe-6.js` to apply the drag-and-drop functionality to the `draggable` elements:

```
$(function(){
    $('.draggable').on("mousedown", function(){
        $(this).addClass('dragging');
    }).on("mousemove mouseout", function(event){
            if ($(this).hasClass("dragging")) {
                //Get the parents position
                var parentPosition = $(this).parent().offset();

                //Don't allow the draggable element to go over the
parent's left and right
                var left = (event.pageX - ($(this).width() / 2));
                var parentRight = parentPosition.left + $(this).
parent().width();
                if (left > (parentRight - $(this).width())){
                    left = (parentRight - $(this).width());
                } else if(left <= parentPosition.left) {
                    left = parentPosition.left;
                }

                //Don't allow the draggable element to go over the
parent's top and bottom
                var top = (event.pageY - ($(this).height() / 2));
                var parentBottom = parentPosition.top + $(this).
parent().height();
                if (top > (parentBottom - $(this).height())) {
                    top = (parentBottom - $(this).height());
                } else if (top <= parentPosition.top) {
                    top = parentPosition.top;
                }

                //Set new position
                $(this).css({
                    top: top + "px",
                    left: left + "px",
                    position: "absolute"
                });
            }
    }).on("mouseup", function(){
        $(this).removeClass('dragging');
    });
});
```

4. Open `recipe-6.html` in a web browser and click on one of the red boxes. This will apply the `dragging` CSS class to the element, allowing you to move it around the page within the frame division.

How it works...

The HTML page provides a container `div` element that acts as the container for the `draggable` elements. There are three additional `div` elements inside the `frame` element. These three elements have the `draggable` class, which jQuery will use to apply the drag-and-drop functionality.

The CSS code used in the recipe creates a border on the `frame` element and sets the height, width, and background color for the `draggable` elements. There is also a `dragging` class, which applies a drop shadow to the `draggable` elements when they are being moved.

Within the jQuery code itself, a series of mouse events are used to create the drag-and-drop functionality. The jQuery `on()` function is used to apply the different event handlers to the `draggable` elements. The first event handler applied to the `draggable` elements is the `mousedown` event as shown in the following code:

```
$('.draggable').on("mousedown", function(){
        $(this).addClass('dragging');
})
```

This simply adds the `dragging` class to the element that has just been clicked (`mousedown`).

The next event handler to be attached is for both the `mousemove` and `mouseout` events. This allows us to update the clicked element's position based on the mouse's position when the user moves the mouse pointer while still clicking on the selected element. We also use the same code for the `mouseout` event for when the user moves too quickly and brings the mouse pointer out of the selected `draggable` box. The box's position will then be updated to the mouse's position thanks to the same code being attached to the `mouseout` event:

```
.on("mousemove mouseout", function(event){
            if ($(this).hasClass("dragging")) {
                //Get the parents position
                var parentPosition = $(this).parent().offset();

                //Don't allow the draggable element to over the
parent's left and right
                var left = (event.pageX - ($(this).width() / 2));
                var parentRight = parentPosition.left + $(this).
parent().width();
                if (left > (parentRight - $(this).width())) {
                    left = (parentRight - $(this).width());
                } else if(left <= parentPosition.left) {
```

```
                left = parentPosition.left;
            }


                //Don't allow the draggable element to go over the
parent's top and bottom
                var top = (event.pageY - ($(this).height() / 2));
                var parentBottom = parentPosition.top + $(this).
parent().height();
                if (top > (parentBottom - $(this).height())) {
                    top = (parentBottom - $(this).height());
                } else if (top <= parentPosition.top) {
                    top = parentPosition.top;
                }


                //Set new position
                $(this).css({
                    top: top + "px",
                    left: left + "px",
                    position: "absolute"
                });
            }
        })
```

The callback function for these two events is where the main functionality is added. This code looks complex, but it is easy to understand once we break it down. First and foremost, nothing will be done unless the clicked element has the dragging class. This is done using the following if statement that checks for the dragging class:

```
if ($(this).hasClass("dragging")) {
    //MAIN FUNCTIONALITY HERE
}
```

Inside this if statement, we first get the clicked element's parent's position (the frame element) so we can work out the boundary for the draggable elements:

```
var parentPosition = $(this).parent().offset();
```

The next block of code looks at the clicked element's position and determines whether or not this is less than the frame element's left position or greater than the container element's right position. If it is either, the dragging element's position is set to the boundary limit instead of the mouse pointer's position, stopping the user from being able to drag the element outside of the left and right boundaries of the container element:

```
//Don't allow the draggable element to over the parent's left and
right
var left = (event.pageX - ($(this).width() / 2));
```

```
var parentRight = parentPosition.left + $(this).parent().width();
if (left > (parentRight - $(this).width())) {
left = (parentRight - $(this).width());
} else if(left <= parentPosition.left) {
left = parentPosition.left;
}
```

If the `draggable` element's position is not over the boundary, its position is updated to the mouse pointer's left position minus the width of the `dragging` element so that the mouse pointer is always in the center of the element while dragging.

Next, the same logic is applied for the top and bottom boundaries:

```
//Don't allow the draggable element to go over the parent's top and
bottom
var top = (event.pageY - ($(this).height() / 2));
var parentBottom = parentPosition.top + $(this).parent().height();
if (top > (parentBottom - $(this).height())) {
    top = (parentBottom - $(this).height());
} else if (top <= parentPosition.top) {
    top = parentPosition.top;
}
```

Finally, now that the new top and left positions for the `draggable` element have been calculated, knowing that it is either the mouse pointer's position minus the width/height of the `draggable` element divided by two or the boundary limits, the jQuery CSS function is used to apply these positions while also setting the CSS `position` attribute to `absolute`:

```
//Set new position
$(this).css({
top: top + "px",
left: left + "px",
position: "absolute"
});
```

And last of all, a final event is used—the `mouseup` event—which is fired when the user releases the click from the `dragging` element. When this happens, the `dragging` CSS class is removed from the dragged element:

```
.on("mouseup", function(){
        $(this).removeClass('dragging');
});
```

See also

▸ *Creating a draggable content pop up*

Creating a dynamic animated tree menu

Tree menus are a great way to display a lot of information in a confined space and allow users to choose the information they wish to see. This recipe will show you how to dynamically create a tree menu based on a set of JSON objects with slide up and down effects.

Getting ready

Create `recipe-7.html`, `recipe-7.js`, and `recipe-7.css` for this recipe, ensuring that they are saved in the same directory as the latest version of jQuery.

How to do it...

To create an animated tree menu, ensure you complete all of the following instructions:

1. Add the following HTML code to `recipe-7.html` to create the basic web page required for this recipe:

```
<!DOCTYPE html>
<html>
<head>
    <title>Chapter 6 :: Recipe 7</title>
    <link href="recipe-7.css" rel="stylesheet" type="text/css" />
    <script src="jquery.min.js"></script>
    <script src="recipe-7.js"></script>
</head>
<body>
<div class="container">
    <div class="list-container"></div>
</div>
</body>
</html>
```

2. Add the following styles to `recipe-7.css`:

```
.list-container {
    width: 800px;
    margin: 20px auto auto auto;
}
ul {
    margin: 0;
    padding: 0;
    list-style: none;
}
ul li {
```

```
            line-height: 25px;
            margin: 5px 0 5px 0;
            position: relative;
            padding: 0 0 0 5px;
            color: #666;
    }
    ul li a {
            display: block;
            background-color: #333;
            padding: 0 0 0 30px;
            margin-left: -5px;
            text-decoration: none;
            color: #FFF;
    }
    .arrow {
            position: absolute;
            width: 20px;
            height: 20px;
            left: 5px;
            top: 2px;
    }
    .right-arrow {
            width: 0;
            height: 0;
            border-top: 10px solid transparent;
            border-bottom: 10px solid transparent;
            border-left: 10px solid white;
    }
    .down-arrow {
            width: 0;
            border-left: 10px solid transparent;
            border-right: 10px solid transparent;
            border-top: 10px solid white;
            top: 7px;
    }
    .list-bg {
            background-color: #F1F1F1;
    }
```

3. Add the following jQuery code to `recipe-7.js`, which provides the data and functionality to create the dynamic tree menu:

```
var tree = [
    {
        name: "Fastolph Bolger",
```

```
            children: []
        },
        {
            name: "Laura Grubb",
            children: [
                {
                    name: "Bungo",
                    children: [
                        {
                            name: "Bilbo",
                            children: []
                        }
                    ]
                },
                {
                    name: "Belba",
                    children: []
                },
                {
                    name: "Longo",
                    children: [
                        {
                            name: "Otho Sackville-Baggins",
                            children: [
                                {
                                    name: "Lotho",
                                    children: []
                                }
                            ]
                        }
                    ]
                }
            ]
        },
        {
            name: "Ponto",
            children: [
                {
                    name: "Rosa",
                    children: [
                        {
                            name: "Peregrin Took",
                            children: []
                        }
```

```
                    ]
                }
            ]
        }
    ];
    $(function(){
        var list = createList(tree, 1);
        $('.list-container').html(list);
        $(document).on('click', '.show-children', function(){
            $(this).next('ul').slideToggle();
            $(this).find('.right-arrow').toggleClass('down-arrow');
        });
    });

    function createList(children, level) {
        var style = "margin-left: " + (10 * level) + "px;"
        if (level > 1) {
            style += "display: none;";
        }
        var list = "<ul style='" + style + "'>";
        level++;
        for (var i = 0; i < children.length; i++) {
            if (children[i].children.length > 0) {
                list += "<li><a href='javascript:void(0)' class='show-
children'><div class='arrow right-arrow'></div> " + children[i].
name + "</a>";
                list += createList(children[i].children, level);
                list += "</li>";
            } else {
                list += "<li class='list-bg'>" + children[i].name +
"</li>";
            }
        }
        list += "</ul>";
        return list;
    }
```

4. Open `recipe-7.html` in a web browser and click on the highlighted list items to expand the list for items that have children, as depicted in the following screenshot:

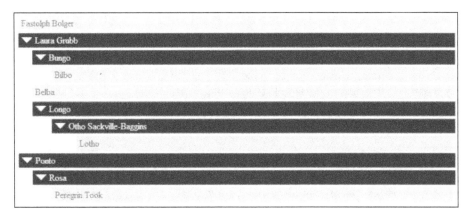

How it works...

The HTML code contains only the basic elements for a valid HTML page and a `list-container` division element that the jQuery code will use to insert the list HTML once it has been created. The CSS code contains basic list styles as well as some styles to create the right and down arrows, as shown in the previous screenshot.

The first part of the JavaScript code is an array of objects that represents a family tree. Each person in the family tree can have children, and there is no limit to the depth of the tree.

The main functionality of the jQuery code is within the `createList()` function. This function takes two arguments: an array of objects (children) and the current list level. Within this function, some inline styles are calculated based on the value of `level`. If the current value of `level` is not 1, meaning the current level is not the topmost level, the list is hidden by default. A left margin is also applied to the list based on the level, so that with each level lower, the list is moved further to the right to create the typical tree view you see in applications. A `list` variable is created and the HTML for an unordered list element is added to it. Next, each of the objects provided are looped through and a list item is created for each one. The length of the object's `children` property is checked to determine whether or not the current object has any children itself. If it has children, a link and right arrow are added to the list. Then, the `createList()` function is called recursively with the updated level and the current object's own children. This function will return the HTML for an unordered list populated with the object's own children. This will happen for each of the objects within the tree variable until the list has been fully created. Then, using `$('.list-container').html(list);`, the list is inserted into the DOM and will become visible on the page.

Because all list items except for the top-level items are hidden, a `click` event handler needs to be attached to each of the list items that have children, as shown in the following code:

```
$(document).on('click', '.show-children', function(){
        $(this).next('ul').slideToggle();
```

```
            $(this).find('.right-arrow').toggleClass('down-arrow');
    });
```

A single event that will listen for clicks on any element with the `show-children` class is attached to the document. When one of these items has been clicked, the `slideToggle()` function is used on the next unordered list element (the children list) to either slide it up or down. The `toggleClass()` function is also used on the `arrow` element to make the arrow point down when the children list is open.

There's more...

This recipe uses a static JavaScript array, but it could easily be adapted to load a set of JSON objects from a web server.

See also

▶ *Creating an accordion content slider*
▶ *Creating tabbed content*

Creating an accordion content slider

An accordion allows the user to easily skip through content. There are many jQuery plugins that provide the accordion functionality. However, this recipe will show you how to create a simple and attractive jQuery accordion content slider from scratch.

Getting ready

Create `recipe-8.html`, `recipe-8.css`, and `recipe-8.js` in the same directory as the jQuery library.

How to do it...

With your newly created files open, complete the following step-by-step instructions:

1. Add the following HTML code to `recipe-8.html` to create a basic web page with the accordion and content:

```html
<!DOCTYPE html>
<html>
<head>
    <title>Chapter 6 :: Recipe 8</title>
    <link href="recipe-8.css" rel="stylesheet" type="text/css" />
    <script src="jquery.min.js"script>
```

```
        <script src="recipe-8.js"></script>
</head>
<body>
<div class="container">
    <div class="accordion">
        <section>
            <a href="#" class="header"><div class='arrow right-
arrow down-arrow'></div> Section 1</a>
            <div class="content">
                <p>Lorem ipsum dolor sit amet, consectetur
adipisicing elit, sed do eiusmod tempor incididunt ut labore
et dolore magna aliqua. Ut enim ad minim veniam, quis nostrud
exercitation ullamco laboris nisi ut aliquip ex ea commodo
consequat. Duis aute irure dolor in reprehenderit in voluptate
velit esse cillum dolore eu fugiat nulla pariatur. Excepteur
sint occaecat cupidatat non proident, sunt in culpa qui officia
deserunt mollit anim id est laborum.</p>
            </div>
        </section>
        <section>
            <a href="#" class="header"><div class='arrow right-
arrow'></div> Section 2</a>
            <div class="content">
                <p>Lorem ipsum dolor sit amet, consectetur
adipisicing elit, sed do eiusmod tempor incididunt ut labore
et dolore magna aliqua. Ut enim ad minim veniam, quis nostrud
exercitation ullamco laboris nisi ut aliquip ex ea commodo
consequat. Duis aute irure dolor in reprehenderit in voluptate
velit esse cillum dolore eu fugiat nulla pariatur. Excepteur
sint occaecat cupidatat non proident, sunt in culpa qui officia
deserunt mollit anim id est laborum.</p>
                <p>Lorem ipsum dolor sit amet, consectetur
adipisicing elit, sed do eiusmod tempor incididunt ut labore
et dolore magna aliqua. Ut enim ad minim veniam, quis nostrud
exercitation ullamco laboris nisi ut aliquip ex ea commodo
consequat. Duis aute irure dolor in reprehenderit in voluptate
velit esse cillum dolore eu fugiat nulla pariatur. Excepteur
sint occaecat cupidatat non proident, sunt in culpa qui officia
deserunt mollit anim id est laborum.</p>
            </div>
        </section>
        <section>
            <a href="#" class="header"><div class='arrow right-
arrow'></div> Section 3</a>
            <div class="content">
```

```
              <p>Lorem ipsum dolor sit amet, consectetur
   adipisicing elit, sed do eiusmod tempor incididunt ut labore
   et dolore magna aliqua. Ut enim ad minim veniam, quis nostrud
   exercitation ullamco laboris nisi ut aliquip ex ea commodo
   consequat. Duis aute irure dolor in reprehenderit in voluptate
   velit esse cillum dolore eu fugiat nulla pariatur. Excepteur
   sint occaecat cupidatat non proident, sunt in culpa qui officia
   deserunt mollit anim id est laborum.</p>
            </div>
         </section>
      </div>
   </div>
</body>
</html>
```

2. Add the following CSS code to `recipe-8.css` to add styles to the accordion:

```
.container {
    width: 800px;
    margin: 20px auto auto auto;
}
.accordion section a.header {
    display: block;
    line-height: 30px;
    /* fallback */
    background-color: #333333;
    background-repeat: repeat-x;
    /* Safari 4-5, Chrome 1-9 */
    background: -webkit-gradient(linear, 0% 0%, 0% 100%,
from(#666666), to(#333333));
    /* Safari 5.1, Chrome 10+ */
    background: -webkit-linear-gradient(top, #666666, #333333);
    /* Firefox 3.6+ */
    background: -moz-linear-gradient(top, #666666, #333333);
    /* IE 10 */
    background: -ms-linear-gradient(top, #666666, #333333);
    /* Opera 11.10+ */
    background: -o-linear-gradient(top, #666666, #333333);
    padding: 0 10px 0 30px;
    position: relative;
    text-decoration: none;
    color: #FFFFFF;
    border-radius: 5px;
}
.accordion section .content {
    padding: 10px;
```

```
        margin: 0 3px 0 3px;
        background-color: #F1F1F1;
        color: #333333;
    }


    .accordion section .content p {
        margin-top: 0;
    }


    .arrow {
        position: absolute;
        width: 20px;
        height: 20px;
        left: 10px;
        top: 5px;
    }
    .right-arrow {
        width: 0;
        height: 0;
        border-top: 10px solid transparent;
        border-bottom: 10px solid transparent;
        border-left: 10px solid white;
    }
    .down-arrow {
        width: 0;
        border-left: 10px solid transparent;
        border-right: 10px solid transparent;
        border-top: 10px solid white;
        top: 10px;
        left: 6px;
    }
```

3. Add the following jQuery code to `recipe-8.js` to ignite the accordion content slider into action:

```
$(function(){
    //Hide all accordion content except the first one
    $('.accordion section:not(:first-child) .content').hide();
    $(document).on("click", ".accordion a.header", function(){
        var _contents = $('.accordion section .content');
        var _currentContent = $(this).parent().find('.content');
        for (var i = 0; i < _contents.length; i++) {
            var content = $(_contents[i]);
            //Only slide the element up if its not the currently
selected element
```

```
            if (content[0] != _currentContent[0]) {
                content.slideUp();
                content.parent().find('.right-arrow').
removeClass('down-arrow');
            }
        }
        _currentContent.slideDown();
        _currentContent.parent().find('.right-arrow').
addClass('down-arrow');
    });
});
```

4. Open `recipe-8.html` in a web browser and you will be provided with the interactive accordion content slider shown in the following screenshot:

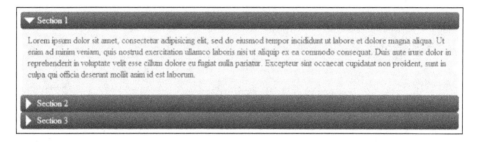

How it works...

The HTML code used in this recipe creates a basic web page that contains the main accordion markup. There is a main accordion division element that contains several sections. Each section contains an anchor tag with the class `header` and a content division element that holds the accordion's content. The jQuery code uses the header anchor element to hide and show the content sections based on the anchor element that was clicked by the user.

The CSS code is very simple and adds basic styles to the accordion. Like in the previous recipe, we are using CSS right and down arrows to indicate whether a section is open or closed. We also use CSS3 gradients to add a gradient background to the accordion headers.

Thanks to the nature of jQuery, we are able to create the entire accordion with only 18 lines of JavaScript. The first part of the jQuery code hides all of the accordion content sections except for the first one:

```
$('.accordion .section:not(:first-child) .content').hide();
```

Then, a `click` event handler is attached to the document to listen for clicks on any of the accordion content headers, as shown in the following code snippet:

```
$(document).on("click", ".accordion a.header", function(){

});
```

Inside the callback function to this event, we select all of the accordion content sections and get the one that belongs to the currently clicked header element:

```
var _contents = $('.accordion .section .content');
var _currentContent = $(this).parent().find('.content');
```

When an accordion section is selected, we only want that one to be displayed. To do this, all of the content sections in the following code are looped through to hide them, apart from the selected section:

```
for (var i = 0; i < _contents.length; i++) {
var content = $(_contents[i]);
//Only slide the element up if it's not the currently selected element
if (content[0] != _currentContent[0]) {
    content.slideUp();
    content.parent().find('.right-arrow').removeClass('down-arrow');
}
}
```

Using the jQuery `slideUp()` function, we can hide the elements with the slide effect. The arrow in the header is also changed to the right arrow, indicating that the content has not been expanded.

Finally, the selected content section is expanded and the down arrow added to indicate that the content has been expanded, as shown in the following code:

```
_currentContent.slideDown();
_currentContent.parent().find('.right-arrow').addClass('down-arrow');
```

See also

- ▶ *Creating a dynamic animated tree menu*
- ▶ *Creating tabbed content*

Creating tabbed content

Similar to an accordion, tabbed content is another great way to display a lot of information on a single page, allowing users to skip through to the sections that are important to them. Like in the previous recipe, there are many jQuery plugins that provide this functionality. This recipe shows you how to create this functionality on your own from scratch, providing you with a deeper understanding of the inner workings of these types of user interfaces.

Getting ready

Create the usual files required for a recipe, `recipe-9.html`, `recipe-9.css`, and `recipe-9.js`, in the same directory as the jQuery library.

How to do it...

Complete all of the following step-by-step instructions:

1. Create a basic web page in `recipe-9.html` using the following HTML code:

```
<!DOCTYPE html>
<html>
<head>
    <title>Chapter 6 :: Recipe 9</title>
    <link href="recipe-9.css" rel="stylesheet" type="text/css" />
    <script src="jquery.min.js"></script>
    <script src="recipe-9.js"></script>
</head>
<body>
</body>
</html>
```

2. In the body tags of the HTML page you just created, add the following HTML code to create the tabbed content:

```
<div class="container">
    <div class="tabs">
        <ul class="tab-nav">
            <li><a href="#section1" class="active">Section
1</a></li><li><a href="#section2">Section 2</a></li><li><a
href="#section3">Section 3</a></li>
        </ul>
        <div class="tab-content">
            <div class="section" id="section1">
                <p><strong>Section 1 content...</strong></p>
```

```
                    <p>Lorem ipsum dolor sit amet, consectetur
adipisicing elit, sed do eiusmod tempor incididunt ut labore
et dolore magna aliqua. Ut enim ad minim veniam, quis nostrud
exercitation ullamco laboris nisi ut aliquip ex ea commodo
consequat. Duis aute irure dolor in reprehenderit in voluptate
velit esse cillum dolore eu fugiat nulla pariatur. Excepteur
sint occaecat cupidatat non proident, sunt in culpa qui officia
deserunt mollit anim id est laborum.</p>
                </div>
                <div class="section" id="section2">
                    <p><strong>Section 2 content...</strong></p>
                    <p>Lorem ipsum dolor sit amet, consectetur
adipisicing elit, sed do eiusmod tempor incididunt ut labore
et dolore magna aliqua. Ut enim ad minim veniam, quis nostrud
exercitation ullamco laboris nisi ut aliquip ex ea commodo
consequat. Duis aute irure dolor in reprehenderit in voluptate
velit esse cillum dolore eu fugiat nulla pariatur. Excepteur
sint occaecat cupidatat non proident, sunt in culpa qui officia
deserunt mollit anim id est laborum.</p>
                    <p>Lorem ipsum dolor sit amet, consectetur
adipisicing elit, sed do eiusmod tempor incididunt ut labore
et dolore magna aliqua. Ut enim ad minim veniam, quis nostrud
exercitation ullamco laboris nisi ut aliquip ex ea commodo
consequat. Duis aute irure dolor in reprehenderit in voluptate
velit esse cillum dolore eu fugiat nulla pariatur. Excepteur
sint occaecat cupidatat non proident, sunt in culpa qui officia
deserunt mollit anim id est laborum.</p>
                </div>
                <div class="section" id="section3">
                    <p><strong>Section 3 content...</strong></p>
                    <p>Lorem ipsum dolor sit amet, consectetur
adipisicing elit, sed do eiusmod tempor incididunt ut labore
et dolore magna aliqua. Ut enim ad minim veniam, quis nostrud
exercitation ullamco laboris nisi ut aliquip ex ea commodo
consequat. Duis aute irure dolor in reprehenderit in voluptate
velit esse cillum dolore eu fugiat nulla pariatur. Excepteur
sint occaecat cupidatat non proident, sunt in culpa qui officia
deserunt mollit anim id est laborum.</p>
                </div>
            </div>
        </div>
</div>
```

3. Open `recipe-9.css` and add the following CSS code to style the tabbed content and display the first set of content on page load:

```
.container {
    width: 800px;
```

```
        margin: 20px auto auto auto;
    }
    .tabs .tab-nav {
        margin: 0;
        padding: 0;
        list-style: none;
        background-color: #E1E1E1;
        border-top-right-radius: 5px;
        border-top-left-radius: 5px;
    }
    .tabs .tab-nav li {
        display: inline-block;
    }
    .tabs .tab-nav li a {
        display: block;
        text-decoration: none;
        text-align: center;
        line-height: 50px;
        color: #FFF;
        background-color: #333;
        padding: 0 20px 0 20px;
        border-right: solid 1px #5c5c5c;
    }
    .tabs .tab-nav li a:hover, .tabs .tab-nav li a.active {
        background-color: #5c5c5c;
    }
    .tabs .tab-nav li:first-child a {
        border-top-left-radius: 5px;
    }
    .tabs .tab-nav li:last-child a {
        border-top-right-radius: 5px;
        border-right: none;
    }
    .tabs .section {
        padding: 10px;
        background-color: #F1F1F1;
        border-bottom-right-radius: 5px;
        border-bottom-left-radius: 5px;
    }
    .tabs .section p {
        margin-top: 0;
    }

    .tabs .section:not(:first-child) {
```

```
        display: none;
    }
```

4. Insert the following jQuery in `recipe-9.js`:

```javascript
$(function(){
    $(document).on("click", ".tabs .tab-nav a", function(){
        var contentId = this.hash;
        $('.tab-nav a').removeClass("active");
        $(this).addClass("active");
        $('.tab-content .section').hide();
        $(contentId).fadeIn();
    });
});
```

5. Open `recipe-9.html` in a web browser and click on the section tabs to switch between the content sections.

How it works...

This is a quick and simple recipe, but it has a powerful outcome. The HTML code in this recipe creates the tab section, which contains navigation and content. Each of the content division elements has an ID that corresponds to the links in the navigation. For example, to link to the `section1` content, there needs to be a corresponding link within the navigation linking to `#content1` as follows: `<a href='#content1'>TITLE HERE</a>`. This allows jQuery to know which section of content to make visible when a tab is clicked.

The CSS in this recipe is very simple and needs no further explanation.

With only nine lines of JavaScript, this is a very simple recipe indeed. The jQuery code attaches a click event handler to the document body, listening for clicks on the tab navigation. When one of these tabs is clicked, the content section ID is collected from the anchor hash as follows:

```javascript
$(document).on("click", ".tabs .tab-nav a", function(){
        var contentId = this.hash;
});
```

Next, the active class is removed from all of the tab navigation items and added to the clicked item. This class is used to show which tab is currently active by changing the background color using CSS as follows:

```javascript
$('.tab-nav a').removeClass("active");
$(this).addClass("active");
```

Finally, all of the content sections are hidden, and then, using the recently acquired content ID of the selected tab, the chosen content is made visible using the `fadeIn()` function, applying an animation as the content appears:

```
$('.tab-content .section').hide();
$(contentId).fadeIn();
```

There's more...

This recipe uses the fade-in animation provided by jQuery to show the selected content. By looking back at *Chapter 4*, *Adding Attractive Visuals with jQuery Effects*, you will be able to use any of the effects and animations described in that chapter to show and hide the content in this recipe.

Creating a modal pop up

A modal is a pop up within a web page that overlays over all other content and focuses the reader's attention. A modal is often opened based on user interaction, such as clicking a button. This recipe will show you how to create a simple modal that is opened at the pressing of a button and can be closed from within the modal.

Getting ready

Once again, create `recipe-10.html`, `recipe-10.css`, and `recipe-10.js` before you start this recipe, ensuring that the latest version of jQuery is available in the same directory as these files.

How to do it...

Perform the following steps to create the modal pop up:

1. Add the following HTML to `recipe-10.html` to create a basic web page and the code that constructs the modal pop up:

```
<!DOCTYPE html>
<html>
<head>
    <title>Chapter 6 :: Recipe 10</title>
    <link href="recipe-10.css" rel="stylesheet" type="text/css" />
    <script src="jquery.min.js"></script>
    <script src="recipe-10.js"></script>
</head>
<body>
```

```
    <button class="openModal">Open Modal</button>
    <p>Lorem ipsum dolor sit amet, consectetur adipisicing elit,
sed do eiusmod tempor incididunt ut labore et dolore magna aliqua.
Ut enim ad minim veniam, quis nostrud exercitation ullamco laboris
nisi ut aliquip ex ea commodo consequat. Duis aute irure dolor
in reprehenderit in voluptate velit esse cillum dolore eu fugiat
nulla pariatur. Excepteur sint occaecat cupidatat non proident,
sunt in culpa qui officia deserunt mollit anim id est laborum.</p>
    <p>Lorem ipsum dolor sit amet, consectetur adipisicing elit,
sed do eiusmod tempor incididunt ut labore et dolore magna aliqua.
Ut enim ad minim veniam, quis nostrud exercitation ullamco laboris
nisi ut aliquip ex ea commodo consequat. Duis aute irure dolor
in reprehenderit in voluptate velit esse cillum dolore eu fugiat
nulla pariatur. Excepteur sint occaecat cupidatat non proident,
sunt in culpa qui officia deserunt mollit anim id est laborum.</p>
        <div class="modal">
            <div class="modal-header">
                <h3>Modal Header Text <a class="close-modal"
href="#">&times;</a></h3>
            </div>
            <div class="modal-body">
                <p>This is some modal content text.</p>
            </div>
            <div class="modal-footer">
                <button class="modalOK close-modal">OK</button>
            </div>
        </div>
        <div class="modal-backdrop"></div>
</body>
</html>
```

2. Add the following CSS code to `recipe-10.css` to style the modal and allow it to cover all other content on the page:

```
.modal-backdrop {
    background-color: rgba(0, 0, 0, 0.61);
    position: absolute;
    top: 0;
    bottom: 0;
    left: 0;
    right: 0;
    display: none;
}
.modal {
    width: 500px;
    position: absolute;
    top: 25%;
```

```
        z-index: 1020;
        background-color: #FFF;
        border-radius: 6px;
        display: none;
    }
    .modal-header {
        background-color: #333;
        color: #FFF;
        border-top-right-radius: 5px;
        border-top-left-radius: 5px;
    }
    .modal-header h3 {
        margin: 0;
        padding: 0 10px 0 10px;
        line-height: 40px;
    }
    .modal-header h3 .close-modal {
        float: right;
        text-decoration: none;
        color: #FFF;
    }
    .modal-footer {
        background-color: #F1F1F1;
        padding: 0 10px 0 10px;
        line-height: 40px;
        text-align: right;
        border-bottom-right-radius: 5px;
        border-bottom-left-radius: 5px;
        border-top: solid 1px #CCC;
    }
    .modal-body {
        padding: 0 10px 0 10px;
    }
```

3. Add the following jQuery code to `recipe-10.js` to open the modal, center it, and allow the user to close it:

```
$(function(){
    modalPosition();
    $(window).resize(function(){
        modalPosition();
    });
    $('.openModal').click(function(){
        $('.modal, .modal-backdrop').fadeIn('fast');
    });
```

```
$('.close-modal').click(function(){
    $('.modal, .modal-backdrop').fadeOut('fast');
});
});
function modalPosition() {
    var width = $('.modal').width();
    var pageWidth = $(window).width();
    var x = (pageWidth / 2) - (width / 2);
    $('.modal').css({left: x + "px"});
}
```

4. Open `recipe-10.html` in a web browser and click on the **Open Modal** button. You should be presented with the modal pop up shown in the following screenshot:

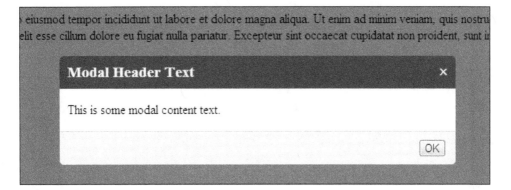

How it works...

The HTML creates the basic web page and code to create the modal. The modal itself consists of a main modal container, a header, a body, and a footer. The footer contains the actions, which in this case is the **OK** button, the header holds the title and the close button, and the body contains the modal content.

The CSS applies the absolute position style to the modal, allowing it to move freely throughout the page without being hindered by other content. To create the modal backdrop, its position is set to `absolute` and its left, right, top, and bottom positions are set to `0`, allowing it to expand and cover the entire page. A `z-index` value is set on the modal and its backdrop elements, ensuring that they always sit above other content and that the modal is above the backdrop.

The jQuery code applies click event handlers to the modal open button and any element that has the `close-modal` class. The `fadeIn()` and `fadeOut()` functions provided by jQuery are used to show the modal. The `fast` argument is passed to both of these functions to speed up the animation.

Additionally, the jQuery code is used to calculate the modal's left position, allowing it to always sit at the center of the screen. The `modalPosition()` function is called on page load and when the browser window is resized as follows:

```
$(function(){
    modalPosition();
    $(window).resize(function(){
     modalPosition();
  });
  });
```

This ensures that the modal will remain in the center of the browser window, even if the user changes the width of the window.

The `modalPosition()` function uses the modal's width and the browser window's width to calculate the modal's left position. The function then uses the jQuery `css()` function to set this value to the modal.

There's more...

Twitter Bootstrap is a very popular HTML framework that comes with a brilliant modal implementation that is ready for use out of the box. Now that you know how modals work, you could benefit from the complete solution that Twitter Bootstrap offers.

See also

▶ *Creating a draggable content pop up*

Creating a draggable content pop up

A draggable content pop up is similar to a modal window. However, it is movable by the user and does not come with a backdrop to focus the user's attention, allowing them to view other content at the same time. This recipe will adapt the modal code used in the preceding recipe and the jQuery code from the *Creating a basic drag-and-drop functionality* recipe that you saw earlier in this chapter.

Getting ready

Even though we will be re-using code from previous chapters, ensure that you have `recipe-11.html`, `recipe-11.css`, and `recipe-11.js` created and ready for use.

How to do it...

Perform the following steps:

1. Add the following HTML code to `recipe-11.html` to create a modal and a basic web page:

```
<!DOCTYPE html>
<html>
<head>
    <title>Chapter 6 :: Recipe 11</title>
    <link href="recipe-11.css" rel="stylesheet" type="text/css" />
    <script src="jquery.min.js"></script>
    <script src="recipe-11.js"></script>
</head>
<body>
<button class="openModal">Open Modal</button>
<p>Lorem ipsum dolor sit amet, consectetur adipisicing elit, sed
do eiusmod tempor incididunt ut labore et dolore magna aliqua. Ut
enim ad minim veniam, quis nostrud exercitation ullamco laboris
nisi ut aliquip ex ea commodo consequat. Duis aute irure dolor
in reprehenderit in voluptate velit esse cillum dolore eu fugiat
nulla pariatur. Excepteur sint occaecat cupidatat non proident,
sunt in culpa qui officia deserunt mollit anim id est laborum.</p>
<p>Lorem ipsum dolor sit amet, consectetur adipisicing elit, sed
do eiusmod tempor incididunt ut labore et dolore magna aliqua. Ut
enim ad minim veniam, quis nostrud exercitation ullamco laboris
nisi ut aliquip ex ea commodo consequat. Duis aute irure dolor
in reprehenderit in voluptate velit esse cillum dolore eu fugiat
nulla pariatur. Excepteur sint occaecat cupidatat non proident,
sunt in culpa qui officia deserunt mollit anim id est laborum.</p>
<div class="modal draggable">
    <div class="modal-header">
        <h3>Modal Header Text <a class="close-modal"
href="#">&times;</a></h3>
    </div>
    <div class="modal-body">
        <p>This is some modal content text.</p>
    </div>
    <div class="modal-footer">
        <button class="modalOK close-modal">OK</button>
    </div>
</div>
</body>
</html>
```

2. Add the following CSS code to `recipe-11.css` to style the modal:

```css
.modal {
    width: 500px;
    position: absolute;
    top: 25%;
    z-index: 600;
    background-color: #FFF;
    border-radius: 6px;
    display: none;
    box-shadow: 3px 3px 5px #CCC;
}
.modal-header {
    background-color: #333;
    color: #FFF;
    border-top-right-radius: 5px;
    border-top-left-radius: 5px;
}
.modal-header h3 {
    margin: 0;
    padding: 0 10px 0 10px;
    line-height: 40px;
}
.modal-header h3 .close-modal {
    float: right;
    text-decoration: none;
    color: #FFF;
}
.modal-footer {
    background-color: #F1F1F1;
    padding: 0 10px 0 10px;
    line-height: 40px;
    text-align: right;
    border-bottom-right-radius: 5px;
    border-bottom-left-radius: 5px;
    border-top: solid 1px #CCC;
}
.modal-body {
    padding: 0 10px 0 10px;
}
```

3. Insert the following jQuery code into `recipe-11.js` to allow the modal to be opened, closed, and dragged:

```javascript
$(function(){
    modalPosition();
```

```
$('.openModal').click(function(){
    $('.modal, .modal-backdrop').fadeIn('fast');
});
$('.close-modal').click(function(){
    $('.modal, .modal-backdrop').fadeOut('fast');
});
$('.draggable').on("mousedown", function(){
    $(this).addClass('dragging');
}).on("mousemove mouseout", function(event){
    if ($(this).hasClass("dragging")) {
        //Don't allow the draggable element to go over the
parent's left and right
        var left = (event.pageX - ($(this).width() / 2));
        if (left > ($(window).width() - $(this).width())) {
            left = ($(window).width() - $(this).width());
        } else if(left <= 0) {
            left = 0;
        }
        //Don't allow the draggable element to go over the
parent's top and bottom
        var top = (event.pageY - ($(this).height() / 2));
        if (top > ($(window).height() - $(this).height())) {
            top = ($(window).height() - $(this).height());
        } else if (top <= 0) {
            top = 0;
        }
        //Set new position
        $(this).css({
            top: top + "px",
            left: left + "px",
            position: "absolute"
        });
    }
}).on("mouseup", function(){
    $(this).removeClass('dragging');
});
});
function modalPosition() {
    var width = $('.modal').width();
    var pageWidth = $(window).width();
    var x = (pageWidth / 2) - (width / 2);
    $('.modal').css({left: x + "px"});
}
```

4. Open `recipe-11.html` in a web browser and click on the **Open Modal** button as in the previous recipe. You will be presented with the same modal pop up without the backdrop, allowing you to clearly see the rest of the page content. You will also be able to drag the modal around the page by clicking and dragging the mouse pointer.

How it works...

The previous recipes that have been adapted to create the `draggable` content modal go into great detail to explain how the modal and the `draggable` elements work, so that will not be repeated in this section.

The main difference with the HTML from the previous modal recipe is that there is no modal backdrop and the modal element has the additional class `draggable`, which is used by jQuery to apply the drag functionality to elements.

The CSS remains very much the same, except that the code for the backdrop has been removed and a drop shadow has been added to the modal using the CSS `box-shadow` attribute.

The jQuery uses the same code as the previous modal recipe with the window resize event handler removed. This event handler was removed because the modal can be moved by the user, so there is no need to keep the modal toward the center of the page. The `modalPosition()` function is only called on page load so that the modal is at the center of the page when it is first opened.

The code used from the basic drag-and-drop recipe is very similar, except that instead of using the `draggable` element's parent as the boundary, the browser window is used. This removes some complexity because we know that the window's left and right positions are always 0.

See also

 ▶ *Creating a basic drag-and-drop functionality*
 ▶ *Creating a modal pop up*

7
User Interface Animation

In this chapter, we will cover the following topics:

- ▶ Creating an animated login form
- ▶ Adding photo zoom
- ▶ Creating an animated content slider
- ▶ Animating background images
- ▶ Creating an animated navigation menu

Introduction

Using jQuery, it is possible to enhance common user interface elements with attractive animations. These animations can supply interactive actions to heighten the user experience of any website or web application. This chapter shows you how to create some popular user interfaces with modern animations, which you can use in new projects or current websites.

Creating an animated login form

The login form is the main entry point to many of the websites and web applications—first impressions are everything. Using jQuery animations, we can create a login form that is animated when it is opened, closed, and there's an error, creating a quality user experience that is reinforced through the animations.

This recipe requires a web server that supports PHP. This sever can be hosted in the cloud or a simple local development server. Before starting with this recipe, ensure that you have this set up.

Getting ready

Create `recipe-1.html`, `recipe-1.js`, and `recipe.css` in the same directory as the latest version of the jQuery library. As we are creating a login form, we are also going to need a PHP script on which to post our login data. Create a PHP file named `index.php` inside the web root of a web server and add the following code:

```php
$response = new stdClass;
$response->success = false;
$response->error = "Username and password must be provided";
if (isset($_POST['username']) && isset($_POST['password'])) {
    $username = $_POST['username'];
    $password = $_POST['password'];
    if ($username == "MyUsername" && $password == "MyPassword") {
        $response->success = true;
    } else {
        $response->error = "Incorrect login credentials";
    }
}
header("Content-type: application/json; charset=UTF-8");
echo json_encode($response);
```

In a real-world implementation, the PHP script would authenticate the user's credentials against a database record. To keep this recipe simple and focus on the jQuery code, our PHP code simply performs a string comparison of the user-submitted username and password for `MyUsername` and `MyPassword`.

How to do it...

To create the animated login form that uses the preceding PHP script, perform the following step-by-step instructions:

1. Add the following HTML code to `recipe-1.html`, which creates the login form and the button to open it:

    ```html
    <!DOCTYPE html>
    <html>
    <head>
        <title>Chapter 7 :: Recipe 1</title>
        <link href="recipe-1.css" rel="stylesheet" type="text/css" />
        <script src="jquery.min.js"></script>
    ```

```
        <script src="recipe-1.js"></script>
    </head>
    <body>
        <button class="open-login">Open Login Box</button>
        <div class="login-frame">
            <div class="login-box">
                <div class="login-msg">Please login below</div>
                <div class="form-group">
                    <label class="form-label">Username:</label>
                    <input type="text" class="form-control" id="username"
/>
                </div>
                <div class="form-group">
                    <label class="form-label">Password:</label>
                    <input type="text" class="form-control" id="password"
/>
                </div>
                <div class="login-actions">
                    <button class="btn login-btn">Login</button>
                    <button class="btn close-login">Cancel</button>
                </div>
            </div>
        </div>
    </body>
</html>
```

2. Add the following CSS code to `recipe-1.css` to add basic styles to the web page:

```
.login-frame {
    position: absolute;
    top: 0;
    bottom: 0;
    left: 0;
    right: 0;
    display: none;
}
.login-box {
    width: 400px;
    height: 165px;
    padding: 20px;
    margin: auto;
    top: -165px;
    box-shadow: 0 0 10px #CCC;
    border-radius: 5px;
    position: relative;
```

```
}
.form-group {
  margin-bottom: 10px;
}
.form-group .form-control {
  margin-left: 55px;
  width: 275px;
  height: 30px;
  padding: 0 5px 0 5px;
  font-size: 16px;
  border-radius: 5px;
  border: solid 1px #CCCCCC;
  color: #999;
}
.form-group .form-label {
  width: 50px;
  font-size: 18px;
  display: block;
  float: left;
  line-height: 30px;
  padding-left: 5px;
  color: #333;
}
.login-msg {
  border: solid 1px #bce8f1;
  text-align: center;
  line-height: 30px;
  margin-bottom: 10px;
  border-radius: 5px;
  color: rgba(58, 135, 173, 0.90);
  background-color: rgba(217, 237, 247, 0.99);
}
.login-msg.success {
  color: rgba(70, 136, 71, 0.96);
  background-color: rgba(223, 240, 216, 0.97);
  border-color: rgba(214, 233, 198, 0.98);
}
.login-msg.error {
  color: rgba(185, 74, 72, 0.98);
  background-color: rgba(242, 222, 222, 0.98);
  border-color: rgba(238, 211, 215, 0.98);
}
.login-actions {
  text-align: right;
```

```
}
.btn {
    height: 40px;
    width: 100px;
    display: inline-block;
    padding: 6px 12px;
    margin-bottom: 0;
    font-size: 14px;
    text-align: center;
    white-space: nowrap;
    vertical-align: middle;
    cursor: pointer;
    border: 1px solid transparent;
    border-radius: 4px;
}

.login-btn {
    color: #ffffff;
    background-color: #5cb85c;
    border-color: #4cae4c;
}
.login-btn:hover {
    background-color: #458a45;
}
.close-login {
    color: #ffffff;
    background-color: #d2322d;
    border-color: #ac2925;
}
.close-login:hover {
    background-color: #ac2c2c;
}
```

3. Add the following jQuery code to `recipe-1.js` to allow the user to open and use the login form:

```
$(function(){
    $(document).on('click', '.open-login', function(){
        $('.login-frame').fadeIn(500);
        $('.login-box').animate({'top' : '50px'}, 500);
    });
    $(document).on('click', '.close-login', function(){
        $('.login-box').animate({'top' : '-165px'}, 500);
        $('.login-frame').fadeOut(500);
    });
```

```
$(document).on('click', '.login-btn', function(){
    var username = $('#username').val();
    var password = $('#password').val();
    $.ajax({
        url: '/index.php',
        type: 'POST',
        data: {
            'username': username,
            'password': password
        },
        success: function(response) {
            var _loginMsg = $('.login-msg');
            if (response.success) {
                _loginMsg.addClass("success").removeClass("error");
                _loginMsg.html("Login was successful!");
            } else {
                _loginMsg.addClass("error").removeClass("success");
                _loginMsg.html(response.error);
                $('.login-box')
                .animate({ left: -25 }, 20)
                .animate({ left: 0 }, 60)
                .animate({ left: 25 }, 20)
                .animate({ left: 0 }, 60);
            }
        }
    });
});
});
```

4. Open `recipe-1.html` in a web browser, click on the **Open Login Box** button, and you will be presented with the interface shown in the following screenshot:

How it works...

A website that allows users to have accounts and log in to them will typically have a login button available somewhere in the main navigation. The HTML code in this recipe creates a very basic web page with a single button to represent where the user can access the login form. The HTML code also provides the basic login form, which by default is hidden using CSS. The CSS code provides the positioning for the login form and the styles for the login errors and form buttons. In addition to the CSS that initially hides the login form, it also sets the value of the login form's top position to a negative number, forcing the login form off the page. This allows us to create slide-in animation to bring the login box into the user's view.

The first part of the jQuery code creates a click event handler that listens for a click on the login button, shown as follows:

```
$(document).on('click', '.open-login', function(){
    $('.login-frame').fadeIn(500);
    $('.login-box').animate({'top' : '50px'}, 500);
});
```

When the button with the `open-login` class is clicked on by the user, the jQuery's `fadeIn()` function is used to fade in the hidden login form and the `animate()` function is used to move the login form onto the screen, creating the slide-in effect.

A click event handler is created to listen for the `close-login` button being clicked on, which then triggers the reverse animation to fade the login box out and move it off the screen, shown as follows:

```
$(document).on('click', '.close-login', function(){
    $('.login-box').animate({'top' : '-165px'}, 500);
    $('.login-frame').fadeOut(500);
});
```

 Both animation functions have the duration set to 500 milliseconds, allowing the fade and position animations to start and finish at the same time.

The main functionality of this recipe is placed within the callback function for the login button's click event handler; this is shown as follows:

```
$(document).on('click', '.login-btn', function(){
    // -- HIDDEN CODE --
});
```

This click event handler, which listens for a click on the login button, takes the input data and submits it to the PHP script we created at the beginning of this recipe. First, the username and password are collected from the form and stored in the `username` and `password` variables, shown as follows:

```
var username = $('#username').val();
var password = $('#password').val();
```

This data is then sent to the PHP script using jQuery's built-in AJAX functionality:

```
$.ajax({
    url: 'http://localhost:8003/index.php',
    type: 'POST',
    data: {
        'username': username,
        'password': password
    },
    success: function(response) {
    // --- HIDDEN CODE
    }
});
```

The previous code creates an AJAX `POST` request by specifying the URL of the PHP file and setting the `type` parameter to `POST`. A data object is also provided, which holds the information from the form.

A callback function is specified for the `success` parameter; this is called on a successful response from the PHP script, which is shown as follows:

```
success: function(response) {
    var _loginMsg = $('.login-msg');
    if (response.success) {
        // -- HIDDEN CODE
    } else {
        // -- HIDDEN CODE
    }
```

By creating our PHP code, we know that the response will hold a success value of either `true` or `false`. If the success value is `false`, there will be an error message to go with it. There is an additional way that an AJAX request can fail; this is caused by a server error, for example, `500 file not found`. To handle these errors, the jQuery AJAX `.fail()` function should be used. Read more about that at `http://api.jquery.com/jquery.ajax/`.

Within the success callback function, we select the `login-msg` element, which will be used to print any messages on screen. The success value provided by the PHP script is evaluated to determine whether or not the login was successful.

If the login was successful, the `login-msg` element is updated with a message informing the user that the login is successful and the `success` class is added to turn the message element green in color, shown as follows:

```
_loginMsg.addClass("success").removeClass("error");
_loginMsg.html("Login was successful!");
```

The `removeClass()` function is used to ensure that the `error` class is not present as a remnant of any previous login attempts. In a real-world situation, you may want to redirect the user to the members' area of the website. This code can be replaced to do just that; see the *There's more...* section of this recipe.

If the login attempt is not successful, the `error` class is added to the `login-msg` element with the message from the PHP script. We use `response.error` to retrieve this data. A series of animation functions are also used to move the login box from left to right to create the shake effect, emphasizing the error to the user; this is shown as follows:

```
_loginMsg.addClass("error").removeClass("success");
_loginMsg.html(response.error);
$('.login-box')
    .animate({ left: -25 }, 20)
    .animate({ left: 0 }, 60)
    .animate({ left: 25 }, 20)
    .animate({ left: 0 }, 60);
}
```

There's more...

The successful login section of the jQuery callback can be easily replaced to redirect the user, if desired. Native JavaScript code can be used to send the user to the desired page using the following code, replacing `/memebers.php` with the appropriate URL, which is shown as follows:

```
window.location.href = "/members.php";
```

See also

▶ *Chapter 5, Form Handling*

Adding photo zoom

Photo zoom is a great effect that can be used in many interfaces to add extra user interaction to a photo gallery or product page so that the user can see smaller images clearly. This recipe will show you how to add the photo zoom effect to four images in a list.

Getting ready

You are going to need four images to use in this recipe. Make sure they are fewer than 800 px wide and 600 px high. Once you have collected the four images that will be used in this recipe, create `recipe-2.html`, `recipe-2.css`, and `recipe-2.js` in the same directory as these images and the jQuery library.

How to do it...

Perform the following instructions to add the zoom effect to your chosen images:

1. Add the following HTML code to `recipe-2.html`; ensure that you update the image references that correspond to the images you have chosen:

```
<!DOCTYPE html>
<html>
<head>
    <title>Chapter 7 :: Recipe 2</title>
    <link href="recipe-2.css" rel="stylesheet" type="text/css" />
    <script src="jquery.min.js"></script>
    <script src="recipe-2.js"></script>
</head>
<body>
    <div class="container">
        <ul class="photos">
            <li><img src="recipe-2-1.jpg" alt="Countryside 1" /></li>
            <li><img src="recipe-2-2.jpg" alt="Countryside 2" /></li>
            <li><img src="recipe-2-3.jpg" alt="Countryside 3" /></li>
            <li><img src="recipe-2-4.jpg" alt="Countryside 4" /></li>
        </ul>
    </div>
</body>
</html>
```

2. Add the following CSS code to `recipe-2.css` to style and position the images:

```
body {
    background-color: #333;
}
.container {
    width: 600px;
    height: 600px;
    margin: 50px auto auto auto;
}
.photos {
```

```
    list-style: none;
    margin: 0;
    padding: 0;
}
.photos li {
    display: inline-block;
    width: 290px;
    height: 250px;
    background-color: #E1E1E1;
    margin: 0 5px 5px 0;
    overflow: hidden;
    position: relative;
        cursor: pointer;
}
.photos li img {
    top: -50%;
    left: -50%;
    position: absolute;
    opacity: 0.5;
}
```

3. Add the following jQuery code to `recipe-2.js` to add the photo zoom animation to the images when the user hovers over them:

```javascript
var images = [];
$(function(){
    $(document).on("mouseover", ".photos li", function(){
        var _image = $(this).find('img');
        _image.finish();
        images[$(this).index()] = {
            width: _image.width(),
            height: _image.height()
        };
        _image.animate({
            width: '290px',
            height: '250px',
            top: 0,
            left: 0,
            opacity: 1.0
        });
    }).on("mouseout", ".photos li", function(){
        var _image = $(this).find('img');
        _image.finish();
        _image.animate({
            width: images[$(this).index()].width + "px",
```

```
          height: images[$(this).index()].height + "px",
          top: '-50%',
          left: '-50%',
          opacity: 0.5
      });
   });
});
```

4. Open `recipe-2.html` in a web browser, and hover over one of the four images to see the zoom animation, shown as follows:

How it works...

The HTML code in this recipe is very basic and simply creates a division element with the class name `container`, which is centered on the page using CSS. Inside the frame division, there is an unordered list element that has four children, each containing an image.

The CSS code removes any margin and padding from the unordered list, sets its children to display inline, and sets each child element's overflow property to `hidden`. This is to allow us to initially load the images larger than the list element without showing any overflow to provide the zoomed-in effect.

The CSS code also sets the image's top and left positions to `-50%` so that they are centered inside the list element. The image's opacity is also set to `0.5` to prevent the images from standing out initially.

At the beginning of the jQuery code, an `images` variable is declared, which is used to store image data that can be reused later in the code. Within the jQuery on-load block, two event handlers are attached to the document to listen for `mouseover` and `mouseout` events on the photo list elements, as shown in the following code:

```
$(document).on("mouseover", ".photos li", function(){
    // --  HIDDEN CODE
}).on("mouseout", ".photos li", function(){
    // --  HIDDEN CODE
});
```

Inside the `mouseover` event handler, `$(this).find('img')` is used to find the image within the hovered list element. With this image selected, its size is stored in the `images` variable using `$(this).index()` to get the list element's index, as follows:

```
images[$(this).index()] = {
    width: _image.width(),
    height: _image.height()
};
```

Then, using the jQuery's `animate()` function, the image's width and height are set to match the size of the list element to create the zoom-out effect. Its top and left positions are also set to 0, overwriting the `-50%` positions set within the CSS to ensure that the image fills 100 percent of the list element. The image's opacity is set to 1 (that is, 100 percent) so that the hovered and zoomed-in image stands out among the other images. The code for this is shown as follows:

```
_image.animate({
    width: '290px',
    height: '250px',
    top: 0,
    left: 0,
    opacity: 1.0
});
```

Inside the `mouseout` event handler, the previously discussed animation is effectively reversed using the stored image information and resets the image back to where it was before the mouse hover, executed as follows:

```
var _image = $(this).find('img');
_image.finish();
_image.animate({
    width: images[$(this).index()].width + "px",
    height: images[$(this).index()].height + "px",
    top: '-50%',
    left: '-50%',
    opacity: 0.5
});
```

In the preceding code, you can see that the `images` array is referenced using `$(this).index()` to get the image's original height and width. Its top and left positions are once again set to `-50%`, centering it inside the list element.

 `_image.finish();` is used in both the event handler callbacks to finish any current animation. This prevents strange results when the user rapidly toggles from one image to the other.

See also

▸ *Creating an animated navigation menu*

Creating an animated content slider

You are probably aware that there is a whole forest of jQuery content slider plugins, tutorials, and downloadable scripts online, which are available for use and most of the content is free of charge. Content sliders are incredibly popular because they are a very attractive and eye-catching way to display important content to a user, such as images, news, and promotions. This recipe will show you how easy it is to create a content slider with jQuery. The slider used in this recipe will allow you to easily customize its look and feel using CSS so you can make it your own.

Getting ready

Create the usual recipe files: `recipe-3.html`, `recipe-3.css` and `recipe-3.js` in the same directory as your jQuery library.

How to do it...

Perform the following step-by-step instructions to create the attractive content slider:

1. Add the following HTML code to `recipe-3.html`, which creates the basic web page and the structure of the content slider:

```
<!DOCTYPE html>
<html>
<head>
    <title>Chapter 7 :: Recipe 3</title>
    <link href="recipe-3.css" rel="stylesheet" type="text/css" />
    <script src="jquery.min.js"></script>
    <script src="recipe-3.js"></script>
</head>
<body>
```

```
                  <div class="slider-frame">
                      <ul class="slider-content">
                          <li>
                              <h1>Section 1</h1>
                              <p>Some content for section one.</p>
                          </li>
                          <li>
                              <h1>Section 2</h1>
                              <p>Some content for section two.</p>
                          </li>
                          <li>
                              <h1>Section 3</h1>
                              <p>Some content for section three.</p>
                          </li>
                          <li>
                              <h1>Section 4</h1>
                              <p>Some content for section four.</p>
                          </li>
                      </ul>
                      <ul class="slider-nav"></ul>
                  </div>
              </body>
          </html>
```

2. Add the following CSS code to `recipe-3.css` to add basic styling and position the content slider:

```
.slider-frame {
    width: 600px;
    height: 250px;
    margin: 50px auto auto auto;
    overflow: hidden;
    position: relative;
}
.slider-content {
    margin: 0;
    padding: 0;
    list-style: none;
    position: relative;
}
.slider-content li {
    float: left;
    width: 600px;
    height: 250px;
    background-color: #E1E1E1;
```

```
    }
    .slider-content li h1 {
       margin: 10px;
    }
    .slider-content li p {
       margin: 10px;
    }
    .slider-nav {
       list-style: none;
       padding: 0;
       margin: 0;
       height: 35px;
       position: absolute;
       bottom: 0;
       left: 0;
       right: 0;
       text-align: center;
    }
    .slider-nav li {
       display: inline-block;
       margin-right: 5px;
    }
    .slider-nav li a {
       display: block;
       color: #FFF;
       text-decoration: none;
       border-radius: 30px;
       background-color: #333;
       width: 25px;
       height: 25px;
       text-align: center;
       line-height: 25px;
    }
    .slider-nav li a:hover {
       background-color: #000;
    }
    .slider-nav li a.active {
       background-color: #FFF;
       color: #333;
    }
```

3. Add the following jQuery code to `recipe-3.js` to allow the user to toggle between the content slides:

```
$(function(){
    var _sliderContent = $('.slider-content li');
    for (var i = 0; i < _sliderContent.length; i++) {
        $('.slider-nav').append("<li><a href='#" + i + "'" + " " +
            ((i == 0) ? "class='active'" : "") + ">" + (i + 1)
            + "</a></li>");
    }
    $('.slider-content').width((600 * _sliderContent.length)
        + "px");
    $(document).on("click", ".slider-nav li a", function(){
        var index = this.hash.replace("#", "");
        $(".slider-nav li a").removeClass("active");
        $(this).addClass("active");
        $('.slider-content').animate({
            left: -(index * 600) + "px"
        });
    });
});
```

How it works...

The slider content is an unordered list whose children contain the content that is to be displayed within each slide. Underneath the content list is another unordered list element, which will be populated dynamically by jQuery to create the navigation between each slide.

The CSS code in this recipe is used to position the slider frame and set its static width and height. The slider frame's overflow value is set to `hidden` so that only one slide is visible at a time. The slider content list item elements are set to `float left` so that they are displayed inline, making it possible to shift them into view using jQuery animations.

The first section of the jQuery code selects all of the slider content children and stores them within a local variable. For each slider content list element, a navigation list item is created and appended to the `slider-nav` unordered list, which links to the slider content's index as shown in the following code; the `active` class is also added to the first navigation anchor:

```
var _sliderContent = $('.slider-content li');
for (var i = 0; i < _sliderContent.length; i++) {
    $('.slider-nav').append("<li><a href='#" + i + "'" + " " + ((i ==
        0) ? "class='active'" : "") + ">" + (i + 1) + "</a></li>");
}
```

In order for the slider content items to float in line with each other, the `slider-content` unordered list element needs to be wide enough to allow it. As the CSS code cannot know how many slides the slider has, jQuery is used to count the number of content items and then multiply this value by the slider's width, applying this result to the `slider-content` element using the jQuery `width()` function, as follows:

```
$('.slider-content').width((600 * _sliderContent.length) + "px");
```

Executing the previous code will ensure that the `slider-content` unordered list element is wide enough to allow for the inline positioning of each of the list elements.

The last part of the jQuery code attaches a click event handler to the document to listen for clicks on the slider navigation. When the user clicks on one of the navigation elements, the callback function for this handler is called as follows:

```
$(document).on("click", ".slider-nav li a", function(){
    var index = this.hash.replace("#", "");
    $(".slider-nav li a").removeClass("active");
    $(this).addClass("active");
    $('.slider-content').animate({
        left: -(index * 600) + "px"
    });
});
```

Within the callback function, the hash value of the clicked link is retrieved using `var index = this.hash.replace("#", "");`, which will result in the index integer of the slide. Using this value, the jQuery `animate()` function can be used to set a negative-left position on the `slider-content` unordered list element; this will animate the slider content to show the selected slide. The `removeClass()` function is used to remove the `active` class from all of the anchor elements within the navigation list. Then, `addClass` is used to add the active class to the clicked element. This will indicate to the user which slide in the navigation has been selected, because it will be lighter in color than the other navigation items.

There's more...

Many of the popular jQuery content sliders have an `auto` mode in which each of the content slides are looped through automatically without any user interaction. This can be easily achieved by adding a little more jQuery code to the recipe. Add the following jQuery code to `recipe-3.js` at the bottom of the `$(function(){});` block if you would like this functionality:

```
var count = 0;
setInterval(function(){
    if (count >= _sliderContent.length) count = 0;
    $('.slider-content').animate({
        left: -(count * 600) + "px"
```

```
    });
    $(".slider-nav li a").removeClass("active");
    $(".slider-nav li").find("a[href='#" + count +
        "']").addClass("active");
    count++;
  }, 3000);
```

Using the native JavaScript function `setInterval()`, it is possible to execute a function continuously for a specified interval. In the preceding example, the specified function will be executed after every 3000 milliseconds.

In the preceding code, a `count` variable is declared to keep track of the current slide. Inside the function provided to `setInterval`, the `count` value is set to `0` if it has reached the maximum amount of available slides. The jQuery animation function is then used in the same way as the click event handler to animate the next content slide into view. Once again, `$(".slider-nav li a").removeClass("active");` is used to remove the `active` class from all of the navigation anchors and then `$(".slider-nav li").find("a[href='#" + count + "']").addClass("active");` is used to add the class only to the element that links to the next content slide. Finally, the count is incremented so that the next iteration animates the next content slide in view.

It is also worth mentioning that every time the jQuery's `append()` function is called, the DOM is redrawn. This can cause the application to slow down if many items are added using the `append()` function, like in this recipe. A simple way to avoid this is by creating a string of all the list elements that are to be added and include a single `append()` function after the loop.

See also

▸ *Animating background images*

Animating background images

Fullscreen image backgrounds can provide a very attractive splash screen for any website. This recipe will show you how to use jQuery to dynamically change the background image of your website.

Getting ready

Create `recipe-4.html`, `recipe-4.css`, and `recipe-4.js` in the same directory as the jQuery library. For this recipe, you will also need a set of images that will be used as the background images. Find three or four large images (upto 1280 X 1024 px in size), and save them in the same directory as the three files you have just created.

How to do it...

Have the three files you have just created open and ready for editing.

1. Add the following HTML code to `recipe-4.html` to create the basic web page and elements to hold the background image and text:

```html
<!DOCTYPE html>
<html>
<head>
    <title>Chapter 7 :: Recipe 4</title>
    <link href="recipe-4.css" rel="stylesheet" type="text/css" />
    <script src="jquery.min.js"></script>
    <script src="recipe-4.js"></script>
</head>
<body>
    <div class="background"></div>
    <div class="text-frame">
        <div class="text-inner">
            <h1>BACKGROUND IMAGE ANIMATION</h1>
            <p>This recipe shows you how to alternate the
                background image of an element using jQuery
                animations.</p>
        </div>
    </div>
</body>
</html>
```

2. Add the following CSS code to `recipe-4.css` to apply basic styles to the newly created web page; ensure that you update the image reference to correspond with one of your chosen images:

```css
body {
    background-color: #333;
}
.background {
    background: url(recipe-4-1.jpg)  no-repeat center center
        fixed;
    -webkit-background-size: cover;
    -moz-background-size: cover;
    -o-background-size: cover;
    background-size: cover;
    position: absolute;
    top: 0;
    bottom: 0;
    left: 0;
```

```
        right: 0;
    }
    .text-frame {
        position: absolute;
        top: 0;
        bottom: 0;
        left: 0;
        right: 0;
    }
    .text-inner {
        width: 600px;
        margin: 15% auto auto auto;
        background-color: rgba(0, 0, 0, 0.78);
        padding: 20px;
        color: #E1E1E1;
        border-radius: 5px;
    }
    .text-inner h1 {
        margin: 0;
        padding: 0;
    }
    .text-inner p {
        font-size: 22px;
        line-height: 30px;
        margin: 5px 0 5px 0;
        color: #CCC;
    }
```

3. Add the following jQuery code to `recipe-4.js` to activate the background animation in the `background` division element that you have just added to `recipe-4.html`:

```
var _images = ['recipe-4-1.jpg', 'recipe-4-2.jpg', 'recipe-4-3.
jpg'];
var index = 1;
$(function(){
    setInterval(function(){
        if (index >= _images.length) index = 0;
        $('.background').animate({
            opacity: 0
        }, 1500, function(){
            $(this).css({
                'background-image': "url('" + _images[index] +
                "')"
            }).animate({
                opacity: 1
```

```
                    }, 1500);
                    index++;
                });
            }, 6000);
        });
```

4. Update the filenames in the _images array at the beginning of `recipe-4.js` to match the filenames of the images you have chosen for this recipe.

How it works...

The basic web page created in this recipe has two main parts. Firstly, there is a division element with the `background` class, which is made to fill the entire screen and use the chosen images as its background. Secondly, there is a `text-frame` division element, which simply holds some text floating in the center of the screen.

The CSS code in `recipe-4.css` sets the background element's position to `absolute` and its left, right, bottom, and top positions to `0`, forcing it to fill the entire screen. Its background property is then set using the following code:

```
background: url(recipe-4-1.jpg)  no-repeat center center fixed;
-webkit-background-size: cover;
-moz-background-size: cover;
-o-background-size: cover;
background-size: cover;
```

The background option sets one of the chosen images as its initial background and ensures that it is centered and fixed. The `background-size` property is used to ensure that the background image always fills 100 percent of the `background` division element.

A similar CSS is used to ensure that the `text-frame` element fills the screen, and using percent and auto margins, the `text-inner` element that holds the text is centered vertically and horizontally.

The _images array at the beginning of `recipe-4.js` holds the references to the chosen background images. The `index` variable is used to keep track of the currently displayed background image. Within the jQuery on-load function, `setInterval` is declared to execute a set of animations to change the background image every six seconds. This is similar to the previous recipe's *There's more...* section.

Because the jQuery's `animate()` function does not support animating the background image directly, we have to provide a workaround. Inside the `setInterval()` function, the `animate()` function is used on the background element's opacity to fade the element out. Then, by specifying a callback for the jQuery's `animate()` function, the background element's `background-image` property is modified using jQuery's `css()` function as soon as the animation is completed. Using `css()`, the background image is changed and the `animate()` function is used again to change the opacity back to `1`, which fades in the element. Using the index value to reference the `_images` array, it is possible to select a different background image for every iteration of the `setInterval()` function, as follows:

```
$(this).css({
    'background-image': "url('" + _images[index] + "')"
}).animate({
    opacity: 1
}, 1500);
index++;
```

Once the last animation is completed, the index value is incremented by one to ensure that the next iteration displays a different image.

See also

► *Creating an animated content slider*

Creating an animated navigation menu

Your website's navigation allows your visitors to easily find the content hosted on your site. Providing the user with a fun and interactive navigation menu that is also easy to use can make a lasting impression on them. This recipe shows you how to create a modern animated navigation menu.

Getting ready

Create `recipe-5.html`, `recipe-5.css`, and `recipe-5.js` in the same directory as the latest version of the jQuery library.

How to do it...

Perform all of the following steps to create a unique and modern animated navigation menu for any site:

1. Add the following HTML to `recipe-5.html` to create the basic web page, and include the newly created files along with the jQuery library:

```
<!DOCTYPE html>
<html>
<head>
    <title>Chapter 7 :: Recipe 5</title>
    <link href="recipe-5.css" rel="stylesheet" type="text/css" />
    <script src="jquery.min.js"></script>
    <script src="recipe-5.js"></script>
</head>
<body>
</body>
</html>
```

2. Inside the body tags of the HTML code you have just added to `recipe-5.html`, add the following code to create the structure for the navigation menu:

```
<div class="container">
    <ul class="navigation">
        <li>
            <a href="#" class="link-base">
                <div class="link-content">
                    <div class="nav-item">HOME</div>
                    <div class="nav-item hover">HOME</div>
                </div>
            </a>
        </li>
        <li>
            <a href="#" class="link-base">
                <div class="link-content">
                    <div class="nav-item">ABOUT <div
                        class="down-arrow"></div></div>
                    <div class="nav-item hover">ABOUT <div
                        class="down-arrow"></div></div>
                </div>
            </a>
            <ul class="sub-nav">
                <li>
                    <a href="#">
```

```
                    <div class="sub-link-content">
                        <div class="sub-nav-item">SECTION
                            1</div>
                        <div class="sub-nav-item
                            hover">SECTION 1</div>
                    </div>
                </a>
            </li>
            <li>
                <a href="#">
                    <div class="sub-link-content">
                        <div class="sub-nav-item">SECTION
                            2</div>
                        <div class="sub-nav-item
                            hover">SECTION 2</div>
                    </div>
                </a>
            </li>
            <li>
                <a href="#">
                    <div class="sub-link-content">
                        <div class="sub-nav-item">SECTION
                            3</div>
                        <div class="sub-nav-item
                            hover">SECTION 3</div>
                    </div>
                </a>
            </li>
        </ul></li>
    <li>
        <a href="#" class="link-base">
            <div class="link-content">
                <div class="nav-item">CONTACT</div>
                <div class="nav-item hover">CONTACT</div>
            </div>
        </a>
    </li>
    </ul>
</div>
```

3. Add the following CSS code to `recipe-5.css` to provide basic styling to the navigation menu and web page:

```
.container {
    width: 800px;
    margin: 100px auto auto auto;
```

```
        }
        .navigation {
            margin: 0;
            padding: 0;
            list-style: none;
            background-color: #333;
            height: 50px;
        }
        .navigation li {
            float: left;
            position: relative;
        }
        .navigation li a {
            display: block;
            text-align: center;
            color: #FFF;
            text-decoration: none;
            overflow: hidden;
            height: 50px;
        }
        .navigation li a .nav-item {
            line-height: 50px;
            padding: 0 15px 0 15px;
            height: 50px;
        }
        .navigation li a .nav-item.hover {
            background-color: #ff3600;
        }
        .sub-nav {
            list-style: none;
            margin: 0;
            padding: 50px 0 0 0;
            opacity: 0;
            position: absolute;
            top: 0;
            left: -10000px;
            opacity: 0;
        }
        .sub-nav li {
            display: block;
            height: 40px;
        }
        .sub-nav li a {
            display: block;
```

```
        width: 120px;
        height: 40px;
        line-height: 40px;
        text-align: center;
        color: #FFF;
        background-color: #333333;
    }
    .sub-nav li a .sub-link-content {
        width: 240px;
    }
    .sub-nav li a .sub-nav-item {
        float: left;
        width: 120px;
    }
    .sub-nav li a .sub-nav-item.hover {
        background-color: #ff3600;
    }
    .down-arrow {
        width: 0;
        border-left: 7px solid transparent;
        border-right: 7px solid transparent;
        border-top: 7px solid white;
        display: inline-block;
        vertical-align: middle;
        margin: -5px 0 0 5px;
    }
```

4. To add the animations to the navigation menu based on user interaction, add the following jQuery code to `recipe-5.js`:

```
$(function(){
    //Base navigation
    $(document).on("mouseenter", "ul.navigation li a.link-
        base", function(){
        $(this).find(".link-content").stop().animate({
            marginTop: -50
        }, 200, function(){
            $(this).parent().parent().find('.sub-nav').css({
                left: 0
            }).animate({
                opacity: 1
            });
        });
    }).on("mouseleave", "ul.navigation li a", function(){
```

```
                    //Only reverse the animation if this link doesn't
                        have a sub menu
                    if ($(this).parent().find('.sub-nav').length == 0) {
                        $(this).find(".link-content").stop().animate({
                            marginTop: 0
                        }, 200);
                    }
                }).on("mouseleave", "ul.navigation li .sub-nav",
                    function(){
                    $(this).animate({
                        opacity: 0
                    }, 200, function(){
                        $(this).css({
                            left: -10000
                    });
                        //When the mouse leaves the sub menu, also reverse
                            the base link animation
                        $(this).parent().find('.link-
                            content').stop().animate({
                            marginTop: 0
                        }, 200);
                    });
                }).on("mouseenter", "ul.sub-nav li a", function(){
                    $(this).find(".sub-link-content").stop().animate({
                        marginLeft: -120
                    }, 200);
                }).on("mouseleave", "ul.navigation li a", function(){
                    $(this).find(".sub-link-content").stop().animate({
                        marginLeft: 0
                    }, 200);
                });
            });
```

5. Open `recipe-5.html` in a web browser, and you will be presented with a simplistic navigation menu. Hovering over the **About** item will activate an animation and present you with the associated submenu as shown in the following screenshot:

How it works...

This recipe's code will be easy to understand when we break it down piece by piece. The HTML code used to create the navigation menu has a division element with the class `frame`, which acts as the menu container to control the width and position.

The menu itself consists of an unordered list element with the navigation class. Within this list, there are multiple first-level list elements with anchors acting as the menu page links.

Each of these first-level links has a `link-content` container element that holds two `nav-item` division elements. Styling two of these `nav-item` elements differently with CSS allows us to create the drop-in animation as we are only showing one of these at once.

The `about` first-level navigation item also has a submenu. To achieve this, the list item contains another unordered list with the `sub-nav` class. Using CSS, this subnavigation element is placed over the original first-level page link when visible so that the cursor is not moved from that area. This allows us to keep the original link in the hovered state and the submenu open until the user's mouse leaves the submenu entirely.

The submenu page links follow the same structure as the first-level links in which they have two item elements with the same text. This is to allow us to create a similar hover animation.

Within `recipe-5.js`, the first part attaches a `mouseenter` event handler to the document to look for the mouse pointer entering one of the navigation first-level links, as follows:

```
$(document).on("mouseenter", "ul.navigation li a.link-base",
function(){
    $(this).find(".link-content").stop().animate({
        marginTop: -50
    }, 200, function(){
        $(this).parent().parent().find('.sub-nav').css({
        left: 0
    }).animate({
        opacity: 1
        });
    });
})
```

When this happens, the `animate()` function is used on the link's `link-content` child to sets its top margin to `-50`. This will move the second `nav-item` class into a view that has its background styled orange with CSS. After 200 milliseconds, when the animation is complete, an additional callback function is called.

This will execute the code to open any subnavigation menus that the currently hovered item contains. Using the `css()` function to first set the subnavigation's left position to `0`, bringing it onto the screen, and then using the `animate()` function to set the opacity of the element to `1`, will fade the image into view. The subnavigation elements are originally positioned off the screen using a left position of `-10000` so that they do not get in the way of any clicks the user may perform on the page.

The second event handler is for the `mouseleave` event. This event handler checks to see whether or not the top-level link, which has just been set to `left`, has a subnavigation menu using `if ($(this).parent().find('.sub-nav').length == 0)`. If it does not, the hover animation is reversed, setting the `link-content` element's top margin back to `0`. This allows us to leave the hovered state active while the user is navigating the submenu.

The next event handler is another `mouseleave` event, which handles the user leaving the submenu, as follows:

```
.on("mouseleave", "ul.navigation li .sub-nav", function(){
    $(this).animate({
        opacity: 0
    }, 200, function(){
        $(this).css({
        left: -10000
    });
    //When the mouse leaves the sub menu, also reverse the base
        link animation
    $(this).parent().find('.link-content').stop().animate({
        marginTop: 0
        }, 200);
    });
})
```

Once the user's mouse has left the submenu, the `animate()` function is used to set the submenu's opacity to `0`, fading it out. Then, after the 200-millisecond animation has been completed, the `css()` function is used to move the submenu -10000 pixels off the screen. Finally, using `find()` to select the first-level `link-content` element, the original hover animation is reversed, putting the menu back to its dormant state.

There are two additional event handlers attached to the document. The additional `mouseenter` and `mouseleave` events are used to create the hover animations for the submenu items. The same code and technique is used for first-level navigation menu, except that instead of changing the top margin, the left margin is changed to animate the `sub-link-content` elements from left to right as opposed to top to bottom.

See also

 ▸ *Creating an animated content slider*
 ▸ *Animating background images*

8
Understanding Plugin Development

In this chapter, we will cover the following topics:

- ▶ Creating a plugin template
- ▶ Creating a tooltip plugin
- ▶ Building a content and image slider plugin
- ▶ Creating an RSS feed reader plugin
- ▶ Coding an image cropper plugin from scratch

Introduction

jQuery plugins allow the developer to write portable code that can be reused within any jQuery project quickly. As part of this book, we have created a lot of functionality that you may want to use in multiple projects. By creating a jQuery plugin with the required functionality, you can abstract the complexity of this functionality and make it simple to include wherever you need it.

Before you start this chapter, create an easily accessible directory called `chapter8`. Within this folder, add the latest version of the jQuery library, which will be used throughout this chapter.

Creating a plugin template

Creating jQuery plugins has become very popular over the years, and there are many articles and discussions online about plugin creation best practices. Many of these articles discuss in depth how to create a plugin template that can be used as the starting point for any jQuery plugin. This recipe will show you how to create your own jQuery plugin template that will be used throughout this chapter.

Getting ready

Inside the `chapter8` folder that was created earlier, create a JavaScript file called `jquery.plugin-template.js`.

How to do it...

To create a basic plugin template that will form the basis of all the plugins used within this chapter, add the following code to `jquery.plugin-template.js`:

```javascript
;(function ($) {
    var name = 'pluginName';
    Plugin.prototype = {
        defaults: {

        }
    };
    // The actual plugin constructor
    function Plugin(element, options) {
        var $scope = this;
        $scope.$element = $(element);
        $scope.element = element;
        $scope.options = $.extend({}, this.defaults, options);
        $scope.init = function () {

        }
    }
    $.fn[name] = function (options) {
        return this.each(function () {
            new Plugin(this, options).init();
        });
    }
})(jQuery);
```

How it works...

Read through the plugin documentation on the jQuery website (`http://learn.jquery.com/plugins/basic-plugin-creation/`) to see a set of guidelines and best practices to adhere to.

The plugin created in this recipe uses simple concepts and best practices to create a lightweight plugin template. There is a popular article (`http://coding.smashingmagazine.com/2011/10/11/essential-jquery-plugin-patterns/`) by Addy Osmani that provides great insight into plugin authoring while adhering to these recommended best practices.

Looking at our plugin template, the first point to note is the semicolon at the start of the document. This is included to ensure that any previously included plugins or scripts have been closed properly.

To conform to the jQuery authoring recommendations, the entire plugin is wrapped inside an **Immediately-Invoked Function Expression (IIFE)** to provide scope to the plugin. jQuery is provided to the IIFE as the local variable $ to allow developers to be able to reference the jQuery library in the usual manner without conflicts.

Within the plugin constructor, a `$scope` variable is declared so that it is clear what represents the plugin's scope. The element that the plugin is being initialized from is then assigned to the plugin's scope along with any provided plugin options. The jQuery `extend()` function is used to merge the `defaults` object with the `options` object, overwriting any defaults that may have been provided within `options`. Finally, the `init()` function is added to the plugin's scope, which is where you will place the plugin's initialization code, as follows:

```
$.fn[name] = function (options) {
    return this.each(function () {
        new Plugin(this, options).init();
    });
}
```

The preceding code makes the plugin available just as any other jQuery object method using the specified plugin name (`$('.element').pluginName();`). Using `this.each()`, it will create a new plugin instance for each of the elements the plugin is initiated on and will call the plugin's `init()` function.

Creating a tooltip plugin

Tooltips are a popular way to show additional information to the user about the UI they are using. This recipe will show you how to create your own basic tooltip plugin that you can easily use in all of your projects.

Copy the `jquery.plugin-template.js` file and create `jquery.tooltip.js`, which will become the plugin file for this recipe. Create `recipe-2.html` and `recipe-2.js` in the same directory as the plugin file and the jQuery library.

How to do it...

To create a simple tooltip plugin and sample web page, perform the following steps:

1. Add the following HTML to `recipe-2.html` to create a very simple web page with elements that can have a tooltip:

```html
<!DOCTYPE html>
<html>
<head>
    <title>Chapter 8 :: Recipe 2</title>
    <script src="jquery.min.js"></script>
    <script src="jquery.tooltip.js"></script>
    <script src="recipe-2.js"></script>
</head>
<body>
<p><input type="text" class="hasTooltip" data-title="This is a
tooltip on an input box" /></p>
<p><a href="http://www.google.com/" target="_blank"
class="hasTooltip" title="External link to http://www.google.
com/">Google.com</a></p>
<button class="hasTooltip" data-title="A button with a
tooltip">Button</button>
</body>
</html>
```

2. At the top of `jquery.tooltip.js`, update the `name` variable and set the plugin defaults to be as follows:

```js
var name = 'tooltip';
Plugin.prototype = {
defaults: {
            'height': 30,
            'fadeInDelay': 200
}

};
```

3. Update the `$scope.init()` function with the following code:

```
$scope.init = function() {
$scope._text = (typeof $scope.$element.data('title') !=
"undefined") ? $scope.$element.data('title') : $scope.$element.
prop("title");
            //Only display the tooltip if a title has been
specified
            if (typeof $scope._text != "undefined") {
                var $html = $("<div class='tooltip-frame'>"
                    + "<div class='tooltip-arrow'></div>"
                    + "<div class='tooltip-text'>" + $scope._
text + "</div>"
                    + "</div>");

                $html.css({
                    'position': 'absolute',
                    'text-align': 'center',
                    'height': $scope.options.height,
                    'line-height': $scope.options.height + "px",
                    'left': $scope.$element.offset().left +
$scope.$element.outerWidth() + 15,
                    'top': $scope.$element.offset().top +
($scope.$element.outerHeight() / 2) - ($scope.options.height / 2),
                    'background-color': 'rgba(0, 0, 0, 0.81)',
                    'color': '#FFF',
                    'padding': '0 10px 0 10px',
                    'border-radius': '5px',
                    'opact': 'none'
                }).find('.tooltip-arrow').css({
                    'width': 0,
                    'height': 0,
                    'border-top': '10px solid transparent',
                    'border-bottom': '10px solid transparent',
                    'border-right': '10px solid rgba(0, 0, 0,
0.81)',
                    'position': 'absolute',
                    'left': '-10px',
                    'top': (($scope.options.height / 2) - 10)
                });

                $scope.$element.on("mouseover", function(){
                    $html.fadeIn($scope.options.fadeInDelay);
                    $scope.$element.after($html);
                }).on("mouseout", function(){
```

```
                    $html.remove();
                });
            }
        }
```

4. Add the following jQuery code to `recipe-2.js` to initialize the tooltip plugin for all the HTML elements with the `hasTooltip` class:

```
$(function(){
    $('.hasTooltip').tooltip();
});
```

5. Open `recipe-2.html` in a web browser and hover over one of the elements on the screen to see a tooltip appear.

How it works...

The HTML page created as part of this recipe is used only to provide a few elements to which a tooltip can be attached.

The first change to the plugin template is to set the default settings. In this case, we have set the tooltip height and the fade-in animation duration. You can introduce additional features of your own by adding these features to the default settings here.

When the plugin is initialized for each of the selected elements, the `init()` function is called, which contains most of the logic for this plugin.

The plugin template makes the "jQueryfied" version of the element available through `$scope.$element`. We can use the `prop()` and `data()` functions to check for a title specified on the element and store this in `$scope._text`, which will be used as the tooltip text.

This variable is then checked to ensure there is some text available to display. If there is no text, we do not show a tooltip.

If `$scope._text` is defined, we create the tooltip HTML using the following code:

```
var $html = $("<div class='tooltip-frame'>"
    +   "<div class='tooltip-arrow'></div>"
    +   "<div class='tooltip-text'>" + $scope._text + "</div>"
    + "</div>");
```

The `var` statement is important to ensure that a new tooltip element is created for each of the selected elements. By wrapping the HTML code within `$()`, it is possible for us to use jQuery functions on this element before we insert it into the DOM. The HTML code for the tooltip adds the title text and creates an element that will display the left arrow.

Using the jQuery `css()` function, a range of CSS styles are applied to the newly created HTML code to position and style the tooltip. The left and top positions of the tooltip are calculated using the offset, width, and height of the selected element on which the tooltip will be displayed. Note that the `outerWidth()` and `outerHeight()` functions are used as opposed to the `width()`/`height()` functions to include the padding and borders and the returned dimensions.

The jQuery `find()` function is also used in conjunction with the `css()` function to add the styles to the left arrow.

Finally, two event listeners are attached to the selected element so that the tooltip is shown when the user's mouse moves over the element and is removed when the user's mouse moves out. The `fadeIn()` function takes the `duration` parameter from the `defaults` object, which can be overridden when the tooltip plugin is initialized.

To initialize the tooltip plugin for all elements that have the `hasTooltip` class, the following jQuery code is added to `recipe-2.js`:

```
$(function(){
    $('.hasTooltip').tooltip();
});
```

This is where you could overwrite the defaults, for example, using the following code:

```
$(function(){
    $('.hasTooltip').tooltip({
        'height': 50,
            'fadeInDelay': 500
    });
});
```

There's more...

This recipe provides a very basic tooltip plugin. You could expand on this recipe to add many additional features, such as positioning, and allow the plugin user to specify which event the tooltip opens on.

Building a content and image slider plugin

In *Chapter 7, User Interface Animation*, you were shown how to create a simple content slider using jQuery. This recipe will show you how to turn that recipe into a reusable jQuery plugin with the addition of being able to add images to the slider. You do not need to read the previous recipe to complete this one, but it is recommended to do so for you to get a better understanding of how the code works.

Getting ready

Copy the `jquery.plugin-template.js` file and rename it to `jquery.slider.js`, which will become the plugin for this recipe. You will also need to find an image 600 pixels wide and 250 pixels high that will be used in the slider. Finally, create `recipe-3.html`, `slider.css`, and `recipe-3.js` in the same directory as the `jquery.slider.js` file and the jQuery library.

How to do it...

Perform the following steps to create your image and a content slider plugin:

1. Add the following HTML to `recipe-3.html`:

```
<!DOCTYPE html>
<html>
<head>
    <title>Chapter 8 :: Recipe 3</title>
    <link href="slider.css" rel="stylesheet" type="text/css" />
    <script src="jquery.min.js"></script>
    <script src="jquery.slider.js"></script>
    <script src="recipe-3.js"></script>
</head>
<body>
<div class="mySlider">
    <div>Slider Content 1</div>
    <img src="british-countryside.jpg" />
    <div>Slider Content 3</div>
    <div>Slider Content 4</div>
</div>
</body>
</html>
```

2. At the top of `jquery.slider.js`, update the plugin name to `slider` and set the defaults as follows:

```
var name = 'slider';
Plugin.prototype = {
    defaults: {
        width: 600,
        height: 250
    }
};
```

3. Update the plugin's `$scope.init()` function to be the following:

```
$scope.init = function () {
$scope.$element.addClass("slider-frame").css({
    width: $scope.options.width,
    height: $scope.options.height
});
$scope.$element.append('<ul class="slider-nav"></ul>');
var _sliderItems = $scope.$element.find('div, img');
_sliderItems.wrapAll("<div class='slider-content'></div>");
$scope.$element.find('.slider-content').css({
    width: $scope.options.width * _sliderItems.length,
    position: 'relative'
});
_sliderItems.css({
    float: 'left',
    width: $scope.options.width,
    height: $scope.options.height
});
var _sliderNav = $scope.$element.find('.slider-nav');
for (var i = 0; i < _sliderItems.length; i++) {
    _sliderNav.append("<li><a href='#" + i + "' " + ((i == 0) ?
"class='active'" : "") + ">" + (i + 1) + "</a></li>");
}
_sliderNav.on("click", "li a", function(){
    var index = this.hash.replace("#", "");
    _sliderNav.find('li a').removeClass("active");
    $(this).addClass("active");
    $scope.$element.find('.slider-content').animate({
        left: -(index * $scope.options.width) + "px"
    });
});
}
```

4. Add the following jQuery code to `recipe-3.js` to initialize the slider plugin:

```
$(function(){
    $('.mySlider').slider();
});
```

5. Add the following CSS code to `slider.css`:

```
.slider-frame {
    overflow: hidden;
    position: relative;
    margin: auto;
    border: solid 1px #CCC;
```

```
        }
        .slider-nav {
            list-style: none;
            padding: 0;
            margin: 0;
            height: 35px;
            position: absolute;
            bottom: 0;
            left: 0;
            right: 0;
            text-align: center;
        }
        .slider-nav li {
            display: inline-block;
            margin-right: 5px;
        }
        .slider-nav li a {
            display: block;
            color: #FFF;
            text-decoration: none;
            border-radius: 30px;
            background-color: #333;
            width: 25px;
            height: 25px;
            text-align: center;
            line-height: 25px;
        }
        .slider-nav li a:hover {
            background-color: #000;
        }
        .slider-nav li a.active {
            background-color: #FFF;
            color: #333;
        }
```

6. Open `recipe-3.html` within a web browser and you will be presented with a dynamically created image and content slider.

How it works...

The HTML page sets up the required HTML for the slider plugin. There is a container division with children that the slider plugin will use as slides. The children can be either division elements or images.

The jQuery code in `recipe-3.js` selects the `mySlider` division element and initializes the slider plugin.

The plugin template we created earlier takes care of the jQuery plugin setup. The functionality for our slider plugin goes inside the `init()` function. At the start of this function, the `slider-frame` class is added to the selected element (`.mySlider`) so that it inherits some basics styles from the `slider.css` stylesheet. Using values from the `options` object, the width and height of the element are set using the jQuery `css()` function as follows:

```
$scope.$element.addClass("slider-frame").css({
width: this.options.width,
height: this.options.height
});
```

After this, `$scope.$element.append('<ul class="slider-nav"></ul>');` is used to insert an empty unordered list into the slider, which is ready for the creation of the slide navigation.

The next section of the code sets up the slider for the animation. As explained in the *Creating an animated content slider* recipe in *Chapter 7, User Interface Animation*, a slider needs the width of its container to be the combined width of its slides so that the slides can float next to each other and be moved into view using an animation, as shown in the following code:

```
var _sliderItems = $scope.$element.find('div, img');
_sliderItems.wrapAll("<div class='slider-content'></div>");
$scope.$element.find('.slider-content').css({
width: $scope.options.width * _sliderItems.length,
position: 'relative'
});
```

To achieve this, the slider's children (the slides) are selected and then wrapped inside a division element using the jQuery `wrapAll()` function. The width of this element is set to be the width of an individual slide times the number of slides in the slider. To float each of the slides, the `css()` function is used to set the `float` property as shown in the following code:

```
_sliderItems.css({
    float: 'left',
    width: $scope.options.width,
    height: $scope.options.height
});
```

With each slide configured, the next step in the code is to add a list item for each slide to the `slider-nav` unordered list element to form the navigation:

```
var _sliderNav = $scope.$element.find('.slider-nav');
for (var i = 0; i < _sliderItems.length; i++) {
```

```
       _sliderNav.append("<li><a href='#" + i + "' " + ((i == 0) ?
    "class='active'" : "") + ">" + (i + 1) + "</a></li>");
    }
```

The final stage of the plugin is to listen for clicks on the anchor elements within the navigation list, which is coded as follows, to allow the user to change the visible slide using this navigation:

```
_sliderNav.on("click", "li a", function(){
    var index = this.hash.replace("#", "");
    _sliderNav.find('li a').removeClass("active");
    $(this).addClass("active");
    $scope.$element.find('.slider-content').animate({
        left: -(index * $scope.options.width) + "px"
    });
});
```

When the user clicks on a link, the `animate()` function is used to change the `slider-content` division element's left position based on the selected link. Read more about this in the *Creating an animated content slider* recipe in *Chapter 7, User Interface Animation*.

There's more...

To add the popular auto-slider effect to this plugin, take a look back to the *Creating an animated content slider* recipe in *Chapter 7, User Interface Animation*.

See also

- The *Creating an animated content slider* recipe in *Chapter 7, User Interface Animation*

Creating an RSS feed reader plugin

RSS feed readers are very popular additions to many websites. This recipe will show you how to create a configurable feed reader plugin utilizing the Google Feed API, allowing you to easily re-use the plugin on any website.

Getting ready

Once again, copy the `jquery.plugin-template.js` file and rename it to `jquery.rssreader.js` to provide the base for this recipe's plugin. Inside the same directory, create `recipe-4.js`, `rssreader.css`, and `recipe-4.html`.

How to do it...

To create the RSS reader plugin, perform the following steps:

1. Add the following HTML code to `recipe-4.html` to create a basic web page and to make the Google Feed API available for use within the page:

```
<!DOCTYPE html>
<html>
<head>
    <title>Chapter 8 :: Recipe 4</title>
    <link href="rssreader.css" rel="stylesheet" type="text/css" />
    <script src="jquery.min.js"></script>
    <script src="https://www.google.com/jsapi"></script>
    <script type="text/javascript">
        google.load("feeds", "1");
    </script>
    <script src="jquery.rssreader.js"></script>
    <script src="recipe-4.js"></script>
</head>
<body>
<div class="myRSSContent"></div>
</body>
</html>
```

2. Add the following CSS code to `rssreader.css` to create the styles for the RSS reader:

```
@import url(http://fonts.googleapis.com/css?family=Source+Sans+P
ro:200,300,400);
.rssreader-frame {
    background-color: #333;
    border-radius: 5px;
    border: solid 1px #1f1f1f;
    padding: 0 10px 10px 10px;
    font-family: 'Source Sans Pro', sans-serif !important;
}
.rssreader-frame h1 {
    margin: 5px 0 5px 0;
    padding: 0;
    font-size: 22px;
    color: #FFF;
    line-height: 30px;
    font-weight: 200;
}
.rssreader-frame ul {
```

```
        margin: 0;
        padding: 0;
        list-style: none;
    }
    .rssreader-frame ul h4 {
        margin: 0;
        position: relative;
        font-weight: 200;
        color: #E1E1E1;
    }
    .rssreader-frame p.description {
        margin: 0 -10px 10px -10px;
        padding: 0 10px 10px 10px;
        color: #CCC;
        font-size: 12px;
        border-bottom: solid 1px #494949;
    }
    .rssreader-frame ul h4 a {
        line-height: 25px;
        margin-right: 110px;
        display: block;
        text-decoration: none;
        color: #8bd;
    }
    .rssreader-frame ul h4 .entry-date {
        width: 100px;
        position: absolute;
        right: 0;
        top: 0;
        height: 25px;
        line-height: 25px;
        text-align: right;
    }
    .rssreader-frame ul li p {
        color: #666;
        margin: 0 0 10px 0;
        padding: 0 0 10px 0;
        border-bottom: dotted 1px #494949;
    }
```

3. At the top of `jquery.rssreader.js`, update the `defaults` object and the `name` variable to be as follows:

```
var name = 'rssreader';
Plugin.prototype = {
```

```
defaults: {
    url: 'http://feeds.bbci.co.uk/news/technology/rss.xml',
    amount: 5,
    width: null,
    height: null
    }
};
```

4. Update the plugin `init()` function to include the following code:

```
$scope.init = function () {
    $scope.$element.addClass("rssreader-frame");
    if ($scope.options.width != null) {
        $scope.$element.width($scope.options.width);
    }
    var feed = new google.feeds.Feed($scope.options.url);
    feed.setNumEntries($scope.options.amount);
    feed.load(function(result) {
        if (!result.error) {
            var _title = $("<h1>" + result.feed.title +
"</h1>");
            var _description = $("<p class='description'>"
+ result.feed.description + "</p>");
            var _feedList = $("<ul class='feed-list'></
ul>");
            for (var i = 0; i < result.feed.entries.
length; i++) {
                var entry = result.feed.entries[i];
                var date = new Date(entry.publishedDate);
                var dateString = date.getDate() + "/" +
(date.getMonth() + 1) + "/" + date.getFullYear();
                var _listElement = $("<li></li>");
                _listElement.append("<h4><a href='" +
entry.link + "'>" + entry.title + "</a><div class='entry-date'>" +
dateString + "</div></h4>");
                _listElement.append("<p>" + entry.content
+ "</p>");

                _feedList.append(_listElement);
            }
            $scope.$element.append(_title);
            $scope.$element.append(_description);
            $scope.$element.append(_feedList);
            if ($scope.options.height != null && (_
feedList.outerHeight() + _title.outerHeight()) > $scope.options.
height) {
                _feedList.css({
```

```
                                        'height': ($scope.options.height - _
        title.outerHeight()),

                                        'overflow-y': 'scroll',
                                        'padding-right': 10
                            });
                    }
                }
            });
        }
```

5. Add the following few lines of jQuery to `recipe-4.js` to initialize the plugin for the `myRSSContent` element:

```javascript
$(function(){
    $('.myRSSContent').rssreader({
        width: 400,
        height: 300
    });
});
```

6. Open `recipe-4.html` in a web browser and you will be presented with the following RSS reader:

How it works...

The HTML code that creates the web page for this recipe has a single `division` element that is used to initialize the RSS reader plugin and acts as the container for the RSS content. Additionally, the Google Feed API is used and included in this page above the `jquery.rssreader.js` file. Using the Google Feed API means that we can easily create a plugin without requiring any server-side work. This also makes the plugin easily portable to any website. Read more about this API at `https://developers.google.com/feed/v1/devguide#hiworld`.

The CSS code styles the RSS reader elements that are created within the plugin itself. No further explanation of this code is needed.

As with the other plugins in this chapter, the template takes care of the plugin setup and our plugin functionality goes inside the `init()` function, which is executed once the plugin has been initialized.

The first part of this function adds the `rssreader-frame` class to the selected element, which the CSS code uses to apply a variety of styles. Then, looking at the `options` variable, a width is set on the selected element if one has been provided.

Using the Google Feed API, the feed request is configured using the `URL` and `amount` values of the `options` object as follows. This will tell the API where to collect the RSS content and how many items to return.

```
var feed = new google.feeds.Feed($scope.options.url);
feed.setNumEntries($scope.options.amount);
```

After this, the `load()` function is used to make the request with a callback function specified, as shown in the following code:

```
feed.load(function(result) {
if (!result.error) {
// -- HIDDEN CODE
}
}
```

If no error has occurred, a header, description, and unordered list elements are created and stored in local variables, as specified by the following code:

```
var _title = $("<h1>" + result.feed.title + "</h1>");
var _description = $("<p class='description'>" + result.feed.
description + "</p>");
var _feedList = $("<ul class='feed-list'></ul>");
```

Using the `result.feed` object, it is possible to extract the feed title and description to be placed within these elements. These elements are created and wrapped inside the jQuery selected (`$()`) so that jQuery's functions will be available on these elements for later use.

We then loop through each of the entries and create a list item for each. Within each list item, we add the feed content, date, title, and link. Using the JavaScript `Date()` function, a more readable date is created to insert into the DOM. To add each of the elements to the unordered list element that was previously created, `_feedList.append(_listElement);` is used.

The title, description, and the list, which is now fully populated with RSS content, can be inserted into the DOM using the following code:

```
$scope.$element.append(_title);
$scope.$element.append(_description);
$scope.$element.append(_feedList);
```

Finally, the following code is used to apply any specified height to the RSS feed reader and add a scrollbar if the content is too big to fit within the specified height:

```
if ($scope.options.height != null && (_feedList.outerHeight() + _
title.outerHeight()) > $scope.options.height) {
    _feedList.css({
    'height': ($scope.options.height - _title.outerHeight()),
    'overflow-y': 'scroll',
    'padding-right': 10
});
}
```

See also

▶   The *Creating a news ticker* recipe in *Chapter 6, User Interface*

Coding an image cropper plugin from scratch

When allowing users to upload their own images, whether it be for a profile picture or some other use, giving them the ability to trim the image down within the browser provides a huge benefit to the user. This is because most users would not know how to alter the image using a third-party application such as Photoshop. There are many image cropper plugins available on the Internet for free and many tutorials to help you use them, but there are very few examples that provide you with the entire solution. This recipe will show you how to create your own image cropper plugin from scratch, how to upload the image to a web server, and how to take data from the image cropper to resize and save the image to the user's specification.

Getting ready

This recipe is quite complex as it includes both client- and server-side code, so ensure you follow each step carefully. Before you begin this recipe, set up the following directory structure in the web root of your web server:

```
▼ www
  ▼ includes
        imagecrop.css
        jquery.imagecrop.js
        jquery.min.js
        recipe-5.css
        recipe-5.js
  ▶ uploads
    index.html
    upload.php
```

Going by the preceding structure, you need to create the `includes` and `uploads` folders in your web root (**www** in the preceding figure). Within the `includes` folder, save the jQuery library and create the following four files:

- ▶ `imagecrop.css`
- ▶ `jquery.imagecrop.js` (copy the `jquery.plugin-template.js` file as before to create the basis of this plugin)
- ▶ `recipe-5.css`
- ▶ `recipe-5.js`

Within the web root itself, you need to create the `index.html` and `upload.php` files.

 This recipe will *not* work in IE9 or below as older browsers do not offer support for the `XMLHttpRequest`, `FormData`, and `FileReader` APIs.

How to do it...

Carefully follow each of the following steps and then read the *How it works...* section to get a full understanding of the plugin and its associated code:

1. Add the following HTML code to `index.html` to create a web page with the image upload form:

```
<!DOCTYPE html>
<html>
```

```
<head>
    <title>Chapter 8 :: Recipe 5 - Image Crop Plugin</title>
    <link href="includes/imagecrop.css" rel="stylesheet"
type="text/css" />
    <link href="includes/recipe-5.css" rel="stylesheet"
type="text/css" />
    <script src="includes/jquery.min.js"></script>
    <script src="includes/jquery.imagecrop.js"></script>
    <script src="includes/recipe-5.js"></script>
</head>
<body>
    <div class="container">
        <h3>#1: Select Image</h3>
        <input type="file" id="selectedImage" />
        <h3>#2: Crop Image</h3>
        <div class="image-preview">
            <div class="preview-msg">Select and image to upload</
div>
            <img id="croppable-image" style="display: none;" />
        </div>
        <h3>#3: Upload</h3>
        <div class="progress-bar"><div class="inner"></div></div>
        <div class="actions">
            <button class="upload-button">Upload</button>
        </div>
    </div>
</body>
</html>
```

2. Put the following CSS code into `recipe-5.css` to style the HTML page and form you just created:

```
@import url(http://fonts.googleapis.com/css?family=Source+Sans+P
ro:200,300,400);
body {
    background-color: #F1F1F1;
    font-family: 'Source Sans Pro', sans-serif !important;
}
h1, h2, h3 {
    font-weight: 300;
    margin: 0;
}
.container {
    width: 800px;
    margin: 50px auto auto auto;
    background-color: #FFFFFF;
```

```css
    padding: 20px;
    border: solid 1px #E1E1E1;
}
.container h3 {
    line-height: 40px;
}
.container .image-preview {
    border: solid 1px #E1E1E1;
    width: 800px;
    height: 600px;
    overflow: hidden;
    margin: auto;
    position: relative;
}
.container .image-preview .preview-msg {
    position: absolute;
    top: 0;
    left: 0;
    right: 0;
    bottom: 0;
    background-color: #F1F1F1;
    text-align: center;
    font-size: 22px;
    line-height: 600px;
    font-weight: 300;
    z-index: 1;
}
#croppable-image {
    position: relative;
    z-index: 2;
}
.container .progress-bar {
    height: 30px;
    border: solid 1px #E1E1E1;
}
.container .progress-bar .inner {
    height: 30px;
    width: 0;
    background-color: #54ee86;
}
.container .actions {
    text-align: right;
    margin-top: 10px;
}
```

```
.container .actions .upload-button {
    height: 30px;
    width: 60px;
}
```

3. Add the following jQuery code to `recipe-5.js`, which will allow the user to select and preview an image from their local filesystem and then initiate the image crop plugin:

```
$(function(){
    var _selectedFile;
    $(document).on("change", "#selectedImage", function(){
        var reader = new FileReader();
        var files = $(this).prop("files");
        if (files.length > 0) {
            _selectedFile = files[0];
            reader.onload = function() {
                var image = new Image;
                image.src = this.result;
                if (image.width > 800 || image.height > 600) {
                    alert("Image cannot be larger that 800x600");
                } else {
                    $('.preview-msg').hide();
                    $('#croppable-image').prop("src", this.
result).fadeIn().imagecrop();
                }
            };
            reader.readAsDataURL(_selectedFile);
        }
    });
    $(document).on("click", ".upload-button", function(){
        var _selectedImage = $('#croppable-image');
        if (_selectedImage.data("selection-width") > 0 && _
selectedImage.data("selection-height") > 0) {
            var data = new FormData();
            data.append("image", _selectedFile);
            data.append("selection-width", _selectedImage.
data("selection-width"));
            data.append("selection-height", _selectedImage.
data("selection-height"));
            data.append("selection-left", _selectedImage.
data("selection-x"));
            data.append("selection-top", _selectedImage.
data("selection-y"));
            var xhr = new XMLHttpRequest();
            xhr.open("POST", "/upload.php");
```

```
                    xhr.onprogress = function(event) {
                        var percent = (event.loaded / event.total * 100);
                        $('.progress-bar .inner').width(percent + "%");
                    }
                    xhr.onload = function() {
                        var response = JSON.parse(this.response);
                        if (response.success == false) {
                            alert(response.error);
                        }
                    }
                    xhr.send(data);
                } else {
                    alert("Please crop the image before upload");
                }
            });
        });
```

4. In `jquery.imagecrop.js`, update the plugin name and defaults as shown in the following code snippet:

```
var name = 'imagecrop';
    Plugin.prototype = {
        defaults: {
            minWidth: 100,
            minHeight: 100
        }
    };
```

5. In the plugin constructor created by the plugin template file, add the following declarations directly after `$scope.options` is declared, as shown in the following code snippet:

```
$scope.options = $.extend({}, this.defaults, options);
$scope.imageSelection = {
    start: {
        x: 0,
        y: 0
    },
    end: {
        x: 0,
        y: 0
    },
    top: 0,
    left: 0
};
var _frame;
```

```
var _overlayLayer;
var _selectionLayer;
var _selectionOutline;
```

6. Update the plugin `$scope.init()` function to include the following code:

```
//Has this element already been initialised?
if (typeof $scope.$element.data("selection-x") != "undefined") {
    //Yes, so reuse the DOM elements...
    _frame = $(document).find('.crop-frame').css({
        width: $scope.$element.width(),
        height: $scope.$element.height()
    });
        _overlayLayer = $(document).find('.overlay-layer');
        _selectionLayer = $(document).find('.selection-layer');
        _selectionOutline = $(document).find('.selection-outline');
} else {
    //No, let's initialise then...
    _frame = $("<div class='crop-frame'></div>").css({
        width: $scope.$element.width(),
        height: $scope.$element.height()
    });
    _overlayLayer = $("<div class='overlay-layer'></div>");
    _selectionLayer = $("<div class='selection-layer'></div>");
    _selectionOutline = $("<div class='selection-outline'></div>");
    //Wrap the image with the frame
    $scope.$element.wrap(_frame);
    _overlayLayer.insertAfter($scope.$element);
    _selectionLayer.insertAfter($scope.$element);
    _selectionOutline.insertAfter($scope.$element);
    /** EVENTS **/
    _selectionLayer.on("mousedown", $scope.onSelectionStart);
    _selectionLayer.on("mouseup", $scope.onSelectionEnd);
    _selectionOutline.on("mouseup", $scope.onSelectionEnd);
    _selectionOutline.on("mousedown", $scope.onSelectionMove);
}
$scope.updateElementData();
/** UPDATE THE OUTLINE BACKGROUND **/
_selectionOutline.css({
    'background': 'url(' + $scope.$element.prop("src") + ')',
    'display': 'none'
});
```

7. Directly after the `$scope.init()` function, add the following additional functions:

```
/**
 * MAKING THE SELECTION
 */
$scope.onSelectionStart = function(event) {
    $scope.imageSelection.start = $scope.getMousePosition(event);
    _selectionLayer.bind({
       mousemove: function(event) {
    $scope.imageSelection.end = $scope.getMousePosition(event);
    $scope.drawSelection();
       }
    });
};
$scope.onSelectionEnd = function() {
    _selectionLayer.unbind("mousemove");
    //Hide the element if it doesn't not meet the minimum specified
dimensions
    if (
        $scope.getSelectionDimentions().width < $scope.options.
minWidth || $scope.getSelectionDimentions().height < $scope.
options.minHeight
    ) {
        _selectionOutline.hide();
    }
    _selectionOutline.css({
        'z-index': 1001
    });
};
$scope.drawSelection = function() {
    _selectionOutline.show();
    //The smallest top value and the smallest left value are used
to set the position of the element
    $scope.imageSelection.top = ($scope.imageSelection.end.y <
$scope.imageSelection.start.y) ? $scope.imageSelection.end.y :
$scope.imageSelection.start.y;
    $scope.imageSelection.left = ($scope.imageSelection.end.x <
$scope.imageSelection.start.x) ? $scope.imageSelection.end.x :
$scope.imageSelection.start.x;
_selectionOutline.css({
    position: 'absolute',
    top: $scope.imageSelection.top,
    left: $scope.imageSelection.left,
    width: $scope.getSelectionDimentions().width,
    height: $scope.getSelectionDimentions().height,
```

```
      'background-position': '-' + $scope.imageSelection.left + 'px
-' + $scope.imageSelection.top + 'px'
});
$scope.updateElementData();
};
  /**
* MOVING THE SELECTION
*/
$scope.onSelectionMove = function() {
   //Prevent trigger the selection events
   _selectionOutline.addClass('dragging');
   _selectionOutline.on("mousemove mouseout", function(event){
      if ($(this).hasClass("dragging")) {
         var left = ($scope.getMousePosition(event).x - ($(this).
width() / 2));
         //Don't allow the draggable element to over the parent's
left and right
         if (left < 0) left = 0;
         if ((left + $(this).width()) > _selectionLayer.width())
left = (_selectionLayer.width() - $(this).outerWidth());
         var top = ($scope.getMousePosition(event).y - ($(this).
height() / 2));
         //Don't allow the draggable element to go over the
parent's top and bottom
         if (top < 0) top = 0;
         if ((top + $(this).height()) > _selectionLayer.height())
top = (_selectionLayer.height() - $(this).outerHeight());
         $scope.imageSelection.left = left;
         $scope.imageSelection.top = top;
         //Set new position
         $(this).css({
            top: $scope.imageSelection.top,
            left: $scope.imageSelection.left,
            'background-position': '-' + $scope.imageSelection.left
+ 'px -' + $scope.imageSelection.top + 'px'
         });
      }
   }).on("mouseup", function(){
   $(this).removeClass('dragging');                $scope.
updateElementData();
   });
}
```

8. Insert the following helper functions under the functions you have added:

```
/**
 * HELPER FUNCTIONS
 */
$scope.getMousePosition = function(event) {
    return {
        y: (event.pageY - _selectionLayer.offset().top),
        x: (event.pageX - _selectionLayer.offset().left)
    };
};
$scope.getSelectionDimentions = function() {
    //Work out the width and height based on the start and end
positions
    var width = ($scope.imageSelection.end.x - $scope.
imageSelection.start.x);
    var height = ($scope.imageSelection.end.y - $scope.
imageSelection.start.y);
    //If any negatives turn them into positives
    if (height < 0) height = (height * -1);
    if (width < 0) width = (width * -1);
    return {
        width: width,
        height: height,
        x: $scope.imageSelection.start.x,
        y: $scope.imageSelection.start.y
    };
}
$scope.updateElementData = function() {
    $scope.$element.data({
        "selection-x": $scope.imageSelection.left,
        "selection-y": $scope.imageSelection.top,
        "selection-width": $scope.getSelectionDimentions().width,
        "selection-height": $scope.getSelectionDimentions().height
    });
}
```

9. Add the following CSS code to `imagecrop.css` to add styles to the elements that are created by the image crop plugin:

```
.crop-frame {
    position: relative;
    margin: auto;
}
.selection-layer {
    position: absolute;
```

```
        top: 0;
        left: 0;
        right: 0;
        bottom: 0;
        z-index: 1000;
    }
    .selection-outline {
        border: dotted 1px #000000;
        z-index: 999;
    }
    .selection-outline:hover, .selection-outline:active {
        cursor: move;
    }
    .overlay-layer {
        background-color: rgba(255, 255, 255, 0.60);
        position: absolute;
        top: 0;
        left: 0;
        right: 0;
        bottom: 0;
        z-index: 998;
    }
```

10. Finally, add the following PHP code to `upload.php`, which will take data from the web form you have just created and then crop the image and save it into the uploads directory:

```php
<?php
if (isset($_FILES['image'])) {
    $response = array(
        "success" => false,
        "error" => ""
    );
    //GET SELECTION DATA
    $selectionWidth = (isset($_POST['selection-width'])) ? $_
POST['selection-width'] : 0;
    $selectionHeight = (isset($_POST['selection-height'])) ? $_
POST['selection-height'] : 0;
    $selectionTop = (isset($_POST['selection-top'])) ? $_
POST['selection-top'] : 0;
    $selectionLeft = (isset($_POST['selection-left'])) ? $_
POST['selection-left'] : 0;
    //GET IMAGE DATA
    $fileName = $_FILES['image']['name'];
    $ext = pathinfo($fileName, PATHINFO_EXTENSION);
    if ($selectionWidth > 800 || $selectionHeight > 600) {
```

```
        $response["error"] = "Image cannot be larger than 800 x
    600";
        } else if (!in_array($ext, array("png", "jpg"))) {
            $response["error"] = "Invalid file type";
        } else {
if ($ext == "png") {
$source = imagecreatefrompng($_FILES['image']['tmp_name']);
        } else {
$source = imagecreatefromjpeg($_FILES['image']['tmp_name']);
        }           $dest = imagecreatetruecolor($selectionWidth,
    $selectionHeight);
    imagecopyresampled($dest, $source, 0, 0, $selectionLeft,
    $selectionTop, $selectionWidth, $selectionHeight, $selectionWidth,
    $selectionHeight);
            $path = "/uploads/";
            if (!imagejpeg($dest, getcwd() . $path . $fileName, 100))
    {
                $response["error"] = "Could not save uploaded file";
            } else {
                $response["success"] = true;
            }
        }
        header("Content-Type: application/json; charset=UTF-8");
        echo json_encode($response);
    }
```

11. Navigate to the `index.html` file in your web browser and you will be presented with a simple web form with three steps. By selecting the **Choose File** button and selecting an image from your computer, you will see the image displayed inside the preview box. In the preview box, you will be able to click-and-drag a selection over the image. Once you have done this, clicking on **Upload** will upload the image to the web server (indicated by the progress bar) and the image will be cropped and saved inside the `uploads` folder you created earlier.

How it works...

It is important to understand the different sections of this recipe. The first element of this recipe is the upload form itself, which provides the ability to view the user-selected image within the browser before upload. The second element of this recipe is the image crop plugin itself, which is what we will focus on the most. Finally, to provide the complete solution, there is the upload element of this recipe, which takes data that the image crop plugin has provided and posts it to a PHP script. This PHP script then takes this data to crop and saves the image to the user's specification.

Image selection and preview

The HTML code in `index.html` creates a basic interface with a file input element. When the user clicks on the **Choose File** button, a browse window will open, allowing them to select a file from their computer. Using JavaScript's `FileReader` class, it is possible for us to read this file and display it within the browser. Looking at `recipe-5.js`, you will see a `change` event handler with the code to do this.

At this point within the code, there is a basic validation check to ensure that the selected image is not bigger than 800 x 600 pixels. If it is, an alert is shown to the user and the image is not loaded.

When the image has finally loaded, the source property for the `#cropableImage` element is updated to be the selected image, displaying it on screen. Finally, the image crop plugin is initialized on the image element as follows:

```
$('#croppable-image').prop("src", this.result).fadeIn().imagecrop();
```

Image crop plugin

The image crop plugin dynamically creates a range of elements that act as layers and containers to allow us to let the user make a selection. To make it easier to understand what each of the layers is trying to achieve, they have been illustrated in the following figure:

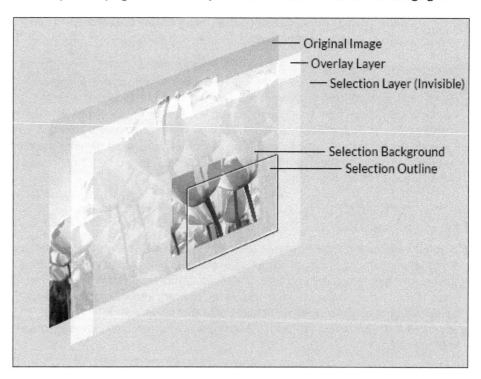

The **Overlay** layer fades out most of the image with a white background and an opacity of 0.6. The **Selection** layer is the layer that listens for mouse events indicating that the user is making a selection. The main reason for this is that if the mouse events were attached to the image itself, we would have difficulty with some browsers that allow you to drag the image away with a visual representation of the image, which would get in the way of our functionality. The **Selection Outline** layer is what is drawn by the plugin as the user is making a selection. Its background is the selected image, except the position is adjusted so it only shows the section of the selected image that has been selected, providing focus over the original image that has the overlay obscuring it.

When the plugin is initialized, there is a set of local variables and defaults declared that the plugin will use throughout its operation; these are shown in the following code snippet:

```
$scope.imageSelection = {
start: {
    x: 0,
    y: 0
},
end: {
    x: 0,
    y: 0
},
top: 0,
left: 0
};
var _frame;
var _overlayLayer;
var _selectionLayer;
var _selectionOutline;
```

The variables prepended with `var` will store the different DOM elements that represent the layers. The `imageSelection` object stores the user's initial click coordinates and then the coordinates when the user finishes making a selection. We can then use these coordinates to calculate the width and position of the selection. The `top` and `left` parameters store the finalized coordinates of the selection once the width and height have been calculated.

Inside the `init()` function of the plugin, there is an initial check to determine if the image has been initialized before. If so, the layer DOM elements have already been created and inserted, as shown in the following code snippet:

```
if (typeof $scope.$element.data("selection-x") != "undefined") {
    // -- HIDDEN CODE
} else {
    // -- HIDDEN CODE
}
```

If the DOM elements are available, the jQuery `find()` function is used to select the elements and store them within the associated variable. If not, they are created and stored. A scenario where the plugin may have already been initialized for the image is when the user decides to change the selected image. The image source changes, but DOM elements can stay in place and be reused with different dimensions.

When the layer elements are first created, a container division element with the `crop-frame` class is created with the same dimensions as the selected image, as shown in the following code snippet:

```
_frame = $("<div class='crop-frame'></div>").css({
    width: $scope.$element.width(),
    height: $scope.$element.height()
});
```

It is very important that the user selection matches the actual image pixel dimensions exactly; otherwise, cropping calculations will be incorrect. The selected image element is then wrapped within this frame using the jQuery `wrap()` function as follows:

```
$scope.$element.wrap(_frame);
_overlayLayer.insertAfter($scope.$element);
_selectionLayer.insertAfter($scope.$element);
_selectionOutline.insertAfter($scope.$element);
```

The other created layers are inserted after the selected image element inside the `crop-frame` division, as shown in the previous code.

The final part of the layer creation attaches various event handler functions that deal will different parts of the selection process:

```
_selectionLayer.on("mousedown", $scope.onSelectionStart);
_selectionLayer.on("mouseup", $scope.onSelectionEnd);
_selectionOutline.on("mouseup", $scope.onSelectionEnd);
_selectionOutline.on("mousedown", $scope.onSelectionMove);
```

Each of the functions specified here are declared later on within the `plugin` class. At the end of the `init()` function, the `updateElementData()` function is called, which sets the initial selection dimensions on the selected image element (for example, `selection-x`) and sets the background image on the Selection Outline layer.

When the user first clicks on the Selection layer, the mouse position is stored as the start coordinates. Then, as the user drags the mouse to make a selection, the new mouse coordinates are stored as end coordinates and the `drawSelection()` function is called. The `drawSelection()` function uses the start and end coordinates to calculate the width and height of the selection and updates the Selection Outline layer's CSS to show this, as follows:

```
$scope.drawSelection = function() {
    _selectionOutline.show();
```

```
    //The smallest top value and the smallest left value are used to
    set the position of the element
    $scope.imageSelection.top = ($scope.imageSelection.end.y < $scope.
    imageSelection.start.y) ? $scope.imageSelection.end.y : $scope.
    imageSelection.start.y;
    $scope.imageSelection.left = ($scope.imageSelection.end.x < $scope.
    imageSelection.start.x) ? $scope.imageSelection.end.x : $scope.
    imageSelection.start.x;
    _selectionOutline.css({
        position: 'absolute',
        top: $scope.imageSelection.top,
        left: $scope.imageSelection.left,
        width: $scope.getSelectionDimentions().width,
        height: $scope.getSelectionDimentions().height,
        'background-position': '-' + $scope.imageSelection.left + 'px -' +
    $scope.imageSelection.top + 'px'
    });
    $scope.updateElementData();
    };
```

As part of this function, the background position of the Selection Outline layer is updated to show the actual selection and the `updateElementData()` function is called to apply the new selection data onto the selected image.

When the user has finished the selection and releases the mouse button, the `onSelectionEnd()` function is called. This function determines whether the selection is smaller than the minimum allowed; if so, the selection is hidden. The mouse move event is unbound from the Selection layer to avoid any conflicts with later functionality, and the Selection Outline layer's `z-index` property is updated so that the Selection Outline layer moves above the Selection layer, allowing for the drag functionality. The drag functionality was covered in detail in the *Creating a basic drag-and-drop functionality* recipe in *Chapter 6, User Interface*. Refer to that recipe for a detailed explanation.

Image upload

In `recipe-5.js`, an event handler is attached to the click event for the **Upload** button. Inside the callback function for this event, it is first determined if a selection has been made by the user. If not, an alert is displayed, asking the user to make a crop selection.

If a valid selection has been made, a new `FormData` object is created to store the data to be uploaded to the PHP script as follows:

```
var data = new FormData();
data.append("image", _selectedFile);
data.append("selection-width", _selectedImage.data("selection-
width"));
```

```
data.append("selection-height", _selectedImage.data("selection-
height"));
data.append("selection-left", _selectedImage.data("selection-x"));
data.append("selection-top", _selectedImage.data("selection-y"));
```

The `_selectedFile` variable contains the reference to the selected file, which is made available within the change event on the file input.

With the required data stored inside the `FormData` object, a new `XMLHttpRequest` object is created to send the data to the PHP upload script as shown in the following code snippet:

```
var xhr = new XMLHttpRequest();
xhr.open("POST", "/upload.php");
xhr.onprogress = function(event) {
    var percent = (event.loaded / event.total * 100);
    $('.progress-bar .inner').width(percent + "%");
}
xhr.onload = function() {
    var response = JSON.parse(this.response);
    if (response.success == false) {
        alert(response.error);
    }
}
xhr.send(data);
```

This code is self-explanatory and simply allows us to POST directly from JavaScript without the need for an HTML form. The `onprogress()` function is called by the XHR request as the image is being uploaded and allows us to update the progress bar on the HTML page to reflect the upload's progress. The `onload()` function is called when the operation has completed, allowing us to display any errors that occurred.

Cropping and saving the image with PHP

The PHP script is relatively simple. It accepts and stores the information provided via the POST request from the JavaScript and does some basic validation on the image width and extension, only allowing JPG and PNG images.

If the image passes validation, either `imagecreatefrompng()` or `imagecreatefromjpeg()` is used to create an image resource in PHP based on the provided image. Then, a blank image is created with the specified crop dimensions as shown in the following line of code:

```
$dest = imagecreatetruecolor($selectionWidth, $selectionHeight);
```

You can think of this blank image as a canvas that PHP will use to paint the modified image on. Then, the provided image is cropped and the new image is stored on the blank canvas using `imagecopyresampled()` as follows:

```
imagecopyresampled($dest, $source, 0, 0, $selectionLeft,
$selectionTop, $selectionWidth, $selectionHeight, $selectionWidth,
$selectionHeight);
```

Finally, the new image is saved to disk in the `uploads` directory that was created at the beginning of this recipe, as follows:

```
imagejpeg($dest, getcwd() . $path . $fileName, 100)
```

You should see the new image when you open the `uploads` directory.

There's more...

This recipe provides a basic complete solution to previewing, cropping, uploading, and saving an image, but there are many improvements that can be made. The validation on both the client and server side could be dramatically improved to allow for additional image types and to check for file size as well as dimensions.

When `FileReader` is reading the local file into the browser, a loader or progress bar could also be added in the same way that the progress bar is implemented for the upload section.

Finally, the drag functionality could be improved so that the selection area's middle does not "snap" to the mouse pointer, since this can be confusing for the user.

See also

▶   The *Creating a basic drag-and-drop functionality* recipe in *Chapter 6, User Interface*

9
jQuery UI

In this chapter, we will cover:

- ▶ Creating stylish and functional buttons
- ▶ Creating dialog boxes for user information and input
- ▶ Implementing progress bars within your application
- ▶ Adding date picker interfaces to input boxes quickly
- ▶ Creating an autocomplete search feature

Introduction

jQuery UI is a user interface library that is built on top of the jQuery JavaScript library. jQuery UI provides many interactive plugins, effects, and interface elements that the developer can use within their interfaces. This chapter will demonstrate jQuery UI's most common elements such as buttons and date pickers and show you how to add them to your website or web application quickly.

Before you start this chapter, ensure that you have visited `http://jqueryui.com/` and downloaded the jQuery UI library. Download the library via the **Download Builder** on their website; make sure all the default options remain selected. The version of jQuery UI that is used in this chapter is v1.10.3, but most recipes will work with newer versions. Their website also provides a wealth of documentation and examples to get you started with jQuery UI.

To start with the recipes in this chapter, create an easily accessible folder named `chapter9` and place the jQuery library inside it. Create a subfolder named `jquery-ui`, and place the `css` and `js` folders from the jQuery UI library inside this subfolder.

Creating stylish and functional buttons

It is relatively easy to create stylish buttons quickly with CSS3, but adding additional functionality often requires more investment in terms of time. jQuery UI provides a button API that can be used to create a wide range of button controls, which can be easily added to UIs and interacted with inside JavaScript code. This recipe shows you how to create common button controls so that you can re-use the code at your convenience.

Getting ready

Inside the `chapter9` folder that was created earlier, create `recipe-1.html` and `recipe-1.js`.

How to do it...

To create a range of different button controls using the jQuery UI library, perform the following steps:

1. Add the following HTML code to `recipe-1.html` in order to add various button elements, ensuring that you update the references to the jQuery and jQuery UI libraries where required:

```
<!DOCTYPE html>
<html>
<head>
    <title>Chapter 9 :: Recipe 1</title>
    <script src="jquery.min.js"></script>
    <script src="jquery-ui/js/jquery-ui-1.10.3.custom.min.js"></script>
    <link type="text/css" rel="stylesheet" href="jquery-ui/css/ui-lightness/jquery-ui-1.10.3.custom.min.css" />
    <script src="recipe-1.js"></script>
</head>
<body>
    <h3>Default buttons: a, button and input</h3>
    <a href="#">Button 1</a>
    <button>Button 2</button>
    <input type="submit" name="button3" value="Button 3" />
    <h3>Button options: Disabled, Custom Label and icons</h3>
    <button class="button4">Button 4: Disabled</button>
    <button class="button5">Button 5</button>
    <button class="button6">Button 6 with icons</button>
    <h3>Button Sets: Radio and Checkbox's</h3>
    <div class="buttonSet1">
```

```
    <button>One</button>
    <button>Two</button>
    <button>Three</button>
</div>
<div class="buttonSet2">
    <input type="checkbox" id="check1" /><label
for="check1">Check 1</label>
    <input type="checkbox" id="check2" /><label
for="check2">Check 2</label>
    <input type="checkbox" id="check3" /><label
for="check3">Check 3</label>
</div>
<h3>Buttons with events</h3>
<button class="enableDisable">Enable/Disable</button>
</body>
</html>
```

2. Add the following jQuery code to `recipe-1.js` in order to apply UI styling and functionality to the button elements:

```
$(function(){
    //Default buttons
    $('a, button, input[type=submit]').button();
    //Button options
    $('#button4').button('option', 'disabled', true);
    $('#button5').button({label: 'Button 5 with custom label'});
    $('#button6').button('option', 'icons', {primary: 'ui-icon-
arrowthick-1-e', secondary: 'ui-icon-circle-arrow-e'});
    //Button sets
    $('.buttonSet1').buttonset();
    $('.buttonSet2').buttonset();
    //Button events
    $('.enableDisable').button().click(function(){
        var _button4 = $('.button4');
        if (_button4.button('option', 'disabled')) {
            _button4.button('option', 'disabled', false);
        } else {
            _button4.button('option', 'disabled', true);
        }
    });
});
```

3. Open `recipe-1.html` in a web browser and you will be presented with various button elements styled with the default jQuery UI theme.

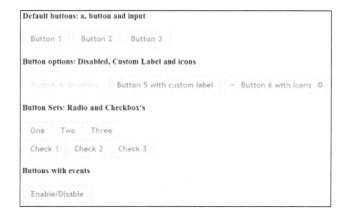

How it works...

HTML provides a range of different button elements that can be used by the jQuery UI button API. By looking at this web page, you will be able to see how the following elements work and re-use the code at your convenience:

▶ Default buttons that include a, `input`, and `button` elements

▶ Default buttons with options such as custom labels, icons, and disabled

▶ Buttons sets that allow for checkbox and radio button functionality

▶ Events on buttons

To initialize the jQuery UI button API, select a button or a set of button elements in the typical jQuery way and use the `button()` function, shown as follows:

```
$('a, button, input[type=submit]').button();
```

This will apply the jQuery UI CSS and additional functionality to the selected buttons. The `button()` function also takes a range of options in order to allow you to individually manipulate the button elements. This is shown in the `Button options` section in `recipe-1.js`.

By grouping buttons within the HTML code and using the `buttonset()` function, you can create a set of buttons that work together to form a checkbox or radio button functionality, shown as follows:

```
<div class="buttonSet1">
    <button>One</button>
    <button>Two</button>
    <button>Three</button>
</div>
```

You can still interact with the HTML button elements using normal jQuery to attach events and perform actions. With this recipe, the button labeled **Enable/Disable** has a click event handler attached, shown as follows:

```
$('.enableDisable').button().click(function(){
    var _button4 = $('.button4');
    if (_button4.button('option', 'disabled')) {
        _button4.button('option', 'disabled', false);
    } else {
        _button4.button('option', 'disabled', true);
    }
});
```

This uses the `button('option')` functionality provided by jQuery UI to check the disabled state of the button and then set it to `true` or `false` based on its current state. With `recipe-1.html` open in a web browser, clicking on this button will visually enable and disable the button labeled **Button 4**. Note that in the above example, the `click()` function can be chained after the `button()` function for convenience.

There's more...

There are more button types available as part of the jQuery UI library. Head over to the documentation provided on their website (`http://jqueryui.com/button/`) for simple examples and more detail.

See also

 ▶ *Creating dialog boxes for user information and input*

Creating dialog boxes for user information and input

In *Chapter 6, User Interface*, you were shown how to create your own modal pop ups. jQuery UI provides an easy-to-use API that helps you to quickly add modals or dialogs to your application. This recipe will look at the default behavior of jQuery UI's dialogs and show you how to use them. Once again, this recipe is designed so that you can easily find the code you need and re-use it at your convenience.

Getting ready

In the `chapter9` folder, create `recipe-2.html` and `recipe-2.js` and have them open and ready for editing.

How to do it...

To understand how to quickly add dialogs or modals to your application, perform the following steps:

1. Add the following HTML to `recipe-2.html` in order to create the button and dialog elements for use within the JavaScript code:

```html
<!DOCTYPE html>
<html>
<head>
    <title>Chapter 9 :: Recipe 2</title>
    <script src="jquery.min.js"></script>
    <script src="jquery-ui/js/jquery-ui-1.10.3.custom.min.js"></script>
    <link type="text/css" rel="stylesheet" href="jquery-ui/css/ui-lightness/jquery-ui-1.10.3.custom.min.css" />
    <script src="recipe-2.js"></script>
</head>
<body>
<div class="actions">
    <button id="openSecondDialog">Open Second Dialog with Animation</button>
    <button id="openModalDialog">Open Modal Dialog</button>
    <button id="openConfirmationDialog">Open Confirmation Dialog</button>
</div>
<div id="default-dialog" title="Default Dialog">
    <p>This is a dialog with default behaviour.</p>
</div>
<div id="second-dialog" title="Second Dialog">
    <p>This is a dialog with animation that is opened by a button.</p>
</div>
<div id="modal-dialog" title="Modal Dialog">
    <p>This is a modal dialog.</p>
</div>
<div id="confirmation-dialog" title="Confirmation Dialog">
    <p>Are you sure you want to close this dialog?</p>
</div>
</body>
</html>
```

2. Add the following JavaScript code to `recipe-2.js` in order to initialize the dialog elements and buttons that open them:

```
$(function(){
    //Set up the dialog elements
    $('#default-dialog').dialog();
    $('#second-dialog').dialog({
        autoOpen: false,
        show: {
            effect: "fade",
            duration: 500
        },
        hide: {
            effect: "explode",
            duration: 1000
        }
    });
    $('#modal-dialog').dialog({
        autoOpen: false,
        modal: true
    });
    $('#confirmation-dialog').dialog({
        autoOpen: false,
        resizable: false,
        buttons: {
            "Yes": function() {
                $(this).dialog("close");
            },
            "No": function() {
                alert("Your dialog will stay open.");
            }
        }
    });
    //Set up button elements
    $('.actions').buttonset();
    $('#openSecondDialog').click(function(){
        $('#second-dialog').dialog("open");
    });
    $('#openModalDialog').click(function(){
        $('#modal-dialog').dialog("open");
    });
    $('#openConfirmationDialog').click(function(){
        $('#confirmation-dialog').dialog("open");
    });
});
```

3. Open `recipe-2.html` in a web browser and you will be presented with the default dialog already open. Use the buttons within the button set to open a variety of other dialog types.

How it works...

As with the previous recipe, the HTML code creates the elements that the jQuery UI library will use to apply the required functionality and styling. There are four dialog elements in the page and three buttons that open the additional dialogs.

The JavaScript code initializes each of the dialog elements, in turn providing different options and settings. The first dialog element, `#default-dialog`, is initialized with no options by simply using the following jQuery UI code:

```
$('#default-dialog').dialog();
```

This will turn the `#default-dialog` HTML element into a jQuery UI dialog and display it on the screen.

The second dialog is initialized with the `autoOpen` option set to `false`, so it will not be automatically opened when the user first visits the page. To open this dialog, the user must click on the button labeled **Open Second Dialog with Animation**. The second dialog has some animation options provided, shown as follows:

```
$('#second-dialog').dialog({
    autoOpen: false,
    show: {
    effect: "fade",
    duration: 500
},
hide: {
    effect: "explode",
     duration: 1000
    }
});
```

This will ensure that the fade animation is used when the dialog is opened and the explode animation is used when the dialog is closed. Read the jQuery UI dialog documentation (`http://api.jqueryui.com/dialog/`) to discover the available animations that you can use.

The third dialog is a modal dialog. By simply adding the `modal: true` option to the `dialog()` function when the modal is opened, a backdrop that obscures the view from the rest of the page is added.

The fourth dialog in this recipe is a confirmation dialog. Using the buttons option, you can specify a number of buttons and callback to hold the button actions, shown as follows:

```
$('#confirmation-dialog').dialog({
    autoOpen: false,
    resizable: false,
    buttons: {
    "Yes": function() {
        $(this).dialog("close");
    },
    "No": function() {
        alert("Your dialog will stay open.");
        }
    }
});
```

The resize option is also set to `false` to override the default behavior of allowing the user to be able to change the size of the dialog.

There's more...

By reading the documentation (`http://api.jqueryui.com/dialog/`), you will find more dialog types at your disposal. The form dialog is particularly useful to quickly retrieve user input with built-in validation functions.

See also

▶ *Creating stylish and functional buttons*

Implementing progress bars within your application

Progress bars allow users to have detailed information regarding a process that your application is performing. Progress bars are the ideal solution to update the user on the progress of a task that they have requested, which could take a long time to complete. This action could be a file upload or some other lengthy server-side process. This recipe will show you how to use the jQuery UI progress bar API to easily add progress bars to your application.

Getting ready

Create `recipe-3.html`, `recipe-3.js`, and `recipe-3.css` in the `chapter9` folder you created earlier.

How to do it...

To learn how to add a progress bar into your application quickly, perform the following steps:

1. Add the following HTML code to `recipe-3.html` in order to create a web page with the required progress bar HTML elements:

```html
<!DOCTYPE html>
<html>
<head>
    <title>Chapter 9 :: Recipe 3</title>
    <script src="jquery.min.js"></script>
    <script src="jquery-ui/js/jquery-ui-1.10.3.custom.min.js"></script>
    <link type="text/css" rel="stylesheet" href="jquery-ui/css/ui-lightness/jquery-ui-1.10.3.custom.min.css" />
    <link type="text/css" rel="stylesheet" href="recipe-3.css" />
    <script src="recipe-3.js"></script>
</head>
<body>
<div class="progress-bar"><div class="progress-label">Press "Start Progress" to begin load...</div></div>
<button class="start-progress">Start Progress</button>
</body>
</html>
```

2. Add the following CSS code to `recipe-3.css` in order to provide some basic styles to the progress bar label:

```css
.progress-bar {
    position: relative;
}
.progress-label {
    position: absolute;
    left: 0;
    top: 0;
    right: 0;
    bottom: 0;
    text-align: center;
    line-height: 35px;
}
```

3. Add the following JavaScript code to `recipe-3.js` to initialize the progress bar and provide functionality to the start progress button:

```javascript
$(function(){
    var progressBar = $('.progress-bar');
```

```
        var progressLabel = $('.progress-label');
        progressBar.progressbar({
            change: function() {
                progressLabel.text(progressBar.progressbar("value") + "%
                    complete...");
            },
            complete: function() {
                progressLabel.text("Completed!");
            }
        });
        $('.start-progress').button().click(doStuff);
        function doStuff() {
            var progressValue =
                ((progressBar.progressbar("value") || 0) + 1);
            progressBar.progressbar("value", progressValue);
            if (progressValue < 100) {
                setTimeout(doStuff, 100);
            }
        }
    }
});
```

4. Open `recipe-3.html` in a web browser and click on the **Start Progress** button. The progress bar will jump to life and begin to show you the progress until it has reached 100 percent.

How it works...

The HTML page creates two elements that jQuery UI will use to create the progress bar and the label:

```
<div class="progress-bar"><div class="progress-label">Press "Start
    Progress" to being load...</div></div>
```

The default label text is added into the label element, which will be displayed when the user first visits the web page. A **Start Progress** button has also been added to the web page so that the user can initiate the load action.

The load action in this recipe is simply a fake process. You could easily reuse this code in conjunction with an `XmlHttpRequest` for image uploads, such as the code that was used in the *Coding an image cropper plugin from scratch* recipe in *Chapter 8, Understanding Plugin Development*.

To initialize the progress bar in the `progress-bar` element that was added to the HTML page, the `progressbar()` function is used:

```
progressBar.progressbar({
    change: function() {
    progressLabel.text(progressBar.progressbar("value") + "%
        complete...");
    },
    complete: function() {
        progressLabel.text("Completed!");
    }
});
```

An object with two properties is provided to this function to set up the change and complete the event callback functions. This allows us to perform actions when the progress value has changed and when the progress has been completed. In this recipe, we simply update the progress label to inform the user of the complete percent value. Ensure that you read the documentation (`http://jqueryui.com/progressbar/`) so that you are aware of all the options available.

By using `progressBar.progressbar("value")`, it is possible to retrieve the progress value from the progress bar element. This value can then be used to update the progress label text.

The `doStuff()` function, which is called when the user clicks on the **Start Progress** button, acts as the progress. It uses `setTimeout()` to recall itself every 100 milliseconds and then increments the progress bar value as follows:

```
var progressValue = ((progressBar.progressbar("value") || 0) + 1);
progressBar.progressbar("value", progressValue);
```

See also

▶ The *Coding an image cropper plugin from scratch* recipe in *Chapter 8, Understanding Plugin Development*

Adding date picker interfaces to input boxes quickly

Date pickers provide the user with an easy-to-use interface to allow them to quickly select the date they require. jQuery UI provides a date picker that can be quickly added to input fields. The date picker provides many configuration options such as date formatting and restrictions, making it easier for the developer to limit the user's input accordingly. This recipe will show you how to add the date picker to two input fields, change the date format of the date pickers, and also apply date limits to each of the fields.

Getting ready

As with the previous recipe, create `recipe-4.html`, `recipe-4.js`, and `recipe-4.css` within the `chapter9` folder you created earlier.

How to do it...

Perform each of the following steps to create a simple interface with two date pickers and configuration options:

1. Insert the following HTML code into `recipe-4.html` to create the basic web page and UI with date picker elements:

```
<!DOCTYPE html>
<html>
<head>
    <title>Chapter 9 :: Recipe 4</title>
    <script src="jquery.min.js"></script>
    <script src="jquery-ui/js/jquery-ui-1.10.3.custom.min.js"></script>
    <link type="text/css" rel="stylesheet" href="jquery-ui/css/ui-lightness/jquery-ui-1.10.3.custom.min.css" />
    <link type="text/css" rel="stylesheet" href="recipe-4.css" />
    <script src="recipe-4.js"></script>
</head>
<body>
    <div class="frame">
        <div class="settings">
            <label>Restrict:</label>
            <select class="restrict">
                <option value="1">1 Year</option>
                <option value="2">2 Years</option>
                <option value="3">3 Years</option>
            </select>
```

```
            <label>Format:</label>
            <select class="formatDate">
                <option value="dd/mm/yy">English Format</option>
                <option value="mm/dd/yy">American Format</option>
            </select>
        </div>
        <div class="datepickers">
            Start: <input type="text" class="start" />
            End: <input type="text" class="end" />
        </div>
    </div>
</body>
</html>
```

2. Add the following CSS to `recipe-4.css` in order to provide a basic style and positioning to the UI:

```css
.frame {
    width: 500px;
    margin: 100px auto auto auto;
    background-color: #494949;
    border-radius: 5px;
    box-shadow: 5px 5px 5px #CCC;
}
.frame .settings {
    line-height: 40px;
    text-align: center;
    background-color: #333;
    color: #FFF;
    border-top-left-radius: 5px;
    border-top-right-radius: 5px;
}
.frame .datepickers {
    line-height: 100px;
    text-align: center;
    color: #CCC;
}
```

3. Add the following jQuery code to `recipe-4.js` in order to set up the date picker elements and provide functionality to the additional elements within `recipe-4.html`:

```javascript
$(function(){
    var _start = $('.start');
    var _end = $('.end');
    var _restrict = $('.restrict');
```

```
    var _formatDate = $('.formatDate');
    var _dateFormat = 'dd/mm/yy';
    _start.datepicker({
        dateFormat: _dateFormat,
        minDate: new Date(),
        onClose: function(selectedDate) {
            _end.datepicker("option", "minDate", selectedDate);
            restrictDates();
        }
    });
    _end.datepicker({
        dateFormat: _dateFormat,
        onClose: function(selectedDate) {
            _start.datepicker("option", "maxDate", selectedDate);
        }
    });
    _formatDate.change(function(){
        _dateFormat = _formatDate.val();
        _start.datepicker("option", "dateFormat", _dateFormat);
        _end.datepicker("option", "dateFormat", _dateFormat);
    });
    _restrict.change(function(){
        restrictDates();
    });
    function restrictDates() {
        var maxDate = _start.datepicker("getDate");
        if (maxDate != null) {
        maxDate.setFullYear(maxDate.getFullYear() + parseInt(_
restrict.val()));
        _end.datepicker("option", "maxDate", maxDate);
    }
    }
});
```

4. Open `recipe-4.html` within a web browser and you will be presented with a simple interface with two inputs and two drop-down menus. The two inputs labeled `start` and `end` will provide you with a date picker interface when you click inside the input fields. You can then use the date picker to select a date to be inserted in the associated input. By using the two dropdowns, you can change the behavior of the dates and the date pickers. The format options will change the date format to either English or American. The restriction dropdown will allow you to select the maximum number of years that the end date picker will allow the user to select past the selected start date.

How it works...

HTML and CSS provides us with a simple interface that can be used with jQuery UI to demonstrate some of the date picker capabilities. At the top of `recipe-4.js`, there are some variables holding references to the different HTML elements that will be used by jQuery and a variable holding the English date format.

To add a date picker to an input element, the jQuery UI `datepicker()` function is used with the required options:

```
_start.datepicker({
    dateFormat: _dateFormat,
    minDate: new Date(),
    onClose: function(selectedDate) {
        _end.datepicker("option", "minDate", selectedDate);
        restrictDates();
    }
});
```

The `dateFormat` option sets the format for the selected date picker. The `minDate` option sets the minimum date that the date picker will allow the user to select; `new Date()` is used to set this restriction to the current date. The function specified for `onClose` will be executed when the date picker has been closed. Within this function, the `minDate` option is set for the end input. This will ensure that the user will not be able to choose an end date that is before the selected start date. The `restrictDates()` function is also being called from here. The `restrictDates()` function is defined as follows:

```
function restrictDates() {
    var maxDate = _start.datepicker("getDate");
    if (maxDate != null) {
        maxDate.setFullYear(maxDate.getFullYear() +
            parseInt(_restrict.val()));
        _end.datepicker("option", "maxDate", maxDate);
    }
}
```

This function applies a restriction to the end date picker so that the user cannot select an end date which is *n* years greater than the selected start date. Here, *n* is the value specified by the **Restrict** drop-down menu. Just as `minDate` is set, the `maxDate` is set using the selected start date plus the amount of specified years. This function is also called using the `change()` function when the user changes the drop-down selection.

When the user chooses to change the date format, the following code is used to update the format for each of the date picker elements:

```
_formatDate.change(function(){
    _dateFormat = _formatDate.val();
    _start.datepicker("option", "dateFormat", _dateFormat);
    _end.datepicker("option", "dateFormat", _dateFormat);
});
```

There are many options available as part of the date picker API. Read the documentation (`http://api.jqueryui.com/datepicker/`) to learn what other options are available.

Creating an autocomplete search feature

This recipe will show you how to suggest search terms to a user as they are typing into a search input. This is a very popular feature and can be very helpful to the user as it provides them with some insight into what search results will be available before they have even made the search. jQuery UI provides the autocomplete functionality that can be quickly added to any input element.

Getting ready

Create `recipe-5.html`, `recipe-5.js`, and `recipe-5.css` in the `chapter9` folder, where you have saved the other recipe files.

This recipe utilizes a quality API provided by Trakt.tv (`http://trakt.tv/api-docs/`). You will need to register (for free) and obtain an API key before you can begin this recipe. Once you have registered, you can find your API key on the following page: `http://trakt.tv/api-docs/authentication`.

At the point of writing this recipe, there is a known bug within Google Chrome, where if you are trying to call an external source using AJAX in jQuery from your local machine (that is, accessing `recipe-5.html` using `file://` instead of `http(s)://`), you may receive an `Access-Control-Allow-Origin` error. If you do experience this problem, either serve your recipe files through a web server or use an alternate browser.

To demonstrate how the autocomplete feature can be used in a real-world situation, this recipe will use the API specified above to create a related TV show search. It will allow the user to search for a TV show (with suggestions from autocomplete), and once the user has selected one, shows related to the selected one will be displayed.

How to do it...

To add the autosearch feature, perform the following instructions:

1. Add the following HTML code to `recipe-5.html` in order to create the basic web page:

```
<!DOCTYPE html>
<html>
<head>
    <title>Chapter 9 :: Recipe 5</title>
    <script src="jquery.min.js"></script>
    <script src="jquery-ui/js/jquery-ui-1.10.3.custom.min.js"></script>
    <link type="text/css" rel="stylesheet" href="jquery-ui/css/ui-lightness/jquery-ui-1.10.3.custom.min.css" />
    <link type="text/css" rel="stylesheet" href="recipe-5.css" />
    <script src="recipe-5.js"></script>
</head>
<body>
<div class="frame">
    <h1>RELATED <span>TV</span> SHOWS</h1>
    <div class="head">
        <p>Find TV shows related to your favorites.</p>
        <div class="search-input-frame">
            <input type="text" id="searchInput"
                placeholder="Search for a TV show..." />
    </div>
    </div>
    <div class="results">
        <div class="searching">Searching for related
            shows...</div>
        <ul id="results-list"></ul>
    </div>
</div>
</body>
</html>
```

2. Place the following CSS in `recipe-5.css` to turn the HTML code into an attractive looking web page:

```
@import url(http://fonts.googleapis.com/
css?family=Roboto:400,300,100);
body {
    background-color: #333;
    font-family: 'Roboto', sans-serif;
```

```
   }
   .frame {
      width: 800px;
      background-color: #FFF;
      margin: 100px auto auto auto;
      padding: 20px;
      border-radius: 5px;
   }
   .frame h1 {
      margin: -93px 0 0 0;
      color: #FFF;
      font-size: 70px;
      text-align: center;
   }
   .frame h1 span {
      color: #00B5B5;
   }
   .search-input-frame #searchInput {
      width: 780px;
      border: none;
      font-weight: bold;
      color: #999;
      background: #373737;
      font-size: 14px;
      height: 40px;
      padding: 0 0 0 10px;
      margin: 0;
      border-radius: 5px;
      line-height: 40px;
   }
   .frame .head p {
      font-style: italic;
      text-align: center;
   }
   .frame .results ul {
      list-style: none;
      margin: 10px 0 0 5px;
      padding: 0;
   }
   .frame .results ul li {
      line-height: 30px;
      font-size: 18px;
   }
   .frame .results .searching {
```

```
        display: none;
        text-align: center;
        font-style: italic;
        font-size: 18px;
        line-height: 100px;
    }
    .frame .results ul li.no-results {
        line-height: 100px;
        text-align: center;
        font-size: 16px;
        font-weight: bold;
    }
```

3. Add the following jQuery to `recipe-5.js` in order to initialize the autocomplete functionality on the search input element:

```
$(function(){
    $('#searchInput').autocomplete({
        minLength: 2,
        source: function(input, response) {
        },
        select: function (event, ui) {
        }
    });
});
```

4. Within the source function you have just added, insert the following code to make a call to the Trakt.tv API based on the user's input to provide the autocomplete functionality with data to display. Ensure that you replace [API KEY HERE] with your Trakt.tv API key, as shown in the following code:

```
$.ajax({
type: 'GET',
url: 'http://api.trakt.tv/search/shows.json/[API KEY HERE]?query='
+ input.term + "&limit=10",
dataType: 'jsonp',
success: function(data) {
    var results = [];
for (var i = 0; i < data.length; i++) {
results.push({
id: data[i].tvdb_id,
label: data[i].title,
value: data[i].title
    });
    }
```

```
        response(results);
    }
});
```

5. To populate the main results list based on the user's autocomplete section, add
    the following jQuery code to the select function you have just added. Once again,
    remember to replace [API KEY HERE] with your API key:

```
var showId = ui.item.id;
var _searchingMsg = $('.searching');
var _resultList = $('#results-list');
_resultList.empty();
_searchingMsg.fadeIn();
$.ajax({
type: 'GET',
    url: 'http://api.trakt.tv/show/related.json/[API KEY HERE]/' +
showId,
    dataType: 'jsonp',
success: function(data) {
_searchingMsg.hide();
for (var i = 0; i < data.length; i++) {
    resultList.append("<li><a target='_blank' href='" +
        data[i].url + "'>" + data[i].title + "</a></li>");
}
}
});
```

6. Open recipe-5.html in a web browser and search for your favorite TV show:

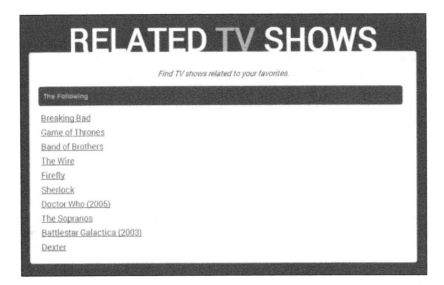

How it works...

The jQuery UI autocomplete function wraps up all the complexity so that the developer only needs to think about providing it with the data and the action after selection, if any.

The HTML page in this recipe creates a web page that provides an input the user can search within. This input is then selected within the jQuery code, and the `autocomplete()` function is used to initialize the autocomplete functionality on the selected element, shown as follows:

```
$('#searchInput').autocomplete({
    minLength: 2,
    source: function(input, response) {

    },
    select: function (event, ui) {

    }
});
```

The `source` property on the object provided to the `autocomplete()` function is the data that is used in the dropdown displayed to the user. The `source` property can either be an array, string, or function. When `source` is a string, it expects the value to be a resource URL providing the data in the expected format. Because we are using an external API that will not provide the data in the expected format, we use the third option and do some additional processing within the function. The `minLength` property allows us to control how many characters the user must input before the autocomplete functionality kicks into action.

First, the data needs to be retrieved from Trackt.tv. To do this, the familiar jQuery `$.ajax()` function is used:

```
$.ajax({
    type: 'GET',
    url: 'http://api.trakt.tv/search/shows.json/[API KEY
        HERE]?query=' + input.term + "&limit=10",
    dataType: 'jsonp',
    success: function(data) {

    }
});
```

The `source()` function takes two arguments: `input` (object) and `response` (function). Using `input.term`, we can get the value that the user entered into the search input text box and insert it into the API URL to search for TV shows. The limit query string variable is set to `10` so that only 10 results will be returned.

Note that on both the AJAX requests within this recipe, the `dataType` attribute has been set to `jsonp`. This is to prevent any cross-domain issues when working with the API. Read more about jQuery's JSONP at `http://www.jquery4u.com/json/jsonp-examples/`.

If the request is successful, we can loop through all the results and create an array in the format that the autocomplete functionality expects, shown as follows:

```
var results = [];
for (var i = 0; i < data.length; i++) {
    results.push({
        id: data[i].tvdb_id,
        label: data[i].title,
        value: data[i].title
    });
}
response(results);
```

The `response()` function is called, which was the second argument to the `source()` function; this will send the results to the autocomplete feature for display.

The next piece of functionality in these recipes occurs when the user selects an option from the autocomplete suggest list. The `select` property on the object provided to the `autocomplete()` function takes a callback function that is executed when the user makes a selection. Using the `ui` argument, it is then possible to retrieve data from the object that represents the user's selection. In this case, we require the ID so that we can pass it back to the Trackt.tv API and retrieve a list of related TV shows:

```
var showId = ui.item.id;
```

This variable is used as a part of another `$.ajax()` request. On the success of this request, the results are looped through and a list item is inserted into the result list for each of the related TV shows. A link to a Trakt.tv web page with more information about each of the shows is also added, shown as follows:

```
for (var i = 0; i < data.length; i++) {
    resultList.append("<li><a target='_blank' href='" + data[i].url
    + "'>" + data[i].title + "</a></li>");
}
```

See also

▶ The *Creating an autosuggest feature* recipe in *Chapter 3, Loading and Manipulating Dynamic Content with AJAX and JSON*

10
Working with jQuery Mobile

In this chapter, we will cover the following topics:

- ▶ Creating a basic mobile website template
- ▶ Building a complete static website
- ▶ Building a dynamic mobile website
- ▶ Implementing the quick call functionality
- ▶ Implementing the send SMS functionality
- ▶ Adding mobile-friendly lists
- ▶ Using touch-oriented events
- ▶ Creating mobile-compatible forms
- ▶ Building a complete registration and login system
- ▶ Building a complete mobile web app

Introduction

jQuery Mobile is a beautifully crafted framework built to make it easier to create mobile-friendly websites and applications. jQuery Mobile incorporates themeable UI elements tailored for the mobile experience and provides custom events targeting special events on touch screen devices.

This chapter provides an introduction to jQuery Mobile and insights into its capabilities. In this chapter, you will learn how to create a basic mobile website that utilizes common elements such as buttons and lists. You will then go on to learn about some of the mobile-specific features such as **Touch to Call**.

Before you start this chapter, ensure you have downloaded the latest release of the jQuery Mobile framework from the jQuery website (http://jquerymobile.com/download). Create a folder named chapter10 where you will save all your recipe files for this chapter. Within this folder, create a folder named jquery-mobile and place the main jQuery Mobile JavaScript and CSS files in it, including the images folder, which will hold all the icon sprites referenced in the CSS.

The version of jQuery Mobile used within this chapter is 1.3.2, but most recipes will work with newer releases.

For some recipes in this chapter, you will require a web server running PHP and MySQL. This web server could be either a local development server or one hosted within the cloud. You will also need access to a MySQL admin interface such as PHPMyAdmin so you can run SQL scripts.

Creating a basic mobile website template

This recipe will show you what the basic layout for a simple jQuery Mobile web page looks like. You will also be able to use this HTML page as a template for future jQuery mobile projects.

Getting ready

Within the chapter10 folder that you created earlier, create recipe-1.html.

How to do it...

Insert the following HTML code into recipe-1.html to create a very basic jQuery Mobile single page website:

```
<!DOCTYPE html>
<html>
<head>
    <title>Chapter 10 :: jQuery Mobile Template</title>
    <meta name="viewport" content="width=device-width, initial-
scale=1" />
    <link rel="stylesheet" href="jquery-mobile/jquery.mobile.min.css"
/>
    <script src="jquery.min.js"></script>
    <script src="jquery-mobile/jquery.mobile.min.js"></script>
</head>
<body>
<div data-role="page">
    <header data-role="header">
```

```
            <h1>Chapter 10 :: Recipe 1 :: jQuery Mobile Webpage Template</
    h1>
        </header>
        <div data-role="content">
            <p>This is where your page content will go.</p>
        </div>
        <footer data-role="footer">
            <h4>Look how easy it is to add a styled footer</h4>
        </footer>
    </div>
    </body>
    </html>
```

Ensure you update references to the jQuery libraries and CSS to reflect your downloaded files. Open `recipe-1.html` in a web browser and you will see how quickly you can create a basic mobile-friendly web page with jQuery Mobile.

How it works...

At first glance, the template page doesn't look much different from a typical HTML web page. The HTML5 standardized document type is declared with `<!DOCTYPE html>` and the required CSS and JavaScript are included within the head of the document.

What does differ is the viewport's `meta` tag, which is not always present in typical HTML pages. This tells the browser how it should set the page dimensions and zoom level. If these are not set, most mobile devices will use a virtual width, making the web page look zoomed out.

> The `data-` attribute is a new HTML5 implementation, allowing for custom element attributes while still providing valid markup. These `data-*` attributes allow you to store arbitrary information about a particular element, and jQuery Mobile utilizes this ability.

With jQuery Mobile, you use the `data-role` attribute to indicate the purpose of elements. In the simple template we created in this recipe, we used the page, header, content, and footer roles to create the structure for a simple page. Each of these roles are self-explanatory, but they will also become clearer throughout this chapter.

There's more...

As with all jQuery implementations, there is a wealth of documentation available (`http://jquerymobile.com`) that all developers should utilize. To get the most out of jQuery Mobile, ensure you read the documentation.

See also

 ▶ *Building a complete static website*

Building a complete static website

This recipe will show you how to quickly create a simple static website using jQuery Mobile. Using the template created in the previous recipe, it only takes adding additional elements with the correct roles to create extra pages and the navigation between them.

Getting ready

Create `recipe-2.html` in the `chapter10` folder you created earlier and ensure you have your newly created jQuery Mobile template ready.

How to do it...

To create a functional mobile website using jQuery Mobile, perform the following steps:

1. Copy the jQuery Mobile template you created earlier into `recipe-2.html` and remove everything within the `<body>` tags as shown in the following code snippet:

```
<!DOCTYPE html>
<html>
<head>
    <title>Chapter 10 :: jQuery Mobile Template</title>
    <meta name="viewport" content="width=device-width, initial-scale=1" />
    <link rel="stylesheet" href="jquery-mobile/jquery.mobile.min.css" />
    <script src="jquery.min.js"></script>
    <script src="jquery-mobile/jquery.mobile.min.js"></script>
</head>
<body>

</body>
</html>
```

2. Insert the following code in between the `<body>` tags to create the home page for the simple static website:

```
<div data-role="page" id="home">
    <header data-role="header">
        <h1>Home Page</h1>
    </header>
```

```
    <div data-role="content">
        <p>This is the content for the home page. You can choose
to go to another page using the buttons below.</p>
        <a href="#about" data-role="button" data-theme="a">About</
a>
        <a href="#contact" data-role="button" data-
theme="a">Contact</a>
    </div>
    <footer data-role="footer">
        <h4>Chapter 10 :: Recipe 2</h4>
    </footer>
</div>
```

3. To create an about page that is linked to the home page, add the following code after the home page declaration but still within the `<body>` tags:

```
<div data-role="page" id="about" data-title="About Page">
    <header data-role="header">
        <h1><a href="#home" data-role="button" data-theme="b"
data-icon="arrow-l" data-inline="true">Back</a> About Page</h1>
    </header>
    <div data-role="content">
        <p>This is the content for the about page.</p>
    </div>
    <footer data-role="footer">
        <h4>Chapter 10 :: Recipe 2</h4>
    </footer>
</div>
```

4. Repeat the previous step with the following code to add the final contact page:

```
<div data-role="page" id="about" data-title="About Page">
    <header data-role="header">
        <h1><a href="#home" data-role="button" data-theme="b"
data-icon="arrow-l" data-inline="true">Back</a> About Page</h1>
    </header>
    <div data-role="content">
        <p>This is the content for the about page.</p>
    </div>
    <footer data-role="footer">
        <h4>Chapter 10 :: Recipe 2</h4>
    </footer>
</div>
```

5. Open `recipe-2.html` in a web browser and you will be presented with the mobile website, and you will be able to use the buttons on the home page to navigate to and from the about and contact pages.

How it works...

In this recipe's code, you will see the data-role attribute used many times to indicate the function of many of the HTML elements. To declare multiple pages, you simply re-use the basic page structure that was used within the template and change the contents as required. Consider the following example:

```
<div data-role="page" id="about" data-title="About Page">
    <header data-role="header">

    </header>
    <div data-role="content">

    </div>
    <footer data-role="footer">

    </footer>
</div>
```

This is the basic structure for the about page used within this recipe. The main div element is indicated as a page using data-role="page". To allow for navigation to this page, a unique ID is defined as about in the same way you would any HTML element (id="about"). There is the additional attribute of data-title on the page division that makes it possible to overwrite the content of the <title> tag in the document head so that the page title can be changed on a per-page basis.

You can use an anchor element to create an internal link to one of the pages created in this way, as shown in the following line of code:

```
<a href="#about" data-role="button" data-theme="a">About</a>
```

When users click on the link, they will be presented with the page that has the unique ID about, indicated within the href attribute as #about. The default page transition will also be used to provide a smooth navigation effect. The data-role="button" attribute is used to style the element into a button and the data-theme="a" attribute specifies which theme to use for styling. Read the mentioned documentation to see what themes are available by default and also how to create your own.

See also

- ▸ *Creating a basic mobile website template*
- ▸ *Building a dynamic mobile website*

Building a dynamic mobile website

In the previous recipe, we created a basic website that would allow you to provide content to a user and update it manually relatively easy. In most situations, this would not be enough. Most websites today rely on some form of database to provide them with rich, new content on a regular basis, and it should be no different with mobile websites. This recipe will show you how to use PHP with jQuery Mobile to create dynamic pages with content served from a web server.

Getting ready

You are going to need to create the following directory structure in the web root of your web server. In the following figure, www is the web root; this may be different for you:

```
▼ www
    ▼ includes
        ▼ jquery-mobile
            ▼ images
                ajax-loader.gif
                icons-18-black.png
                icons-18-white.png
                icons-36-black.png
                icons-36-white.png
            jquery.mobile.min.css
            jquery.mobile.min.js
        jquery.min.js
        script.js
    categories.php
    index.html
```

In the web root of your web server (www), create an `includes` folder and the files `index.html` and `categories.php`. Within the `includes` folder, create a subfolder named `jquery-mobile` and ensure all the jQuery Mobile library files have been copied into it. Also, within the `includes` folder, create `script.js` and add the jQuery library (`jquery.min.js`).

How to do it...

To create a dynamic mobile website using PHP, carefully perform the following steps:

1. Re-using the structure that was created as part of the template in the first recipe, add the following code to `index.html`. This will create a home page and an additional blank page with the ID of `categorypage`.

    ```
    <!DOCTYPE html>
    <html>
    ```

```
<head>
    <title>Chapter 10 :: Recipe 3</title>
    <meta name="viewport" content="width=device-width, initial-
scale=1" />
    <link rel="stylesheet" href="includes/jquery-mobile/jquery.
mobile.min.css" />
    <script src="includes/jquery.min.js"></script>
    <script src="includes/jquery-mobile/jquery.mobile.min.js"></
script>
    <script src="includes/script.js"></script>
</head>
<body>
<div id="home" data-role="page">
    <header data-role="header"><h1>Dynamic page creation demo</
h1></header>
    <div data-role="content">
        <h2>Select a category:</h2>
        <a href="#categorypage?cat=colours" data-
role="button">Colours</a>
        <a href="#categorypage?cat=shapes" data-
role="button">Shapes</a>
        <a href="#categorypage?cat=sounds" data-
role="button">Sounds</a>
    </div>
</div>
<div id="categorypage" data-role="page">
    <div data-role="header"><h1></h1></div>
    <div data-role="content"></div>
</div>
</body>
</html>
```

2. Add the following PHP code to `categories.php` to be able to provide content on request to the jQuery Mobile site:

```php
<?php
$categories = array(
    "colours" => array(
        "title" => "Colours",
        "description" => "Some of my favorite colours",
        "items" => array(
            "Black",
            "Green",
            "Red",
            "Blue",
            "Purple"
```

```
                )
            ),
        "shapes" => array(
            "title" => "Shapes",
            "description" => "Some shapes I really like",
            "items" => array(
                "Triangle",
                "Circle",
                "Square"
            )
        ),
        "sounds" => array(
            "title" => "Sounds",
            "description" => "Some crazy sounds",
            "items" => array(
                "Buzz",
                "Swish",
                "Boom!",
                "Tick"
            )
        )
    );
    if (isset($_POST['category'])) {
        $response = array(
            "success" => true,
            "data" => array()
        );
        $category = $_POST['category'];
        if (isset($categories[$category])) {
            $response["data"] = $categories[$category];
        } else {
            $response["success"] = false;
            $response["data"] = "Invalid category provided";
        }
        header("Content-Type: application/json; charset-UTF-8");
        echo json_encode($response);
    }
```

3. To catch the user request for one of the dynamic pages, add the following jQuery code to `script.js`, which will listen for the `pagebeforechange` event. This allows us to intercept just before the user is sent to the category page.

```
$(document).bind("pagebeforechange", function(e, data) {
    if (typeof data.toPage === "string") {
        var urlObject = $.mobile.path.parseUrl(data.toPage);
```

```
            if (urlObject.hash.search(/^#categorypage/) !== -1 &&
urlObject.hash.search(/cat=*/) !== -1) {
                displayCategory(urlObject, data.options);
                //We are handling the change page event ourselves so
prevent the default behaviour
                e.preventDefault();
            }
        }
    });
```

4. To be able to generate the dynamic page, content from the PHP script is required. Add the following JavaScript function to the end of `script.js` to make an AJAX request to collect this data and generate the markup for the dynamic page:

```javascript
function displayCategory(urlObject, options) {
    var catName = urlObject.hash.replace(/.*cat=/, "");
    var pageId = urlObject.hash.replace( /\?.*$/, "");
    var _page = $(pageId);
    var _header = _page.children(":jqmData(role=header)");
    var _content = _page.children(":jqmData(role=content)");
    $.ajax({
        url: 'categories.php',
        type: 'POST',
        data: {
            category: catName
        },
        success: function(response) {
            if (response.success) {
                var category = response.data;
                //Add title to header
                _header.find("h1").html(category.title);
                //Create content HTML
                var contentHtml = "<p>" + category.description +
":</p><ul>";
                for (var i = 0; i < category.items.length; i++) {
                    var item = category.items[i];
                    contentHtml += "<li>" + item + "</li>";
                }
                contentHtml += "</ul>";
                _content.html(contentHtml);
                //Update the URL to reflect the page the user is
actually on
                _page.data("url", urlObject.href);
                $.mobile.changePage(_page, options);
            } else {
                alert(response.data);
```

```
            }
          }
      });
  }
```

5. Go to your newly created mobile website via your web browser (for example, `http://localhost/`) and you will be presented with the home page, which provides a button for three different categories. Click on one of these buttons to be taken to a new page with the content displayed served from the PHP script you have just created.

How it works...

The HTML code that is used to create the mobile site in this recipe differs little from the previous static mobile site. The only difference is that there is only one additional page with no title or content. This is because the additional page will be re-used to create multiple pages dynamically, and its title and content will be set based on the user request.

The HTML code within `index.html` creates the home page with three buttons labeled **Colours**, **Shapes**, and **Sounds**. Each of these buttons is a link to the same internal page with some additional information, as shown in the following line of code:

```
#categorypage?cat=colours
```

Each of the buttons provide a different value for the `cat` variable representing the different category pages. When the user clicks on one of these pages, the default behavior is for jQuery Mobile to navigate the user to this internal page. As we are creating these internal pages dynamically, we need to intercept this behavior, collect the requested category content from a PHP script, and then generate the page. To do this, we bind to the `pagebeforechange` event as follows:

```
$(document).bind("pagebeforechange", function(e, data) {
    if (typeof data.toPage === "string") {
        var urlObject = $.mobile.path.parseUrl(data.toPage);
        if (urlObject.hash.search(/^#categorypage/) !== -1 &&
urlObject.hash.search(/cat=*/) !== -1) {
            displayCategory(urlObject, data.options);
            //We are handling the change page event ourselves to
prevent the default behaviour
            e.preventDefault();
        }
    }
});
```

As we only want to intercept certain page requests, there are a few checks we perform before we ask for the dynamic content. We can get the request URL from the `data` object provided to the event handler function. We first check that the URL is a string as follows:

```
if (typeof data.toPage === "string") {
```

If it is a string, it is parsed to a URL object as follows:

```
var urlObject = $.mobile.path.parseUrl(data.toPage);
```

Once the URL object has been created, it is possible to perform two final checks to see if the requested page is one of the category pages, as follows:

```
if (urlObject.hash.search(/^#categorypage/) !== -1 && urlObject.hash.
search(/cat=*/) !== -1) {
```

Using the `search()` function, it is possible to search for the string `#categorypage` to check if it is the category page being requested, and then again to check that a `cat` variable has also been provided.

If these checks pass, the `displayCategory()` function is called to collect and render the content for the dynamic page. `e.preventDefault()` is also used to stop jQuery Mobile from navigating the user to the requested page before it has been generated with the dynamic content.

At the top of the `displayCategory()` function, there are a series of variables declared as follows:

```
var catName = urlObject.hash.replace(/.*cat=/, "");
var pageId = urlObject.hash.replace( /\?.*$/, "");
var _page = $(pageId);
var _header = _page.children(":jqmData(role=header)");
var _content = _page.children(":jqmData(role=content)");
```

The first two take values from the request URL, the requested category, and the page ID (that is, `#categorypage`).

The page ID is then used to select the page DOM element from `index.html` using the typical jQuery selector. Then, using the `page` element, it is possible to find and store the DOM elements for the page header and content, which we can manipulate later using standard jQuery.

An AJAX request using jQuery's `$.ajax()` function is then used to make a POST request to `categories.php`, specifying the value of `catName`, which was taken from the request page URL.

This `categories.php` PHP script holds a multidimensional array that stores data for the three different categories. This PHP script takes the posted category and checks to see if there is a matching category within the `$categories` array using `isset()`. If there is, the `$response` array's data value is updated to include the data for the requested category. If there is no data for the requested category, the `$response` array's success value is set to `false` and an error message is provided.

Finally, the PHP script sets the content type and charset before it encodes the `$response` array as JSON and outputs it.

The AJAX request made from the `displayCategory()` function will receive this JSON data and process it accordingly.

By checking if `response.success` is true, it is possible to determine if there is some data to display for the requested category. If there is, the page's title can be added along with the HTML code created for the content, as shown in the following code:

```
var category = response.data;
//Add title to header
_header.find("h1").html(category.title);
//Create content HTML
var contentHtml = "<p>" + category.description + ":</p><ul>";
for (var i = 0; i < category.items.length; i++) {
var item = category.items[i];
contentHtml += "<li>" + item + "</li>";
}
contentHtml += "</ul>";
_content.html(contentHtml);
```

To ensure that the URL reflects the page the user is viewing, the jQuery `data()` function is used to set the `url` attribute on the `categorypage` element as follows:

```
_page.data("url", urlObject.href);
```

Finally, the `changePage()` function is called to navigate the user to the newly generated page, where they will be presented with the requested content served from the PHP script. The `changePage()` function will also insert an entry into the browser history to provide typical browser navigation behavior.

There's more...

The PHP script in this recipe that provides the content to populate the additional category pages holds this content within a PHP array. This is just for demonstrative purposes and could easily be the content that is stored within a database accessible by the PHP script.

 ▶ *Building a complete static website*

Implementing the quick call functionality

HTML5 allows developers to tell the browser to launch an application to make a phone call in the same way you would do for an e-mail. This recipe will show you how to do this with a jQuery Mobile button so that when users click on this button, their default call application will open with a prepopulated telephone number.

Getting ready

Within the `chapter10` folder, create `recipe-4.html` for use within this recipe.

How to do it...

To allow users to be able to click on a button to make a phone call without having to copy and paste a number into their call application, perform the following simple steps:

1. Re-using the mobile website template, add the following HTML code into `recipe-4.html`:

```
<!DOCTYPE html>
<html>
<head>
    <title>Chapter 10 :: jQuery Mobile Template</title>
    <meta name="viewport" content="width=device-width, initial-scale=1" />
    <link rel="stylesheet" href="jquery-mobile/jquery.mobile.min.css" />
    <script src="jquery.min.js"></script>
    <script src="jquery-mobile/jquery.mobile.min.js"></script>
</head>
<body>
<div data-role="page">
    <header data-role="header">
        <h1>Chapter 10 :: Recipe 4</h1>
    </header>
    <div data-role="content">

    </div>
    <footer data-role="footer">
```

```
        <h4>The HTML5 tel: attribute allows you to provide
    interaction to telephone numbers</h4>
        </footer>
    </div>
    </body>
    </html>
```

2. Add a button into the `content` section of the home page with the `tel:` attribute that will launch the call application once pressed as follows:

```
<p>This is my simple mobile website, click the button below to
call me!</p>
<a href="tel: 01234 567891" data-role="button">Call Me!</a>
```

3. Opening `recipe-4.html` in Google Chrome and pressing the **Call Me!** button will present you with an alert informing you that the website is requesting an external application to be opened. Opening the web page on your mobile browser will open your device's default call application, allowing you to make a call with the number specified on the button element.

How it works...

For many years, the `mailto:` attribute has been available to allow websites to open the user's default mail client. An example is shown in the following line of code:

```
<a href="mailto:name@domain.com">E-Mail Me</a>
```

HTML5 allows some additional attributes that work in a similar way to allow for additional functionality. The `tel:` attribute is one of them. Browsers that support this attribute will open the default calling application installed on the device or computer when the user clicks on the link. Note that to open Skype, a popular VOIP application, you may need to use an alternative attribute called `callto:`.

See also

 ▸ *Implementing the send SMS functionality*

Implementing the send SMS functionality

The previous recipe covered making a call directly from your mobile website. Making it easy for the user to send an SMS is also a useful feature. This recipe will show you how to add a button that, when clicked, will open the default SMS client on the user's device.

Getting ready

Create `recipe-5.html` in the `chapter10` folder you created before starting this chapter.

How to do it...

It is easy to allow users to be able to quickly send an SMS message to you via your mobile website. Perform the following simple steps to learn how:

1. Once more, using the jQuery Mobile template created in the first recipe of this chapter, create a simple mobile website within `recipe-5.html` using the following code:

```
<!DOCTYPE html>
<html>
<head>
    <title>Chapter 10 :: Recipe 5</title>
    <meta name="viewport" content="width=device-width, initial-
scale=1" />
    <link rel="stylesheet" href="jquery-mobile/jquery.mobile.min.
css" />
    <script src="jquery.min.js"></script>
    <script src="jquery-mobile/jquery.mobile.min.js"></script>
</head>
<body>
<div data-role="page">
    <header data-role="header">
        <h1>Chapter 10 :: Recipe 5</h1>
    </header>
    <div data-role="content">

    </div>
    <footer data-role="footer">
        <h4>Use the HTML5 sms: attribute to open the default SMS
client on click</h4>
    </footer>
</div>
</body>
</html>
```

2. Add the following text and anchor element within the `content` section of the home page in `recipe-5.html`:

```
<p>This is my simple mobile website, click the button below to
send me an SMS message!</p>
<a href="sms:01234 567891" data-role="button">SMS Me!</a>
```

3. Open `recipe-5.html` on a mobile device and click on the **SMS Me!** button. Your default SMS client will open with the recipient field already populated with the number specified in the HTML.

How it works...

In addition to the new `tel:` attribute provided by HTML5, the `sms:` attribute is also available. This will tell compatible devices to open the default SMS client with the telephone number specified. An example is shown in the following line of code:

```
<a href="sms:01234 567891" data-role="button">SMS Me!</a>
```

This anchor element also has the `data-role` attribute and the value of a button so that jQuery Mobile adds the appropriate styling for a simple button.

There's more...

In addition to the telephone number, it is also possible to specify some text to be automatically added to the message body; change the anchor element as follows to add this functionality:

```
<a href="sms:01234 567891?body=This is some text in the body" data-role="button">SMS Me!</a>
```

See also

▶ *Implementing the quick call functionality*

Adding mobile-friendly lists

There have been various recipes throughout this cookbook that utilize HTML lists to present data in a simple and effective way. jQuery Mobile allows developers to quickly add mobile-and touch-friendly lists to their jQuery Mobile website. This recipe provides you with multiple examples of the more common types of lists made available by jQuery Mobile. You can copy and re-use the code for these lists at your convenience.

Getting ready

Within the `chapter10` folder you created earlier, create a single HTML file called `recipe-6.html`.

How to do it...

To understand how to add different types of lists that are mobile-friendly, perform the following steps:

1. Create a basic jQuery Mobile site by adding the following HTML to `recipe-6.html`:

```html
<!DOCTYPE html>
<html>
<head>
    <title>Chapter 10 :: Recipe 6</title>
    <meta name="viewport" content="width=device-width, initial-scale=1" />
    <link rel="stylesheet" href="jquery-mobile/jquery.mobile.min.css" />
    <script src="jquery.min.js"></script>
    <script src="jquery-mobile/jquery.mobile.min.js"></script>
</head>
<body>
<div data-role="page">
    <header data-role="header">
        <h1>Chapter 10 :: Recipe 6 :: Lists</h1>
    </header>
    <div data-role="content">

    </div>
</div>
</body>
</html>
```

2. To create the most common list type—a basic linked list—add the following code in the `content` division element in `recipe-6.html`:

```html
<p>This page contains a selection of list examples for you to
reuse at your convenience.</p>
<h2>Basic linked list</h2>
<ul data-role="listview">
<li><a href='#'>Linked Item 1</a></li>
<li><a href='#'>Linked Item 2</a></li>
<li><a href='#'>Linked Item 3</a></li>
</ul>
```

3. To create a nested list, add the following HTML structure within the `content` division element. Make note of the comment within the HTML that, for this list to work correctly, you will need to serve `recipe-6.html` from a web server. The reason for this is given in the *How to do it...* section of this recipe.

```
<h2>Nested list</h2>
<p>Please note that the sub-list will not work if you have
opened recipe-6.html directly in a web browser. For the sub-
list navigation to work you must serve this HTML file from a web
server. i.e. http://localhost/recipe-6.html.</p>
<ul data-role="listview">
<li><a href='#'>Top Level Item 1</a></li>
<li><a href='#'>Top Level Item 2</a></li>
<li><a href='#'>Top Level Item 3 - With Sub-Level</a>
<ul data-role="listview">
<li><a href='#'>Second Level Item 1</a></li>
<li><a href='#'>Second Level Item 2</a></li>
</ul>
</li>
</ul>
```

4. When displaying content within a list, there may be a need to allow the user to interact with each list item in multiple ways. jQuery Mobile allows the developer to easily add buttons alongside the list elements with icons to reinforce their functionality. Use the `data-split-icon` attribute to add this functionality to a list as shown in the following code:

```
<h2>List items with buttons</h2>
<ul data-role="listview" data-split-icon="delete">
<li><a href='#'>Jane Doe</a><a href='#'></a></li>
<li><a href='#'>John Doe</a><a href='#'></a></li>
<li><a href='#'>James Mathews</a><a href='#'></a></li>
</ul>
```

5. Long lists can become cumbersome to navigate. jQuery Mobile allows the developer to quickly add a filter option to any list, which will allow the user to look for the list items they require. To add a list with this functionality, use the following code:

```
<h2>List with filter</h2>
<ul data-role="listview" data-filter="true">
<li><a href='#'>Cat</a></li>
<li><a href='#'>Dog</a></li>
<li><a href='#'>Lizard</a></li>
<li><a href='#'>Rabbit</a></li>
</ul>
```

6. Opening `recipe-6.html` within a web browser will present you with a range of list examples, as shown in the following screenshot, that you can use at your convenience in future projects:

How it works...

Using the `data-role="listview"` attribute and value, it is possible to turn a basic HTML list into a mobile-friendly implementation. jQuery Mobile, as it does with buttons and other elements, will automatically add the styling.

If you refer to the documentation (`http://jquerymobile.com/demos/1.2.1/docs/lists/docs-lists.html`), you will get a complete list of all of the available list types along with detailed examples.

The majority of the examples used in this recipe are simple and self-explanatory. The nested list part of the recipe has some additional functionality that may not be obvious. With most mobile devices, the screen space is very limited, especially in portrait mode. Because of this, it would not make sense to allow nested lists to act in their traditional way, which is to expand to the right with a different indentation, as illustrated in the following list:

- ► Top Level Item 1
- ► Top Level Item 2
- ► Top Level Item 3 – With Sublevel

    - ❏ Second Level Item 1
    - ❏ Second Level Item 2

To save space and provide a better user experience, when you add a nested list, jQuery Mobile will create an additional page with the sublist items within. When the user selects a list item that has a list within itself, they are taken to an additional page where the sublevel items are displayed.

At the time of writing this recipe, the additional page created for the sublevel items does not work unless the page is served from a web server using HTTP.

One of the more powerful examples within this recipe is the ability to quickly add a filter to your lists. Simply by adding the `data-filter="true"` attribute and value on the HTML list, jQuery Mobile automatically adds the filter input to the top of the list, allowing the user to filter out unwanted list items.

Using touch-oriented events

Along with typical events available with jQuery, such as `click` and `hover`, jQuery Mobile makes touch-centric events available to the developer. Using these events, it is possible to add extra functionality to your mobile application for these additional user interactions. This recipe provides samples for many of these useful events that will allow you to re-use them at your convenience.

Getting ready

Within the web root of your web server, create `recipe-7.html` and `recipe-7.js`.

How to do it...

To learn which touch-centric events are available and how to use them, perform the following steps:

1. Create a basic mobile website with an empty list by adding the following HTML to `recipe-7.html`. Make sure you update the references to the included libraries where required.

```
<!DOCTYPE html>
<html>
<head>
    <title>Chapter 11 :: Recipe 1</title>
    <meta name="viewport" content="width=device-width, initial-scale=1" />
    <link rel="stylesheet" href="includes/jquery-mobile/jquery.mobile.min.css" />
    <script src="includes/jquery.min.js"></script>
    <script src="includes/jquery-mobile/jquery.mobile.min.js"></script>
    <script src="recipe-7.js"></script>
</head>
<body>
<div data-role="page">
    <header data-role="header">
```

```
        <h1>Chapter 10 :: Recipe 7 :: jQuery Mobile Touch Events</
h1>
    </header>
    <div data-role="content">
        <p>Perform various touch events and watch the output
below.</p>
        <ul id="touch-event-response" data-role="listview"></ul>
    </div>
</div>
</body>
</html>
```

2. At the top of `recipe-7.js`, add the following function, which will add a new list item to the list you have just created within `recipe-7.html`:

```
function addEvent(msg) {
    var _list = $('#touch-event-response');
    _list.append("<li>" + msg + "</li>");
    _list.listview('refresh');
}
```

3. To add a new list item when the user performs a tap, add the following JavaScript code to `recipe-7.js`:

```
$(function(){
    $(document).bind('tap', function(){
        addEvent("Tap");
    });
});
```

4. To listen for the `taphold` event and add a new list item, add the following code directly under the previous `.bind()` statement within the `$(function(){})` block:

```
$(document).bind('taphold', function(){
addEvent("Tap & Hold");
});
```

5. The same can be done to listen for the `swipe` event. Append the following `.bind()` definition:

```
$(document).bind('swipe', function(){
addEvent("Swipe");
});
```

6. To clear the list when the user swipes left, append the following JavaScript code:

```
$(document).bind('swipeleft', function(){
$('#touch-event-response').empty();
});
```

7. Finally, to detect when the user changes the device's orientation, add the following code after the `swipeleft` bind definition:

```
$(window).bind('orientationchange', function(event){
addEvent("Orientation changed to: " + event.orientation);
});
```

8. With a mobile- and touch-compatible device, open `recipe-7.html` and perform a range of touch events to see the appropriate responses added to the list. When you swipe left, the list should empty, and when you change the device's orientation, a new list item will be added, indicating the new orientation (portrait or landscape).

How it works...

By using the following code, it is possible to listen for various events that jQuery Mobile makes available:

```
$(document).bind('[EVENT]', function() {
});
```

To see the full list of events that are available, read the documentation (http://jquerymobile.com/demos/1.2.1/docs/api/events.html) on the jQuery Mobile website, which provides a comprehensive list with examples.

Within this recipe, the `addEvent()` function takes a string that it will append to the list element created within the simple mobile website in `recipe-7.html`. When you manipulate a jQuery Mobile list with JavaScript, you must call the `refresh` method to ensure that the styling is reapplied to the newly added elements. This is shown in the following code:

```
var _list = $('#touch-event-response');
_list.append("<li>" + msg + "</li>");
_list.listview('refresh');
```

Knowing when the user changes the device's orientation can be useful to rearrange elements on the page to improve the user experience. With jQuery Mobile, this is very easy to do. Simply bind to the `orientationchange` event and ready the `orientation` property of the `event` object to determine what the new orientation is, as shown in the following code:

```
$(window).bind('orientationchange', function(event){
addEvent("Orientation changed to: " + event.orientation);
});
```

Note that unlike the other events in this recipe, this had been bound to `window` and not `document`, as `document` is unaware of the browser or device orientation.

See also

▶ *Chapter 2, Interacting with the User by Making Use of jQuery Events*

Creating mobile-compatible forms

jQuery Mobile provides a wide array of form components that are similar to the jQuery UI offering but optimized for mobile devices. This recipe provides examples of the more commonly used form elements so that you can re-use them at your convenience.

Getting ready

Within the `chapter10` folder you created earlier, create `recipe-8.html`.

How to do it...

To learn what form elements are made available by jQuery Mobile and how to use them, perform each of the following steps:

1. Create a simple jQuery Mobile website to hold all the examples. Add the following HTML code to `recipe-8.html`:

```
<!DOCTYPE html>
<html>
<head>
    <title>Chapter 10 :: Recipe 8</title>
    <meta name="viewport" content="width=device-width, initial-
scale=1" />
    <link rel="stylesheet" href="jquery-mobile/jquery.mobile.min.
css" />
    <script src="jquery.min.js"></script>
    <script src="jquery-mobile/jquery.mobile.min.js"></script>
</head>
<body>
<div data-role="page" id="home">
    <header data-role="header" data-theme="b">
        <h1>Chapter 10 :: Recipe 8</h1>
    </header>
    <div data-role="content">
    </div>
</div>
</body>
</html>
```

2. Add the following code inside the `content` division element you have just added to create a range of text input elements:

```
<h1>Text Input</h1>
<div data-role="fieldcontain">
<label for="textInput">Text input:</label>
<input type="text" name="textInput" id="textInput" />
</div>
<div data-role="fieldcontain">
<label for="textArea">Text area:</label>
<textarea id="textArea" name="textArea"></textarea>
</div>
<div data-role="fieldcontain">
<label for="textSearch">Text search:</label>
<input type="text" name="textSearch" id="textSearch" data-
type="search">
</div>
```

3. To create two different varieties of select menus, add the following code under the text inputs:

```
<h1>Select Menu</h1>
<div data-role="fieldcontain">
<label for="simpleSelect">Simple select:</label>
<select id="simpleSelect">
<option value="1">Option 1</option>
<option value="2">Option 2</option>
        <option value="3">Option 3</option>
</select>
</div>
<div data-role="fieldcontain">
<label for="customSelect">Custom select:</label>
<select id="customSelect" data-native-menu="false">
<option value="1">Option 1</option>
<option value="2">Option 2</option>
        <option value="3">Option 3</option>
</select>
</div>
```

4. To create checkboxes and radio buttons, use the following code:

```
<h1>Selection</h1>
<h2>Checkboxes</h2>
<fieldset data-role="controlgroup">
<input type="checkbox" name="checkbox-1" id="checkbox-1">
<label for="checkbox-1">Option 1</label>
```

```
<input type="checkbox" name="checkbox-2" id="checkbox-2">
<label for="checkbox-2">Option 2</label>
<input type="checkbox" name="checkbox-3" id="checkbox-3">
<label for="checkbox-3">Option 3</label>
</fieldset>
<h2>Radio buttons</h2>
<fieldset data-role="controlgroup">
<input type="radio" name="radio-1" id="radio-1">
<label for="radio-1">Option 1</label>
<input type="radio" name="radio-1" id="radio-2">
<label for="radio-2">Option 2</label>
<input type="radio" name="radio-1" id="radio-3">
<label for="radio-3">Option 3</label>
</fieldset>
<h2>Inline selection</h2>
<fieldset data-role="controlgroup" data-type="horizontal">
<input type="checkbox" name="checkbox-1" id="checkbox-4">
<label for="checkbox-4">Option 1</label>
<input type="checkbox" name="checkbox-2" id="checkbox-5">
<label for="checkbox-5">Option 2</label>
<input type="checkbox" name="checkbox-3" id="checkbox-6">
<label for="checkbox-6">Option 3</label>
</fieldset>
<fieldset data-role="controlgroup" data-type="horizontal">
<input type="radio" name="radio-2" id="radio-4">
<label for="radio-4">Option 1</label>
<input type="radio" name="radio-2" id="radio-5">
<label for="radio-5">Option 2</label>
<input type="radio" name="radio-2" id="radio-6">
<label for="radio-6">Option 3</label>
</fieldset>
```

5. Finally, to create some additional elements—a switch and slider—add the following code:

```
<h1>Additional</h1>
<div data-role="fieldcontain">
<label for="switch">Switch:</label>
<select id="switch" data-role="slider">
<option value="1">On</option>
      <option value="0">Off</option>
</select>
</div>
<div data-role="fieldcontain">
```

```
<label for="slider">Slider:</label>
<input type="number" data-type="range" name="slider" id="slider"
value="50" min="0" max="100" data-highlight="true">
</div>
```

6. Opening `recipe-8.html` in a web browser will present you with a range of different form elements. You can then easily select and re-use the code for any of the element types, as shown in the following screenshot:

How it works...

Each type of jQuery Mobile element used within this recipe is explained in detail in the following sections.

Text input

jQuery Mobile provides different text input elements. The typical text input and text area elements are easily created by adding a label and either an `input` or `textarea` element inside a `div` element with the `fieldcontain` class, as shown in the following code:

```
<div data-role="fieldcontain">
<label for="textInput">Text input:</label>
<input type="text" name="textInput" id="textInput" />
</div>
```

To create a search input, simply add `data-type="search"` to the `input` element. This adds a search icon to the `input` element and also provides a clear button once the user has entered some text.

Select menu

The two select menus provided as examples in this recipe look identical at face value. When you select the first simple example, you are provided with a dropdown that looks like a typical select menu on a normal non-mobile-optimized website.

The second example, which has the additional `data-native-menu="false"` attribute added, provides a different selection menu once clicked. This additional menu makes it easier to make a selection using a touch interface. The following screenshot provides a comparison of the two types of select menus:

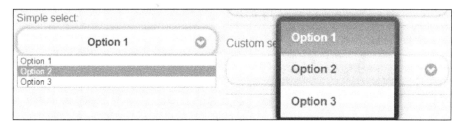

Checkboxes and radio buttons

Using a `fieldset` element with the `data-role="controlgroup"` attribute, it is very easy to create checkboxes and radio buttons, as shown in the following code snippet:

```
<fieldset data-role="controlgroup">
<input type="checkbox" name="checkbox-1" id="checkbox-1">
<label for="checkbox-1">Option 1</label>
<input type="checkbox" name="checkbox-2" id="checkbox-2">
<label for="checkbox-2">Option 2</label>
<input type="checkbox" name="checkbox-3" id="checkbox-3">
<label for="checkbox-3">Option 3</label>
</fieldset>
```

To create a set of radio buttons, you can re-use the preceding code, changing the `type` attribute to `radio` and ensuring they all have the same value within the `name` attribute.

In addition to these interface elements, jQuery Mobile makes it possible to have an inline equivalent. Simply add the `data-type="horizontal"` attribute onto the `fieldset` element to get the inline version of either checkboxes or radio buttons.

Additional

The final two elements provided as part of this recipe are a switch and a slider. The `switch` element is essentially a select menu with only two options, but presented in a more touch-friendly manner. The `slider` element is created by adding the `data-type="range"` attribute to a number input (as shown in the following code), which allows a user to easily enter and change a numeric value on a form:

```
<div data-role="fieldcontain">
<label for="slider">Slider:</label>
<input type="number" data-type="range" name="slider" id="slider"
value="50" min="0" max="100" data-highlight="true">
</div>
```

There's more...

All of the examples provided as part of this recipe are displayed at the default size. jQuery Mobile provides all its form elements with an additional smaller size for situations where the default is a little too large.

To use the mini equivalent, add the attribute `data-mini="true"` to elements requiring the smaller size.

Building a complete registration and login system

This recipe shows you how to create a simple register and login system from scratch using jQuery Mobile and PHP with a MySQL database. This recipe will form the base for a complete web application in the next recipe of this chapter.

Getting ready

You should already have a PHP and MySQL server available that will be utilized to complete this recipe. Within the web root of your web server, create `index2.html` and `script2.js`, which will hold the main functionality of the application.

How to do it...

To create a complete registration and login system, ensure you follow each of the following instructions carefully:

1. Add the following HTML code to `index2.html` to create a simple jQuery Mobile website and home page:

   ```
   <!DOCTYPE html>
   <html>
   ```

```html
<head>
    <title>Chapter 10 :: Register & Login</title>
    <meta name="viewport" content="width=device-width, initial-
scale=1" />
    <link rel="stylesheet" href="includes/jquery-mobile/jquery.
mobile.min.css" />
    <script src="includes/jquery.min.js"></script>
    <script src="includes/jquery-mobile/jquery.mobile.min.js"></
script>
    <script src="script2.js"></script>
    <link rel="stylesheet" href="styles.css" />
</head>
<body>
<div data-role="page" id="home">
    <header data-role="header" data-theme="b">
        <h1><a href="#home" data-role="button" data-icon="home"
data-iconpos="notext" data-inline="true"></a> Home Page</h1>
    </header>
    <div data-role="content">
        <p>Welcome to my community.</p>
        <a data-role="button" href="#login">Login</a>
        <a data-role="button" data-theme="a"
href="#register">Register</a>
    </div>
</div>
</body>
</html>
```

2. Use the following HTML to add a login page to `index2.html`:

```html
<div data-role="page" id="login" data-title="Login">
    <header data-role="header" data-theme="b">
        <h1><a href="#home" data-role="button" data-icon="home"
data-iconpos="notext" data-inline="true"></a> Login</h1>
    </header>
    <div data-role="content">
        <div data-role="fieldcontain">
            <label for="login-username">Username:</label>
            <input type="text" name="username" id="login-username"
value="" />
        </div>
        <div data-role="fieldcontain">
            <label for="login-password">Password:</label>
            <input type="password" name="password" id="login-
password" value="" />
        </div>
```

```
        <button data-role="button" id="login-account" data-
theme="a">Login</button>
        <p>Don't have an account? <a href='#register'>Register</
a>.</p>
    </div>
</div>
```

3. A registration page can also be created using the following HTML code, ensuring the page code is added within the body section of the HTML document in index2. html:

```
<div data-role="page" id="register" data-title="Register">
    <header data-role="header" data-theme="b">
        <h1><a href="#home" data-role="button" data-icon="home"
data-iconpos="notext" data-inline="true"></a> Register</h1>
    </header>
    <div data-role="content">
        <div data-role="fieldcontain">
            <label for="register-username">Username:</label>
            <input type="text" name="username" id="register-
username" value="" />
        </div>
        <div data-role="fieldcontain">
            <label for="register-password">Password:</label>
            <input type="password" name="password" id="register-
password" value="" />
        </div>
        <div data-role="fieldcontain">
            <label for="register-passwordagain">Password Again:</
label>
            <input type="password" name="register-passwordagain"
id="register-passwordagain" value="" />
        </div>
        <button data-role="button" id="register-account" data-
theme="a">Register</button>
        <p>Already have an account? <a href='#login'>Login</a>.</
p>
    </div>
</div>
```

4. The final page to add is the member page. Create this using the following HTML code:

```
<div data-role="page" id="member">
    <header data-role="header" data-theme="b">
        <h1><a href="#home" data-role="button" data-icon="home"
data-iconpos="notext" data-inline="true"></a> Member's Page</h1>
    </header>
```

```
        <div data-role="content">
            <p>You're logged in.</p>
            <button data-role="button" data-theme="a"
id="logout">Logout</button>
        </div>
</div>
```

5. Using the following SQL code, create a database called `chapter10` and a table called `user` within your MySQL database:

```
SET SQL_MODE="NO_AUTO_VALUE_ON_ZERO";
SET time_zone = "+00:00";


--
-- Database: `chapter10`
--
CREATE DATABASE `chapter10` DEFAULT CHARACTER SET latin1 COLLATE
latin1_swedish_ci;
USE `chapter10`;


-- -------------------------------------------------------


--
-- Table structure for table `user`
--

CREATE TABLE IF NOT EXISTS `user` (
  `id` bigint(20) unsigned NOT NULL AUTO_INCREMENT,
  `username` varchar(128) DEFAULT NULL,
  `password` varchar(512) DEFAULT NULL,
  UNIQUE KEY `id` (`id`),
  UNIQUE KEY `username` (`username`)
) ENGINE=InnoDB  DEFAULT CHARSET=latin1 AUTO_INCREMENT=8;
```

6. Create `connect.db.php` in the web root of your web server and add the following PHP code to connect to the `chapter10` database. Update the database username and password if required.

```
<?php
$mysqli = new mysqli("localhost", "root", "", "chapter10");
if ($mysqli->connect_errno) {
    die("Failed to connect to MySQL: (" . $mysqli->connect_errno .
") " . $mysqli->connect_error);
}
$pwsalt = "TH1SISF0RCHAPTER10";
```

7. To be able to add new users to the `user` table, create `register.php` within the web root of your web server and add the following PHP code:

```php
<?php
require_once("connect.db.php");
$username = isset($_POST['username']) ? strtolower($_
POST['username']) : "";
$password = isset($_POST['password']) ? $_POST['password'] : "";
$passwordAgain = isset($_POST['passwordagain']) ? $_
POST['passwordagain'] : "";

$response = array(
    "success" => false,
    "errors" => array()
);

if (strlen($username) < 3 || strlen($username) > 32) {
    $response["errors"]["username"] = "Username must be between 3
and 64 characters in length";
} else {
    $query = "SELECT `id` FROM `user` WHERE `username` = ? LIMIT
1";
    $stmt = $mysqli->stmt_init();
    if ($stmt->prepare($query)) {
        $stmt->bind_param("s", $username);
        if ($stmt->execute()) {
            $stmt->store_result();
            if ($stmt->num_rows > 0) {
                $response["errors"]["username"] = "Username has
already been taken";
            }
        } else {
            $response["errors"]["username"] = "Could not execute
query";
        }
    } else {
        $response["errors"]["username"] = "Could query database
for existing usernames";
    }
    $stmt->close();
}

if (strlen($password) < 6 || strlen($password) > 32) {
    $response["errors"]["password"] = "Password must be between 6
and 32 characters in length";
}
```

```php
    if ($password != $passwordAgain) {
        $response["errors"]["passwordagain"] = "Passwords must match";
    }

    if (empty($response["errors"])) {
        $query = "INSERT INTO `user` (`username`, `password`) VALUES
(?, ?)";
        $stmt = $mysqli->stmt_init();
        if ($stmt->prepare($query)) {
            $password = crypt($password, $pwsalt);
            $stmt->bind_param("ss", $username, $password);
            if ($stmt->execute()) {
                $stmt->close();
                $response["success"] = true;
            } else {
                $response["errors"]["username"] = "Could not execute
query";
            }
        } else {
            $response["errors"]["username"] = "Could not insert new
user, please try again";
        }
    }
    $mysqli->close();
    header("Content-Type: application/json; charset=UTF-8");
    echo json_encode($response);
```

8. To allow users to log in with their newly created account, create `login.php` within the web root of your web server and add the following PHP code:

```php
<?php
session_start();
require_once("connect.db.php");
$username = isset($_POST['username']) ? strtolower($_
POST['username']) : "";
$password = isset($_POST['password']) ? $_POST['password'] : "";

$response = array(
    "success" => false,
    "error" => "",
    "user" => array()
);

$query = "SELECT `id` FROM `user` WHERE `username` = ? AND
`password` = ? LIMIT 1";
$stmt = $mysqli->stmt_init();
```

```php
if ($stmt->prepare($query)) {
    $password = crypt($password, $pwsalt);
    $stmt->bind_param("ss", $username, $password);
    if ($stmt->execute()) {
        $res = $stmt->get_result();
        if ($res->num_rows > 0) {
            $row = $res->fetch_assoc();
            $response["success"] = true;
            $_SESSION['uid'] = $response["user"]["id"] =
$row["id"];
            $_SESSION['username'] = $response["user"]["username"]
= $username;
        } else {
            $response["error"] = "Incorrect username or password";
        }
    } else {
        $response["error"] = "Could not execute query";
    }
} else {
    $response["error"] = "Could not query database";
}
$stmt->close();
$mysqli->close();
header("Content-Type: application/json; charset=UTF-8");
echo json_encode($response);
```

9. For the logout functionality, create logout.php within the same directory as login.php and add the following code:

```php
<?php
session_start();
$response = array(
    "success" => false,
    "error" => ""
);
if (isset($_SESSION["uid"]) && isset($_SESSION["username"])) {
    $_SESSION = array();
    session_destroy();
    $response["success"] = true;
} else {
    $response["success"] = false;
    $response["error"] = "Not logged in";
}
header("Content-Type: application/json; charset=UTF-8");
echo json_encode($response);
```

10. To allow a user to be able to submit their information for registration, add the following JavaScript code to `script2.js` within the jQuery on-load block (`$(function(){});`):

```javascript
$('#register-account').click(function(){
        $('.input-error').remove();
        var data = {
            username: $('#register-username').val(),
            password: $('#register-password').val(),
            passwordagain: $('#register-passwordagain').val()
        };
        $.ajax({
            type: 'POST',
            url: 'register.php',
            data: data,
            beforeSend: function() {
                $.mobile.loading('show');
            },
            success: function(data) {
                $.mobile.loading('hide');
                if (data.success) {
                    $.mobile.showPageLoadingMsg("b", "Registration
successful! You may now login.", true);
                } else {
                    $.each(data.errors, function(key, value){
                        $('#register-' + key).parent().after("<div
class='input-error'>" + value + "</div>");
                    });
                }
            }
        });
    });
```

11. To react when the user attempts to log in from the login page, add the following JavaScript code to `script2.js` under the code you have just added for registration:

```javascript
$('#login-account').click(function(){
        var data = {
            username: $('#login-username').val(),
            password: $('#login-password').val()
        };
        $.ajax({
            type: 'POST',
            url: 'login.php',
            data: data,
            beforeSend: function() {
```

```
                        $.mobile.loading('show');
                },
                success: function(data) {
                    $.mobile.loading('hide');
                    if (data.success) {
                        $.mobile.showPageLoadingMsg("b", "Login
Successful", true);
                        localStorage.setItem("user", JSON.
stringify(data.user));
                        $.mobile.changePage("#member");
                    } else {
                        $.mobile.showPageLoadingMsg("b", data.error,
true);
                    }
                }
            });
        });
```

12. To allow the user to be able to click on the logout button and be logged out, add the following code to `script2.js`:

```
$('#logout').click(function(){
        $.ajax({
            type: 'POST',
            url: 'logout.php',
            beforeSend: function() {
                $.mobile.loading('show');
            },
            success: function(data) {
                $.mobile.loading('hide');
                if (data.success) {
                    localStorage.removeItem("user");
                    $.mobile.changePage("#home");
                } else {
                    $.mobile.showPageLoadingMsg("b", data.error,
true);
                }
            }
        });
    });
```

13. To prevent access to the members page, add the following code to check if the user is logged in when they try to navigate to this page:

```
$(document).bind("pagebeforechange", function(e, data) {
        if (typeof data.toPage === "string") {
            var urlObject = $.mobile.path.parseUrl(data.toPage);
```

```
          if (urlObject.hash.search(/^#member/) !== -1) {
             if (getUser() === false) {
                e.preventDefault();
                $.mobile.showPageLoadingMsg("b", "You must be
logged in to access this page", true);
                setTimeout(function(){
                    $.mobile.hidePageLoadingMsg();
                    $.mobile.changePage("#home");
                }, 1500);
             }
          }
       }
    });
```

14. The preceding code uses the `getUser()` function to determine if the user has been logged in or not. Add the following function to the end of `script2.js`, ensuring it is added outside the `$(function(){})`; block:

```
function getUser() {
    var user = localStorage.getItem("user");
    if (user == null) {
        return false;
    } else {
        return JSON.parse(user);
    }
}
```

15. To add some basic styling to the error messages within the web root of your web server, create a file named `styles.css` and add the following CSS code:

```
.input-error {
    position: absolute;
    font-size: 10px;
    color: #ff0800;
}
```

16. Visiting your web server that is serving `index2.html` will allow you to register an account. If you attempt to visit the members page without being logged in, you will get a message saying you must be logged in and will then be sent back to the home page.

How it works...

Each section of code created within this recipe is explained in detail in the following sections.

HTML

The HTML within `index2.html` creates a simple jQuery Mobile website with the following four pages:

- The home page
- The register page
- The login page
- The members page

The home page provides links to both the login and register pages, and each of these pages link to each other respectively. The members page has a logout button that allows the user to log out once they have gotten access to the members page. The HTML code is simple, and each element has been explained in detail in the previous recipes of this chapter.

SQL

The SQL code that is provided as part of this recipe can be used to create the required `chapter10` database and the `user` table, which stores the user accounts.

PHP

There are four PHP files created within this recipe. The first is `connect.db.php`, which establishes a connection to the MySQL database and is included within the other three PHP files. The PHP `mysqli` class is used to connect and query the MySQL database throughout the PHP files in this recipe. You can find more information about this class on PHP.net (http://www.php.net/mysqli).

The `register.php` file takes a set of values via a POST request. These values are as follows:

- Username
- Password
- Password again

The PHP script performs basic validation for all three inputs to ensure that the username specified is between 3 and 32 characters long and that a password has been provided that is at least 6 characters in length. It also ensures that both passwords match and queries the database to ensure the requested username has not already been taken.

If it passes all validations, a new user is inserted into the database, which will then allow this user to log in using the specified details. It is important to note that the password is encrypted using the PHP `crypt()` function with the default settings. This is a simple encryption method, and greater encryption techniques should be used in a production environment.

The `login.php` script takes a username and password via a POST request and queries the user table to see if there are any matching user credentials; if so, a PHP session is created for that user and a user object returned to the client.

The `logout.php` script simply destroys the PHP session if one exists, logging out the user.

Each of these PHP scripts return data in a standard format that has been used multiple times throughout this cookbook. At the top of each script, an array is created as shown in the following code:

```
$response = array(
    "success" => false,
    "errors" => array()
);
```

If the script is successful and no errors are needed to be output, the success value is changed to `true` and the `errors` array left empty. In the case of the `register.php` script, when one of the inputs fail validation, an associative array is returned with the key matching the input. The following is an example:

```
$response["errors"]["username"] = "Username has already been taken";
```

This is so that the JavaScript on the client knows which input to place the error message under, making it easier for the user to understand what changes they need to make.

When the response array is output, it is converted to a JSON object, and the content type and charset is set appropriately using the PHP `header()` function, as shown in the following code:

```
header("Content-Type: application/json; charset=UTF-8");
echo json_encode($response);
```

JavaScript

The JavaScript used within this recipe is simple and nothing new. There are three `click` event handlers created for the register, login, and logout buttons. The callback function provided to each of these event handlers collects data from the associated form and uses the jQuery `$.ajax()` function to make a POST request to the `register.php`, `login.php`, or `logout.php` scripts respectively. AJAX with jQuery has been covered extensively in *Chapter 3, Loading and Manipulating Dynamic Content with AJAX and JSON*.

For each of the AJAX requests, the `beforeSend()` function is used to open and show a spinner image to the user, indicating a request is being made. This spinner image is then removed on the success of the AJAX request. This is shown in the following code:

```
$.ajax({
type: 'POST',
url: 'register.php',
data: data,
beforeSend: function() {
$.mobile.loading('show');
},
success: function(data) {
```

```
        $.mobile.loading('hide');
// -- HIDDEN CODE
    }
});
```

Also, as shown in the following code, within the `success()` function for each of the AJAX requests, the `$.mobile.showPageLoadingMsg()` function is used to display a message to the user for various reasons, either on error or for information regarding a successful registration:

```
$.mobile.showPageLoadingMsg("b", "Registration successful! You may now
login.", true);
```

The first argument to the function is the theme, the second is the message you wish to display, and setting the third argument to `true` will remove the spinner image, just displaying the simple text message.

As previously mentioned, the `login.php` script returns an object that represents the newly logged-in user. As the client JavaScript has no sense of PHP sessions, this user object needs to be stored locally so that the client is aware of the logged-in user. To do this, local storage is used, as shown in the following line of code:

```
localStorage.setItem("user", JSON.stringify(data.user));
```

Local storage will only allow you to store a string, but we need to store an entire object. To get around this, we convert the object to a JSON string, which can then be converted to an object again when retrieved from local storage. The preceding example uses the `JSON.stringify()` function to convert the user object to a string and stores it in local storage under the name `user`.

The `getUser()` function is then used to retrieve and convert the string value to an object, or return `false` if there is no currently logged-in user:

```
function getUser() {
    var user = localStorage.getItem("user");
    if (user == null) {
        return false;
    } else {
        return JSON.parse(user);
    }
}
```

When the AJAX call to the `logout.php` script that destroys the server session is successful, `localStorage.removeItem("user")` is also used to remove the user object on the client.

The final element of the JavaScript within this recipe is restricting access to the members page. Note that any restriction enforced using client-side code can be bypassed by any user with the right knowledge. This type of client-side restriction is only used to enhance the user experience, and it is always a requirement that the server side prevent access to any actions that users shouldn't be able to perform.

Within the *Building a dynamic mobile website* recipe, the jQuery Mobile `pagebeforechange` event was used to detect the user trying to access a certain page. This same functionality is used within this recipe to catch when the user is trying to access the members page. The `getUser()` function is then used to determine if the user is logged in or not. If they are not logged in, they are prevented from navigating to the members page and sent back to the home page after being told they must be logged in to access the members page.

There's more...

Currently, to submit any of the forms on the website, the user is required to click on or press the associated button. To improve on this, it would be beneficial if the user could press the *Enter* key or the mobile-equivalent go button from within any of the inputs in the form.

See also

  ▸   *Building a dynamic mobile website*

Building a complete mobile web app

This recipe shows you how to create a simple but complete web app that allows registered users to write notes that can be accessed on all devices. The notes app extends upon the previous login and register recipe to allow the logged-in user to create and manage a note or a to-do list.

Getting ready

Before you start this recipe, ensure you have completed the previous recipe, *Building a complete register and login system*. You will still need a web server running PHP and MySQL to complete this recipe.

How to do it...

To create a complete mobile web app that can be accessed on all mobile and desktop devices, perform the following steps:

  1.   To store the user-created notes, another database table is required. Use the following SQL code to create a table within the `chapter10` database called `note`:

```
CREATE TABLE IF NOT EXISTS `note` (
  `id` bigint(20) unsigned NOT NULL AUTO_INCREMENT,
  `user_id` bigint(20) unsigned NOT NULL,
  `text` varchar(2048) DEFAULT NULL,
  `added` datetime DEFAULT NULL,
  UNIQUE KEY `id` (`id`),
  KEY `user_id` (`user_id`)
) ENGINE=InnoDB  DEFAULT CHARSET=latin1;

ALTER TABLE `note`
  ADD CONSTRAINT `note_ibfk_1` FOREIGN KEY (`user_id`) REFERENCES
`user` (`id`) ON DELETE CASCADE ON UPDATE CASCADE;
```

2. While most of the pages defined within `index2.html` stay the same, we need to update the members page to have a button that takes the user to their current notes. Update the members page with the following HTML in `index2.html`:

```html
<div data-role="page" id="member">
    <div data-role="header" data-theme="b">
        <h1><a href="#home" data-role="button" data-icon="home"
data-iconpos="notext" data-inline="true"></a> Member's Page</h1>
    </div>
    <div data-role="content">
        <p>Welcome <strong><span class="username"></span></
strong>, what would you like to do?</p>
        <a href="#notes" data-role="button" data-inline="true"
data-icon="arrow-r">View Notes</a>
        <button data-role="button" data-theme="a" id="logout"
data-inline="true" data-icon="delete">Logout</button>
    </div>
</div>
```

3. We now need to create the notes page that this new button takes the user to. Use the following HTML code to create the notes page, adding it after the members page in `index2.html`:

```html
<div data-role="page" id="notes">
    <div data-role="header" data-theme="b">
        <h1><a href="#home" data-role="button" data-icon="home"
data-iconpos="notext" data-inline="true"></a> Your Notes</h1>
    </div>
    <div data-role="content">
        <h1>Your Notes <a href="#add-note" data-icon="plus" data-
role="button" data-inline="true">Add note</a><a href="#member"
data-theme="e" data-icon="back" data-role="button" data-
inline="true">Back</a></h1>
        <ul data-role="listview" data-filter="true" id="current-
notes" data-icon="delete"></ul>
```

```
        </div>
    </div>
```

4. With the notes page, the user will be able to view their current notes, so there needs to be a way to create new notes. Using the following HTML code, add the create note page to `index2.html`:

```html
<div data-role="page" id="add-note" data-title="Add new note">
    <div data-role="header" data-theme="b">
        <h1>Add new note</h1>
    </div>
    <div data-role="content">
        <textarea id="note-text"></textarea>
        <div class='input-error' style="display: none;" id="note-error"></div>
        <div class="actions">
            <button data-role="button" id="save-new-note" data-theme="a" data-icon="check" data-inline="true">Save</button>
            <a href="#notes" data-role="button" data-theme="e" data-icon="delete" data-inline="true">Cancel</a>
        </div>
    </div>
</div>
```

5. With the new database table created and the HTML UI updated for the additional functionality, we now need to create the PHP that provides the interaction to the database. To enable a user to create a new note, within the web root of your web server, create a file named `addNote.php` and insert the following code:

```php
<?php
session_start();

require_once("connect.db.php");
$text = isset($_POST['text']) ? $_POST['text'] : "";

$response = array(
    "success" => false,
    "error" => "",
    "note" => array()
);

if (!isset($_SESSION['uid'])) {
    $response["error"] = "You must be logged in to add a new note";
} else if (strlen($text) <= 0 || strlen($text) > 1024) {
    $response["error"] = "A note must be between 1 and 1024 characters in length";
```

```php
    } else {
        $query = "INSERT INTO `note` (`user_id`, `text`, `added`)
VALUES (?, ?, ?)";
        $stmt = $mysqli->stmt_init();
        if ($stmt->prepare($query)) {
            $now = date("Y-m-d H:i:s");
            $stmt->bind_param("sss", $_SESSION['uid'], $text, $now);
            if ($stmt->execute()) {
                $stmt->close();
                $response["success"] = true;
                $response["note"] = array(
                    "id" => $mysqli->insert_id,
                    "text" => $text,
                    "added" => $now
                );
            } else {
                $response["error"] = "Could not execute query";
            }
        } else {
            $response["error"] = "Could not insert new note, please
try again";
        }
    }
}
$mysqli->close();
header("Content-Type: application/json; charset=UTF-8");
echo json_encode($response);
```

6. To populate the notes page with the user's current notes, we need to be able to retrieve the notes from the database. Create a file named `getNotes.php` and add the following PHP code:

```php
<?php
session_start();
require_once("connect.db.php");

$response = array(
    "success" => false,
    "error" => "",
    "notes" => array()
);

if (!isset($_SESSION['uid'])) {
    $response["error"] = "You must be logged in to add a new
note";
} else {
```

```php
$query = "SELECT * FROM `note` WHERE `user_id` = ? ORDER BY
`added` DESC";
    $stmt = $mysqli->stmt_init();
    if ($stmt->prepare($query)) {
        $stmt->bind_param("s", $_SESSION['uid']);
        if ($stmt->execute()) {
            $res = $stmt->get_result();
            $response["success"] = true;
            if ($res->num_rows > 0) {
                while ($row = $res->fetch_assoc()) {
                    $response["notes"][] = array(
                        "id" => $row["id"],
                        "text" => $row["text"],
                        "added" => $row["added"]
                    );
                }
            }
        } else {
            $response["error"] = "Could not execute query";
        }
    } else {
        $response["error"] = "Could not query database";
    }
    $stmt->close();
}
$mysqli->close();
header("Content-Type: application/json; charset=UTF-8");
echo json_encode($response);
```

7. The user also needs to be able to remove unwanted notes. For this, within the web root of your web server, create a file named deleteNote.php and add the following code:

```php
<?php
session_start();

require_once("connect.db.php");
$id = isset($_POST['id']) ? (int)$_POST['id'] : 0;

$response = array(
    "success" => false,
    "error" => ""
);

if (!isset($_SESSION['uid'])) {
```

```
        $response["error"] = "You must be logged in to delete a note";
    } else if ($id <= 0) {
        $response["error"] = "Invalid note ID specified";
    } else {
        $query = "DELETE FROM `note` WHERE `id` = ?";
        $stmt = $mysqli->stmt_init();
        if ($stmt->prepare($query)) {
            $stmt->bind_param("i", $id);
            if ($stmt->execute()) {
                $stmt->close();
                $response["success"] = true;
            } else {
                $response["error"] = "Could not execute query";
            }
        } else {
            $response["error"] = "Could not insert new note, please
try again";
        }
    }
    $mysqli->close();
    header("Content-Type: application/json; charset=UTF-8");
    echo json_encode($response);
```

8. With all the backend code in place, we can now add JavaScript to link the user interface and this backend code together. First of all, we need to make a few changes to the original JavaScript code from the previous recipe within `script2.js`. At the top of `script2.js`, but still within the jQuery on-load block `$(function(){});`, add the following line of code:

```
var _currentNotes = $('#current-notes');
```

9. Within the `success()` function for the logout AJAX call, just before `$.mobile. changePage("#home");`, add the following line of code:

```
_currentNotes.data("initialized", false);
```

10. Within the `pagebeforechange` event handler, we need to add some code so that we can display the currently logged-in user's username within the members page. Update the code as follows, adding `$('.username').html(user.username);`:

```
if (urlObject.hash.search(/^#member/) !== -1) {
var user = getUser();
if (user === false) {
        e.preventDefault();
$.mobile.showPageLoadingMsg("b", "You must be logged in to access
this page", true);
setTimeout(function(){
```

```
$.mobile.hidePageLoadingMsg();
$.mobile.changePage("#home");
}, 1500);
} else {
        $('.username').html(user.username);
}
}
```

11. With the required JavaScript updates made, we need to add the additional
    functionality. To allow the user to add a new note, insert the following code into
    `script2.js` to catch when the user clicks on the save note button:

```
$('#save-new-note').click(function(){
        $('#note-error').hide();
        var _text = $('#note-text');
        $.ajax({
            type: 'POST',
            url: 'addNote.php',
            data: {
                'text': _text.val()
            },
            beforeSend: function() {
                $.mobile.loading('show');
            },
            success: function(data) {
                $.mobile.loading('hide');
                if (data.success) {
                    _text.val("");
                    _currentNotes.prepend(createNoteItem(data.
note));
                    //If the list view has already been
initialized then we need to refresh it
                    if (_currentNotes.hasClass('ui-listview')) {
                        _currentNotes.listview('refresh');
                    }
                    $.mobile.changePage("#notes");
                } else {
                    $('#note-error').html(data.error).fadeIn();
                }
            }
        });
    });
```

12. To populate the notes page with any currently available notes, we need to add some additional functionality to the `pagebeforechange` event handler. Update the code as follows (some code has been hidden for illustrative purposes):

```
$(document).bind("pagebeforechange", function(e, data) {
 if (typeof data.toPage === "string") {
  var urlObject = $.mobile.path.parseUrl(data.toPage);
  if (urlObject.hash.search(/^#member/) !== -1) {
   //HIDDEN CODE - DO NOT REMOVE
  } else if(urlObject.hash.search(/^#notes/) !== -1) {
   if (_currentNotes.data("initialized") != true) {
    e.preventDefault();
    _currentNotes.empty();
    _currentNotes.data("initialized", true);
    $.ajax({
     type: 'GET',
     url: 'getNotes.php',
     beforeSend: function() {
      $.mobile.loading('show');
     },
     success: function(data) {
      $.mobile.loading('hide');
      if (data.success) {
       for (var i = 0; i < data.notes.length; i++) {
        _currentNotes.append(createNoteItem(data.notes[i]));
       }
       //If the list view has already been initialized then we
need to refresh it
       if (_currentNotes.hasClass('ui-listview')) {
_currentNotes.listview("refresh");
       }
       $.mobile.changePage("#notes");
      } else {
       alert(data.error);
      }
     }
    });
   }
  }
 }
});
```

13. The currently available notes that are listed need to be clickable to allow users to delete them. Add the following code within `script2.js` to listen for a click on one of the current note list items to then make an AJAX call to the `deleteNote.php` script:

```
$(document).on('click', '.delete-note', function(){
        var _listItem = $(this).closest('li');
        var id = _listItem.data("id");
        var response = confirm("Are you sure you want to delete
this note?");
        if (response) {
            $.ajax({
                type: 'POST',
                url: 'deleteNote.php',
                data: {
                    'id': id
                },
                beforeSend: function() {
                    $.mobile.loading('show');
                },
                success: function(data) {
                    $.mobile.loading('hide');
                    if (data.success) {
                        _listItem.remove();
                        _currentNotes.listview("refresh");
                    } else {
                        alert(data.error);
                    }
                }
            });
        }
});
```

14. Finally, add the following function outside the jQuery on-load block (`$(function() {}) ;`), which constructs a list item for a note:

```
function createNoteItem(note) {
    return "<li data-id='" + note.id + "'><a
href='javascript:void(0);' class='delete-note'>" + note.text + "</
a></li>";
}
```

15. By visiting `index2.html` served from a web server, you will be able to register an account and then log in, just as with the previous recipe. Once logged in, tapping on the **View Notes** button will take you to a page with an empty list. Click on the **Add note** button to add a new note. Once a new note has been added, you will be taken back to the current note's list with your new note showing. You can remove this note by clicking on it and confirming that you wish to delete it. You can access your notes on multiple devices across logged-in sessions.

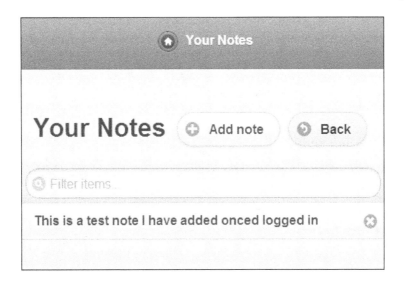

How it works...

Each section of the code for this recipe is explained in detail in the following sections.

HTML

The HTML code within this recipe adds a few extra pages so that the logged-in user can create a note and view the previous ones. The notes page uses a listview with a filter that was shown within the *Adding mobile-friendly lists* recipe of this chapter.

SQL

The simple SQL code within this recipe creates an additional table called note that is used to store all of the user's notes. A foreign key relationship is also defined between the user_id field on the note table and the id field on the user table.

PHP

All PHP scripts within this recipe use the same database connection file and structure as the previous recipe. There are an additional three PHP scripts created for this recipe, as follows:

- addNote.php: This script takes a POST request with the text for a note. It then checks to see if there is a currently logged-in user using the PHP $_SESSION super global. If there is a logged-in user, the provided text is validated to ensure it is between 0 and 1024 characters in length. If it is, it is inserted into the database with the logged-in user's ID and an added date. To get the database ID for the newly created note item, $mysqli->insert_id is used. This is then returned within the note object, which is sent back to the requesting script.

- deleteNote.php: This script, like addNote.php, takes a POST request with a note ID as a parameter. It also checks to ensure there is a logged-in user and, if so, will then use a simple SQL query to delete the specified note from the database.

- getNotes.php: By using the logged-in user's ID, all notes for that user are retrieved from the database and converted to JSON so that they can populate a list element using JavaScript.

 If a PHP script requires access to session data, the session_ start() function must be called at the top of the script, before any other code.

JavaScript

At the top of script2.js, the _currentNotes variable is declared as shown in the following line of code:

```
var _currentNotes = $('#current-notes');
```

This is because the current note's list is required throughout the code, and by re-using the same variable, jQuery is not forced to reselect the element multiple times.

To dynamically populate the #current-notes list element with the currently logged-in user's notes from the database, the pagebeforechange event is exploited once again. With an additional check as part of an if...else statement, it is possible to determine when the user tries to go to the notes page, as illustrated by the following line of code:

```
else if(urlObject.hash.search(/^#notes/) !== -1) {
```

When the user does visit this page using _currentNotes.data("initialized"), it is possible to check if the list has already been populated. If the initialized data attribute has already been set, then it has been populated, and there is no need to go and get all the data from the database again. If the initialized attribute has not been set to true, an AJAX call is made to collect the current notes and populate the list as shown in the following code:

```
_currentNotes.empty();
    _currentNotes.data("initialized", true);
    $.ajax({
      type: 'GET',
      url: 'getNotes.php',
      beforeSend: function() {
        $.mobile.loading('show');
      },
      success: function(data) {
        $.mobile.loading('hide');
        if (data.success) {
```

```
            for (var i = 0; i < data.notes.length; i++) {
             _currentNotes.append(createNoteItem(data.notes[i]));
            }
            //If the list view has already been initialized then we need to
        refresh it
        if (_currentNotes.hasClass('ui-listview')) {
        _currentNotes.listview("refresh");
            }
            $.mobile.changePage("#notes");
            } else {
             alert(data.error);
            }
          }
         });
```

The `_currentNotes.data("initialized", true);` line is used to set the initialized attribute to `true` so that when the user returns to the page, the script knows not to recollect the data. The AJAX call is made to the `getNotes.php` script and then a new list item is created using the `createNoteItem()` function for every returned `note` object.

If jQuery Mobile has already initiated the #current-notes list (meaning the user has already been to the page once before), the listview will need to be refreshed. This is done using the following code, taken from the `success()` function of the AJAX call:

```
//If the list view has already been initialized then we need to
refresh it
if (_currentNotes.hasClass('ui-listview')) {
    _currentNotes.listview("refresh");
        }
```

The create note and delete note functionalities within this recipe are very simple and have been covered numerous times throughout this book. As an overview, when either the save note button or the note list item is clicked, an AJAX call is made to the `addNote.php` or `deleteNote.php` script respectively.

When adding a new note, the following code is used to prepend the new note item to the current note's list and send the user back to the notes page:

```
_currentNotes.prepend(createNoteItem(data.note));
//If the list view has already been initialized then we need to
refresh it
if (_currentNotes.hasClass('ui-listview')) {
_currentNotes.listview('refresh');
}
$.mobile.changePage("#notes");
```

When deleting a note, the following code is used to remove the deleted note item:

```
var _listItem = $(this).closest('li');
_listItem.remove();
```

Because jQuery Mobile adds a lot of additional elements to the DOM for styling the list, the `closest()` function is used to find the list element when the anchor (within the list) is clicked. Additionally, note that `$(document).on('click', '.delete-note'` is used as opposed to `$('.delete-note').click()` so that the `click` event handler is triggered for dynamically added elements. This was covered in *Chapter 2, Interacting with the User by Making Use of jQuery Events*.

There's more...

This recipe provides a very simple example of a complete mobile web application. There are many aspects that could be improved upon but were left out to ensure this recipe was kept as concise as possible.

One element that could be improved upon would be the security aspects of the `deleteNote.php` script. The script will currently allow the logged-in user to delete any note provided the correct ID is specified. A user with some knowledge could hijack the request by specifying a note ID of their choice, potentially deleting a note from another user. This can easily be avoided by checking if the specified note ID belongs to the logged-in user.

See also

- *Chapter 2, Interacting with the User by Making Use of jQuery Events*
- *Building a complete registration and login system*

Index

U

updateElementData() function 306, 307
updateList() function 36
user element clicks
  detecting 47, 48

V

valdiateNumber() function 165
val() function 23
validateAntiSpam() function 185
validateCreditCard function 170
validateDate() function 172

validateEmail() function 174
validateNumber function 167
validatePasswords() function 179, 182
validateRequired() function 163, 167
View Notes button 384

W

website elements
  clicking on 44
wrapAll() function 285
wrap() function 306

Thank you for buying
jQuery 2.0 Development Cookbook

About Packt Publishing

Packt, pronounced 'packed', published its first book "*Mastering phpMyAdmin for Effective MySQL Management*" in April 2004 and subsequently continued to specialize in publishing highly focused books on specific technologies and solutions.

Our books and publications share the experiences of your fellow IT professionals in adapting and customizing today's systems, applications, and frameworks. Our solution based books give you the knowledge and power to customize the software and technologies you're using to get the job done. Packt books are more specific and less general than the IT books you have seen in the past. Our unique business model allows us to bring you more focused information, giving you more of what you need to know, and less of what you don't.

Packt is a modern, yet unique publishing company, which focuses on producing quality, cutting-edge books for communities of developers, administrators, and newbies alike. For more information, please visit our website: www.packtpub.com.

About Packt Open Source

In 2010, Packt launched two new brands, Packt Open Source and Packt Enterprise, in order to continue its focus on specialization. This book is part of the Packt Open Source brand, home to books published on software built around Open Source licences, and offering information to anybody from advanced developers to budding web designers. The Open Source brand also runs Packt's Open Source Royalty Scheme, by which Packt gives a royalty to each Open Source project about whose software a book is sold.

Writing for Packt

We welcome all inquiries from people who are interested in authoring. Book proposals should be sent to author@packtpub.com. If your book idea is still at an early stage and you would like to discuss it first before writing a formal book proposal, contact us; one of our commissioning editors will get in touch with you.

We're not just looking for published authors; if you have strong technical skills but no writing experience, our experienced editors can help you develop a writing career, or simply get some additional reward for your expertise.

jQuery UI 1.10:
The User Interface Library for jQuery

Build highly interactive web applications with ready-to-use widgets

Alex Libby   Dan Wellman   [PACKT] open source ✦

jQuery UI 1.10: The User Interface Library for jQuery

ISBN: 978-1-78216-220-9   Paperback: 502 pages

Build highly interactive web applications with ready-to-use widgets

1. Packed with clear explanations of how to easily design elegant and powerful frontend interfaces for your web applications.

2. A section covering the widget factory including an in-depth example of how to build a custom jQuery UI widget.

3. Revised with updated code and targeted at both jQuery UI 1.10 and jQuery 2.

jQuery Game Development Essentials

Learn how to make fun and addictive multi-platform games using jQuery

Selim Arsever   PACKT

jQuery Game Development Essentials

ISBN: 978-1-84969-506-0   Paperback: 244 pages

Learn how to make fun and addictive multi-platform games using jQuery

1. Discover how you can create a fantastic RPG, arcade game, or platformer using jQuery!

2. Learn how you can integrate your game with various social networks, create multiplayer experiences, and also ensure compatibility with mobile devices.

3. Create your very own framework, harnessing the very best design patterns and proven techniques along the way.

Please check **www.PacktPub.com** for information on our titles

www.ingramcontent.com/pod-product-compliance
Lightning Source LLC
LaVergne TN
LVHW081329050326
832903LV00024B/1090